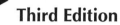

Third Edition

Creative Interviewing

The Writer's Guide to Gathering Information by Asking Questions

Ken Metzler
University of Oregon

Allyn and Bacon

Boston • London • Toronto • Sydney • Tokyo • Singapore

Vice President, Humanities: Joseph Opiela
Editorial Assistant: Kate Tolini
Executive Marketing Manager: Sandi Kirshner
Editorial-Production Administrator: Rob Lawson
Editorial-Production Service: Ruttle, Shaw, & Wetherill, Inc.
Composition Buyer: Linda Cox
Manufacturing Buyer: Suzanne Lareau
Cover Administrator: Suzanne Harbison
Illustrator: Thomas H. Bivins

Copyright © 1997 by Allyn & Bacon
A Viacom Company
Needham Heights, MA 02194

Internet: www.abacon.com
America Online: Keyword: College Online

Library of Congress Cataloging-in-Publication Data

Metzler, Ken.
    Creative interviewing / by Ken Metzler. — 3rd ed.
        p.   cm.
    Includes bibliographical references and index.
    ISBN 0–205–26258–9
    1. Interviewing in journalism.   I. Title.
PN4784.I6M4   1997
070.4'3—dc20   96–12079
                                                          CIP

Printed in the United States of America

10 9 8 7 6 5 4 3 2 1   00 99 98 97 96 95

For Betty Jane
"Look up there—a patch of blue. I do believe it's brightening up."

Contents

Preface

One word distinguishes this third edition of *Creative Interviewing* from the two previous editions: "truth." Or "pursuit of truth," if I'm allowed three. In the twenty-five years I have concentrated on journalistic interviewing as a topic of inquiry, I've become increasingly concerned about truth. What is it? How do you define it? How do you apply it to journalism? Most important, is it enhanced or impeded by the variety of interview practices common to journalism? What inspired this change? Mostly the fact that the public today sees much more of interviewers in action than ever before. Ever more broadcast shows employ questions and answers. These include acerbic talk shows— shouting matches oftentimes. Or you can watch clever people use the Q-A dialogue to match wits just for laughs. Occasionally you can even watch serious forums for discussion of public events. In all such examples, the public has come to recognize that the nature of the question often dictates the nature of the answer. Jocular questions beget jocular answers. Belligerent questions beget defensive answers. How does truth fare in that arena? How does truth fare under the long-standing premise that the work of the journalist is essentially adversarial? The premise suggests that reporters and sources are enemies and that the journalistic interview represents a grand chess game of thrust and counterthrust, advance and retreat, win or lose. We may want to rethink those tactics if our journalistic objective is to tell the truth without fear or favor.

I like to think of the changes in the third edition as a slight course correction, like a ship captain steering three or four degrees left or right. The changes might seem slight at first, but some of the scenery will be different. Among the changes is an increasing concern for the ethics of the journalistic interview. It's a concern fueled by increasingly prevalent examples, primarily on television, of such shady tactics as the hidden camera sting, the ambush interview, and the *screaming meemies*, the term I use to cover television's more boisterous talk shows. The new emphasis on pursuit of truth drew further inspiration from a research project I undertook in 1990. I talked with frequently interviewed news sources, particularly those who had risen from obscurity to moments of fame. One "reward" of fame—*true* celebrityhood—is that tabloid journals will talk about you without bothering to interview you. Consider the ethics of that. And what does it mean when an interviewer tells a source, "Just between you and me—whisper the answer to me," when the whispered answer is heard by millions? Interviewing behavior represents what one journalism professor, Lee Wilkins of Missouri, calls the "great black hole of journalism ethics" because it has received so little attention. So two new chapters deal with the ethics of the interview. Chapter 20 deals specifically with ethics; Chapter 21 adds some thoughts about truth: how some show business celebrities and others see it, and how interviewers can come closer to it.

Another change embraces new technology. The computer network known as the Internet has opened journalistic horizons in spectacular ways. And this has brought another new chapter to this book, Electronic Aids to Interviewing (Chapter 15), depicting not only a dramatic example of an E-mail interview with a scientist at the South Pole, but dealing with a new journalistic beat—the Internet. Talk about new journalistic horizons—it's a whole new world out there.

Another innovation of this third edition comes as a result of my extensive interviews with news media sources. Quite a few case histories depict how interviews feel from the other side of the fence—the source's side. I'm indebted to many erstwhile celebrities for their insights and their descriptions of interview experiences. One of them is a young woman named Melissa Rathbun Coleman, the U.S. Army's first female enlisted prisoner of war who enjoyed neither her celebrity status nor the media attention. "I would rather be back in the Iraqi prison than be in the prison the media have created for me," she once remarked. She flatly turned down more than 100 requests for interviews including Phil Donahue's and Maury Povich's, but granted a few interviews, including one with me. Her experience dramatizes the best and the worst practices in journalistic information-gathering methods. Her story appears in Chapter 20.

In this new edition you'll find updated examples and references to new research, including three new studies that focus directly on the journalistic interview. Some examples have not changed since the first edition, however, because responses from readers suggest that they contain useful lessons. We are still talking about achieving greater candor among sources by spilling your coffee. This has become a symbol that suggests one journalistic truth—show a little of your own human vulnerability if you expect sources to show theirs.

The original idea for this book came from the discovery that college journalism students have a dread of talking with people in what they perceive as the "formal" interview situation. That is why the stories they wrote for the magazine writing classes I taught then came out so dull and flat, representing the barren snowfields of abstraction rather than the warm enclaves of human experience. I hope this book, and classroom experiences based on this book, will persuade you to remove the "formal" from the interviewing experience. Interviewing is just people talking, sometimes barefooted people. I hope the experiences will introduce you to the wonderful world of—well, to the wonderful world, period. Journalism is the last "cool" profession. It's fun. It encourages you to meet new people—people you'd never meet under ordinary circumstances, from kings on their thrones to prisoners in the lockup, as Mark Twain suggested.

SOURCES AND ACKNOWLEDGMENTS

Information in this book comes from a wide variety of sources—so wide that I'm awed by the prospect of winnowing into manageable chapters the mountains of material derived from people ranging from ministers to child killers in addition to reporters, editors, and social science researchers. Sources of any nonfiction book have remained standard despite the new technology. You consult primary (unpublished) or secondary (published) documents. You talk to people—the right people, the ones who can introduce you to new horizons. You ask lots of questions. You immerse yourself in relevant experiences. You observe. You experiment, informally or systematically, and you record the results of the experimentation. You then synthesize the diverse bits of information to form a mosaic that represents the thrust of your message.

Immersion? For more than forty years of professional journalism I have gathered information by asking questions. I've been interviewed a good deal myself, both by student interviewers and by the media.

Experiments? I have constantly experimented in interviewing classes at the University of Oregon, even to the point of encouraging students to "fail" (and obtain good grades in the process) by trying special approaches to interviews such as asking questions in a loud, arrogant manner to see if kicking information out of sources works better than the softer, more permissive approaches recommended in this text. (It doesn't.) Some experiments failed miserably. Several times I tried to arrange with newspaper reporters to recall their innermost thoughts while conducting interviews—in much the same way reporters ask athletes, "What were you thinking as you approached the finish line en route to a new American record in the 5,000-meter race?" Well, reporters like to ask those questions, but I guess they don't like to answer them.

Talking to people? I talked to journalists who suddenly found themselves thrust into the media spotlight, and almost without exception they became quite nervous about being interviewed. Some confessed feelings bordering on terror. "A request for an interview is a red alert for me," says Jon Franklin, a two-time Pulitzer Prize winner. Such reactions offer new meaning to the word "irony."

Observation? Easy. Watching TV—every night on television brings the best and worst of interviewing techniques. Viewing videotapes of interviews. Listening to print reporters' tape-recorded sessions or reading transcripts where available. Watching news conferences. Even noting the way ordinary citizens ask questions of one another (often poorly, with wretchedly biased assumptions).

Documentation? The bibliography continues to grow as the result of continued reports of interviewing experiences and experiments. Most of the research comes from fields other than journalism/mass communication, namely social science fields such as psychology and anthropology. However, some new research relates directly to journalism.

Synthesis? The new perspectives have merely confirmed principles that have remained largely the same throughout these three editions. Good preparation for interviews, sympathetic nonjudgmental listening, and responding with interest and questions to what is being said—those in a nutshell remain the appropriate patterns.

Every author owes a debt of gratitude to others who have generously assisted in the preparation of his or her material. The list could reach thousands, especially if you consider the students and professional journalists who have participated in interviewing seminars and workshops over the past twenty-five years. I've conducted many—from New York to New Zealand—and have learned from every one.

And I've read widely. Books and documents consulted for this work are listed in the bibliography.

I calculate that I've interviewed about 300 news sources over a course of twenty-five years on the topic of relationships with the media. About 200 of them were interviewed since 1990 by phone with the financial assistance of the Freedom Forum, for which I offer thanks. Those whose comments I found directly useful in the content of this new edition are listed in the back of the book. Specifically, I'd also like to thank the following:

Michael Thoele, Oregon author, former newspaperman, extraordinary interviewer. Down through the years I've absorbed so many of the Thoele principles of interviewing that I confess I'm not always sure which are mine and which are borrowed from Mike.

Also Don Bishoff, columnist at *The Register-Guard* in Eugene, Oregon; Jack Hart of *The Oregonian*; and Melody Ward Leslie, of Eugene, journalist and quintessential interview respondent.

Jim Upshaw, Alan Stavitsky, and Karl Nestvold, all University of Oregon faculty colleagues who specialize in broadcast reporting and interviewing—they offered advice on broadcast interviewing methods. Tom Bivins, another faculty colleague—thanks for the illustrations. John Russial, also a faculty colleague, former newspaper copyeditor—editor to the end, he combed through several chapters of this book correcting typos and offering useful suggestions. Steve Ponder, my river rafting buddy—many thanks for surfing the Internet and finding choice items for textbook display.

Sharon Brock of Ohio State University—thanks for reading chapters and offering valuable suggestions. (We had lovely e-mail discussions on "What is truth?" a topic on which we never could agree.)

Lisa McCormack, former Washington newspaper writer—thanks for helping me meet lots of important people.

Thanks to the readers of previous editions—John L. Griffith, Del Brinkman, Al Hester, Kenneth S. Devol, David Rubin, and John F. Dillon.

Special thanks to Joe Opiela of Allyn & Bacon, an encouraging kind of editor—the best kind if you're a writer.

Though many years have passed, I remain grateful to *The Honolulu Advertiser*, which generously took me on as a "special writer" during a sabbatical leave in 1974–75, an experience that led to the first edition of *Creative Interviewing* (1977).

My wife, Betty Jane—thanks for being my life-long pal.

And special thanks to our three children. In earlier years, I thanked them for trying to be quiet around the house while I wrote. Now they've grown up, have become productive citizens, and have developed splendid expertise in their respective fields. Barbara, the first-born, works for a business consulting firm called Strategic Decisions Group at Menlo Park, California. She served as consultant for Chapter 8, which deals with preparation for an important interview with a prominent if hypothetical business executive. Scott is a civil engineer in Eugene, Oregon, who runs a branch office of a California engineering firm called Biggs Cardoza. He provided insight into the nature of "tech-talk," the kind reporters must learn if they are to cover public affairs. And Doug, the youngest, works for Microsoft Corporation near Seattle; he patiently led me through the twisted streets and backroads of the Internet and thus provided valuable assistance for Chapter 15, Electronic Aids to Interviewing. Also helping in that task were Doug's computer pal, Eric (Cygnus) Swanson of San Francisco, and Mick Westrick, computer genius for the School of Journalism and Mass Communication at the University of Oregon.

Many others who contributed to this book are quoted by name in the succeeding pages. Let it be emphasized that the author takes full responsibility for any errors that may appear in this book.

Ken Metzler

▶ 1

What's Your Interviewing Problem?

Q. What are your views on the future of humanity?

A. Why should I care? I have just swallowed a cyanide pill. I'll be dead in twenty seconds.

Q. Uh-huh. Okay. . . . Now I'd like to ask about your hobbies—uh, do you engage in any kind of athletic activities?

You think you have interviewing problems? Consider the plight of a young woman named Nora Villagrán. She was about to begin her first assignment on her new job as entertainment writer for the *San Jose Mercury News:* to interview folk singer Joan Baez. She put on a white dress that morning, complete with hose and high heels, and she hurried to her rendezvous with her first celebrity.

A problem intervened. She fell down a flight of steps en route to the interview. She received only minor scratches and bruises, but she was bleeding through her white dress, and her stockings were torn. Now what? Change clothes and repair the damage? No time for that. Cancel the interview? She might not get another chance.

She decided to plunge ahead. She appeared at Joan Baez's doorstep in her disheveled condition. The singer, answering the door in her bare feet, glanced at Villagrán and remarked, "You've either been mugged or been in a car accident—which was it?"

"Neither," she replied. Her recounting of events led Baez to invite her to use the bathroom to repair the damage. Baez prepared an ice pack for the swollen ankle.

Then she suggested that Villagrán take off her shoes and her torn stockings. They wouldn't have an interview, she said. Rather they'd be, in Joan Baez's words, "just two barefooted women talking."

Just two barefooted women talking. Recounting the incident later, Villagrán concluded that it had been one of her best interviews, one that involved great candor on both sides. What seemed like a disaster turned out precisely the opposite. She saw a barefooted celebrity exhibiting an unusual degree of candor—not in spite of the reporter's disheveled condition but possibly because of it.

This is not unusual. Villagrán, having taken a course in interviewing, had already heard of similar incidents through the class discussions, and she says her decision to go on with the interview drew inspiration from the "spilled coffee" story.

We've been discussing that story for years in the interviewing classes I teach at the University of Oregon. It concerns another young woman, Ann Curry, who later became anchor-correspondent for NBC News in New York. For a class assignment, Curry interviewed a prominent businesswoman. The conversation, though, failed to develop the candor that Curry had hoped for. She suggested that they repair to a nearby coffee shop. Sitting side by side at a counter, they conversed more amiably. Then Curry—in a gesture to emphasize a point—spilled her coffee. Mortified, she thought she had blown the interview. But, to her astonishment, the woman began talking more candidly. It was almost as though Curry's social gaffe had allowed the woman to drop her own facade of dignity. Suddenly they could become just a couple of women talking.

The story illustrates something unpredictable and ironic about human nature. We can discern at least two truths from the incident: One suggests that if you want candor—you want human responses rather than defensive exaggerations and false facades—try revealing a little of yourself in the conversation. The other suggests that striving for technical perfection can intrude on candor. Better to have just two people talking. The relaxed informality allows the full dimension of human nature to emerge. The best journalists savor the unpredictability of human response, and they pass it along to their audiences when they can.

The spilled-coffee story inspired a tradition in those interview classes: Can you top that story? Several former students have reported similar incidents. In Florida, reporter Scott Martell showed up at a black-tie occasion wearing blue jeans, ratty tennis shoes, and a smudged T-shirt. He'd dressed for a ride on a fishing boat in pursuit of a story, but stormy weather forced a cancellation. The paper reassigned him to a furniture store opening. Nobody told him it was a formal occasion. Yet he looks back on it as one of his best interviews. He still wonders why.

Such stories suggest that a higher level of candor emerges in the context of "two barefooted women talking" than from the formal interview. The interviews we see on television have become so strained that an authority on oral history interviewing claimed that he'd learned quite a bit about interviewing by watching "Meet the Press." He studied the reporters' questioning techniques, he said, and then he did just the opposite.

You do indeed sometimes find reporters aloof and hostile—maybe that's how they believe they must act with celebrities and high-level government officials. But most people respond most candidly to an amiable and friendly approach. Reporters often ask questions in an adversarial manner, yet research studies on questioning techniques suggest that the nonjudgmental approach works best to enhance rapport and candor. It shows that you have come not to judge, not to argue, not to destroy, but to listen, to ascertain the facts, to learn. When people discover that you have come not as judge and jury but as a student of human affairs, they become more candid.

Under such circumstances, the professional interviewer should be able to talk with practically anybody about practically anything, to paraphrase the title of a book by TV interviewer Barbara Walters. Name the most despicable of human beings—a rapist or a child molester, perhaps—and ask yourself: Could you interview this person without displaying your contempt? To the extent that you can answer "yes," consider yourself a professional journalistic interviewer. Professionalism requires not that you win arguments or display moral superiority but that you learn something from the encounter that you can share with an unseen audience.

Given what seems to be a reasonably valid truth from the episodes described here, it seems remarkable that so many young journalists claim to have problems in interviewing. "I just hope that my source will do all the talking," said one student, "so that I won't have to ask any questions."

In the twenty-five years I have taught classes in interviewing, the technology has changed but the problems have not. Interviewers who take their notes on tiny laptop computers still profess inability to cope with a taciturn or garrulous interviewee (henceforth called "respondent" in this text). How do you avoid that awkward silence when you can't think of a question to follow an unexpected answer? Do you just go to your next question on the list? That could lead to non sequiturs almost as silly as the one illustrated at the head of this chapter.

Some 1,500 students attending interviewing classes at the University of Oregon over the years have filled out questionnaires identifying their most serious interviewing problems. The exercise defines two sets of problems, actually: the ones that novice interviewers know about and the ones they don't.

THE OBVIOUS PROBLEMS

First consider the problems that young journalists identify in their responses to the classroom surveys.

Lack of Self-Confidence.   Students have many colorful ways of expressing it. "Basically I am a chicken," said a woman. "I wish I could find a way to avoid breaking out in a cold sweat during an interview," said a man. By whatever label, it remains the number one problem of novice interviewers. A tally of comments over the years reveals that almost a third of the women and 20 percent of the men confess to having some form of the problem. "Most people are, I think, inherently uncomfortable in an interview situation," suggests one student. "Although they are normally quite capable of carrying on a pleasant conversation with others, when it comes to what they consider a *formal* interview, they tend to become tense and unnatural."

This appears to be a temporary problem. Most students find that the social skills that lead to pleasant conversation also serve in interviews. You'd be astounded to learn how many famous interviewers confess to shyness—Barbara Walters, Phil Donahue, and Gay Talese, to name a few. (Huber and Diggins 1991. For full citations, see listing by author in the bibliography.)

Getting Complete Information.   "I had a wonderful conversation with my source," complained one student reporter, "but when I sat down to write a story, I realized I had nothing new or interesting to write about." You'll find no easy solution to this one. But as you gain experience you will learn that the following elements help—preparation for interviews, careful listening, and, most important, the ability to recognize something "new and different" when it whizzes past you in conversation.

Knowing What Questions to Ask Next.   A student explained: "Let's say I ask a question, and the answer I get is something totally unexpected—I never know what to say next." How about something like this? "What a wonderful answer! Please tell me more!"

Taking Notes.   Journalistic note-taking differs from notes you take in the classroom. You must identify and record the major points. That's not easy during informal conversations in which people just talk rather than organizing their thoughts into formal lectures. Second, you must record evidence—colorful quotations, illustrative anecdotes, facts, figures—all necessary to support the points. It's hard to listen, make notes, and keep the conversation going at the same time. The conscious human mind doesn't work on three tracks; it works on only one. The solutions, never easy, range from learning shorthand (or developing your own shorthand) to using recording devices or some combination of taping and note-taking. More about this in Chapter 12.

Coping with Taciturn Respondents. Students consider this their worst nightmare—you ask all the right questions but receive only short answers or none at all. The dynamics of human conversation are never simple. Who can say why a particular respondent seems sullenly uncommunicative? Respondents' reactions to being interviewed often reflect the attitude of the interviewer. Who can blame them if they meet news media arrogance with their own brand of arrogance—clamming up? One truth may predominate, however. Most people have a keen interest in *something*—politics, sports, investments, fishing, travel, whatever—that can assist in starting the conversational ball rolling.

Coping with Nonstop Talkers. Some motor mouths become mired in trivia or otherwise fail to address the questions posed. Interrupting may not work. A more creative solution may be necessary. One interviewer contrived to interview an official, a noteworthy big talker, while the latter was being shaved by his barber. He managed to get in quite a few questions as the barber worked around the mouth. The respondent was Theodore Roosevelt. (Marcosson 1919.)

These six by no means exhaust the list of problems perceived by students. The others include:

1. Beginning and ending an interview
2. Asking sensitive or potentially embarrassing questions

"Can I quote you on that, Senator?"

3. Preparing for an interview
4. Establishing an easy-going rapport with respondents
5. Securing interviews with busy and important people
6. Formulating, in the words of one student, "the perfect question that will unlock the interviewee and cause him to rattle off enormously candid and heretofore unpublished insights without my having to think up a single additional question."

Good topics all, and they'll receive attention in later chapters.

THE HIDDEN PROBLEMS

Most problems perceived by students stem from issues that lie unrecognized beneath the surface. Here, based on a quarter century of watching student interviewers in action, is a list of hidden problems.

A General Aversion to Asking Questions for Fear of Being Labeled Ignorant. True learning is accompanied by pain, said the Greek philosopher Aristotle. People tend to cover up gaps in knowledge because they're uneasy about learning. How many men (more than women) drive blocks out of their way rather than stop to ask directions? A natural, childlike curiosity seems, unfortunately, to go out of style as people reach a certain age.

Too bad that asking is so painful. But not asking can be worse. *He who is afraid of asking is ashamed of learning.* That wisdom emerged from a fortune cookie. Another Chinese proverb offers similar insight: *He who asks is a fool for five minutes. He who does not is a fool forever.*

Failure to Define Clearly and State the Purpose of the Interview. Consider the problem of nudging a garrulous person back onto the interview track. This requires that *you* know what the track is—that is, the precise purpose of your interview. Had you understood the purpose and explained it candidly, your garrulous performer might not have strayed so recklessly. Or if the conversation did stray, you'd have brought it back on course sooner.

When our interviewing laboratory exercises call for pairing students to interview one another, this emerges as the number one problem—at least on the first few pairings. About half of the respondents in those first interview pairs complained that while they answered questions to the best of their ability, they never understood why the interviewers asked a certain sequence of questions. As a result they felt vaguely uncomfortable: What was it, precisely, that the interviewer wanted to know? And why? Some respondents tried to guess at the purpose. When they guessed wrong, as they often did, their answers were irrelevant. They had strayed off the track and didn't know it. How could they know? They were never informed.

A Lack of Enthusiasm and Natural Curiosity about People and the World at Large.   Most respondents quickly sense an interviewer's level of interest in the subject. When they perceive low interest, they often turn to terse answers to avoid the pain of addressing indifferent ears. The term *curiosity* emerged as a common denominator among nineteen nationally noted interviewers who commented on their work in a book, *Interviewing America's Top Interviewers*, published in 1991 (Huber and Diggins). ABC's Barbara Walters cites three elements of a good interview: curiosity, listening, and homework. "In interviewing," says author Gay Talese, "curiosity is step one."

Failure to Listen.   Respondents who seem taciturn or evasive may simply be responding to clues that suggest you're not listening. Often the clues are obvious. They include lack of eye contact, slumped body posture, excessive note-taking, talking too much, excessive and gratuitous argumentation, absence of follow-up questions, deadpan demeanor, and an array of nervous mannerisms such as drumming fingers or sitting cross-legged and jiggling a foot. More about listening in Chapter 10.

Lack of Preparation.   Who can blame you for being nervous about an interview when you haven't done your homework? How would you know what questions to ask? You would feel as unarmed as a college student who had not bothered to study for an exam. Preparation involves learning what has come before—the historical context. This can range from reading previous articles about your respondent or topic to conducting preliminary interviews with people who know your respondent. Preparation also involves deciding what information you're seeking and what questions might logically draw out that information.

Failure to Probe.   Experienced reporters know that the best questions in any interview are the ones they didn't know they were going to ask. It's not question one—the one you've prepared—that yields the best answer. The answer to question one leads to question two and so on until you arrive at the essence of the topic. The more you've prepared for the interview, the easier you'll find it to improvise subsequent questions on the spot. It doesn't matter that those subsequent questions aren't as nicely phrased as the planned questions. It's more important that you're listening and thinking during the interview and asking new questions based on those thoughts.

Vagueness.   College students tend to generalize and intellectualize. Their interviewing and writing thus fail to realize the drama and impact that concrete details could provide. They're forever asking academic kinds of questions, such as this one of a reformed alcoholic: "Do you think alcoholism is a disease?" Such a question prompts the respondent to give an equally abstract and dull answer. Journalists, by contrast, need specifics low on the abstraction ladder, *concrete visual imagery* as one editor calls it. A group of students followed a more productive track when asking this question of a reformed alcoholic: "How much alcohol, all told, did you consume over the fifteen years of your alcoholism?" It took a while to make the calculations, but the answer emerged dramatically: nearly 2,000 gallons of wine, beer, and whiskey, consumed at a cost of forty jobs, two wives, eleven wrecked cars, and "a hell of a lot of self-esteem."

Careless Appearance.   A college student complained that she kept getting brush-offs from counselors and doctors in her attempt to conduct interviews for an article on the emotional problems of college women. Someone suggested she dress for the occasions—stop wearing to interviews the tattered blue jeans and faded sweatshirt that were her campus uniform. Dress "professionally," they suggested. When she did, her success rate improved dramatically.

Defining before Seeing.   Some reporters have a tendency to see a story first and then seek only the information that confirms their ideas. A Honolulu businessman separates reporters into two categories: the "listeners" and the "dogmatists." The dogmatic reporters, he says, "always put you on the defensive. They seem to have all the answers and they merely want you to confirm what they've decided. The listeners really listen. They take the issue from various angles, get underneath it and over it and around it. Then they want to know who else they should talk to about it."

Laziness.   Some reporters—possibly the same ones who complain about boring sources—expect brilliant, dramatic, highly entertaining answers to dumb, fumbling questions. It happens occasionally, particularly when you encounter respondents sufficiently zealous or egotistical to burst forth no matter what—politicians, maybe, or civic boosters or authors or ax grinders. But usually reporters have to do their homework and set their goals lest the results become aimless and superficial.

▶ 2

What Is an Interview?

Q. May I interview you?

A. No way! How about we just talk?

Whatever an interview is, you'd be wise not to call it by that name. To many people, the term *interview* portrays an aggressive journalist interrogating a stuffy bureaucrat or perhaps a whole contingent of loud reporters pursuing a hapless newsmaker across a courthouse corridor shouting questions: "Did the jury's verdict shock you? . . . Do you plan to appeal? . . . How does it feel? . . ." and so on.

Such experiences, as witnessed on television news, have obscured the reality of the journalist interview. Small wonder young people have trouble with the concept. The truth about interviewing offers wider dimensions. Just about any conversation in which someone offers information in response to questions can be called an interview. For journalistic purposes, we need only to add the words "on behalf of an unseen audience." The interview, then, is a *conversation designed to elicit (or exchange) information on behalf of an unseen audience.*

Interviewing, however, does involve more than simple technique: if this problem then that solution. Students frequently ask, "How do you handle the respondent who gives just yes or no answers?" or "What do you say to a hostile source who keeps complaining about an editorial our newspaper published two years ago?"

Such questions defy simple answers because an interview is a multidimensional human conversation. It runs on several levels, conscious and unconscious, verbal and nonverbal. It may *seem* mostly one-way talk, long answers to simple questions. But nonverbal communication often overrides the verbal. Respondents will take note of certain signals: a frown, an averted glance, a smile, a nod. It should be obvious to all—though clearly it's not—that frowns, averted glances, and deadpan expressions dampen responses, whereas smiles and nods and eye contact enhance them. That and a hundred other factors could influence a source's answers and even cause the yes–no response limitation.

So this is not a book of simple techniques—if this problem then that solution. Nor is it a book that will encourage you to indulge in "fill in the blanks" interviewing. You know the type—ask a prepared question, receive an answer, ask your next question (no matter what the answer), and so on. You'll soon run out of things to talk about by that format. It's one-dimensional interviewing at its worst, something a computer can do. Some computer programs already assist newspaper sports departments by handling routine sports reports.

NONJUDGMENTAL DEMEANOR: THE BASIC PRINCIPLE

What makes human communication successful? Carl Rogers, counseling psychotherapist, and an associate, F. J. Roethlisberger, proposed two theories in a classic article for the *Harvard Business Review* entitled "Barriers and Gateways to Communication." (Rogers 1952.)

The first theory suggests that communication becomes successful when Party A convinces Party B that what he or she says is true. The second suggests that communication becomes successful when Party B makes it possible for Party A to say what he or she really thinks and feels, regardless of whether B believes it's true.

Apply the second theory to journalistic interviewing. Make it possible for respondents to say what they really think and feel rather than having to think twice about what they say. Apply the principle to the most extreme examples you can imagine—an interview with that convicted rapist or child molester, for example. On television, talk show hostess Oprah Winfrey once "interviewed" a child molester at the state penitentiary via telephone. After a short discussion she expressed disdain for the molester. "You ain't letting me say nothing," he protested. She shouted, "You're a scumbag!" The audience burst into lively applause. Splendid showmanship. Wretched interviewing.

Why bother with an interview whose only purpose is to dramatize your own moral superiority? Learning something worthwhile to share with an audience—that's the goal of a good interview. And, yes, we can even learn from the pariahs of society if we seek to understand, not to accuse and judge. A good interviewer, suggests a therapist, tries to ensure that both parties emerge with their self-esteem intact.

HOW JOURNALISTS OBTAIN INFORMATION

The interview, a uniquely American invention, dominates the newsgathering methods of today's media. Reporters estimate that they gain 75 to 80 percent of their information through interviews. It wasn't always that way. In the nearly 300-year history of American newspapers, the interview became a recent innovation—and not a respected one at first. The earliest reporters relied heavily on documents and public speeches for their information. Though reporters talked frequently with public officials, they seldom mentioned those conversations in print. The origin of the first interview has caused some disagreement among historians: Was it in 1836 with James Gordon Bennett (*New York Herald*) or in 1859 with Horace Greeley (*New York Tribune*)?

It's safe to say that newspaper reporting based on interviews—questioning officials and quoting their answers by name—grew to significance in the 1860s. Not everyone approved. One contemporary observer, E. L. Godkin, editor of *The Nation*, eschewed the idea as "the joint production of some humbug of a hack politician and another humbug of a newspaper reporter"—a common reaction, especially overseas. The idea caught fire, however, particularly after President Andrew Johnson allowed himself to be interviewed and quoted. It attained further fame—and a little notoriety—when a reporter from the *New York World* interviewed Pope Pius IX in 1871, presumably a journalistic first. "The Church and the Press have kissed each other," exclaimed the *World*. (Schudson 1995.) Use of the interview continued to grow through the years even while its practitioners acknowledged its shortcomings such as interviewer bias, manipulation by sources, and the inherent perils in accurately portraying the spoken word through quoted fragments.

The other two methods of newsgathering have been documentary research and observation. Journalists continue to write from documents or to use them to prepare for interviews. But the documents tend to supplement interviews, not replace them. The same holds true for observation: alone, it seldom produces news stories (even sportswriting relies heavily on postgame interviews) but it's particularly useful in providing touches of description or action.

Many other professions use interviews, of course. The field includes interviews used for counseling, employment, oral history, opinion surveys, medicine, law enforcement, academic research, and countless business and personal conversations conducted to elicit information. It includes even something called the "persuasive" interview, the kind you normally encounter in automobile sales rooms. Most of these interviews rely on similar principles. In fact, most of our knowledge of journalistic interviews comes from research in academic areas other than journalism.

ILLUSTRATING THE JOURNALISTIC INTERVIEW

We've called the journalistic interview a "conversation between two parties to gather information on behalf of an unseen audience." Here's how it works:

A television reporter calls the state highway patrol office to inquire about a fatal auto accident. The reporter asks questions based on the information required by a typical accident story, one that begins, "A fatal car crash took the life of a local resident this afternoon. . . ." The traditional news criteria are Who, What, When, Where, How, and Why, so the telephone conversation follows that pattern: What happened? (Details given of how a car spun out of control and plunged down a steep bank into the river.) Who was involved? (Source gives names, ages, and addresses of dead and injured.) When? (This afternoon about three.) Where? (Location cited.) How? (Driver lost control on slick, wet pavement.) Why? (Slick pavement a factor and the driver had been drinking.)

The reporter may ask several cleanup questions. Were any citations issued or arrests made? Are police continuing to investigate? Will charges be filed against the drinking driver? Were any unusual circumstances involved? ("Why, yes, good thing you asked. Seems that a young passerby dove into the river to rescue a child trapped inside the car. . . .") This new information will change the story's emphasis on tonight's six o'clock news: "A dramatic river rescue amid a highway tragedy—next, after these messages . . . ."

THE CREATIVE INTERVIEW

The term *creative* has been added to this book's title to reshape the definition of the journalistic interview. Let it now read: "A two-person conversational *exchange* of information on behalf of an unseen audience to produce a level of enlightenment neither participant could produce alone."

Most beginning journalists assume that they start at zero knowledge and that through preparation and questions they learn enough about a topic or event to permit them to form questions. As you gain experience, however, you bring a higher level of knowledge to the conversation. A veteran sportswriter probably has more overall knowledge of football than the young college quarterback being interviewed. The writer can thus bring a certain historical perspective to the interview—the quarterback has many of the same passing qualities of Joe Namath, let's say, and the writer's questions will reflect that perspective.

A second aspect of creative interviewing centers on use of the imagination in picking the people you interview and in developing the overall plan for asking questions. When a group of women's magazines agreed to publish articles in support of the Equal Rights Amendment, one of them, *Woman's Day*, decided to focus on just one person: a woman who had changed her mind from being mildly against the ERA to becoming strongly in favor of it. How did the change take place? What incidents contributed to her change of heart? Anyone who has studied the techniques of dramatic literature—the characterization, suspense, and irony within a series of incidents that lead to a climax—will recognize the narrative possibilities in interviewing and writing about such a person.

So we are talking here about a form of creative writing—the kind of writing that reads like fiction in that it shows life in action, but has the impact of reality because it depicts real people involved in real events. Because we cannot fabricate the episodes that happened, we employ the interview to supply the details.

To summarize, *creative* interviewing involves two points: first, an exchange of ideas and information that creates a higher level of enlightenment, and second, seeking elements of personality and drama through the interview, such as identifying and portraying a main character confronted with a problem that's resolved after one or more dramatic incidents.

THE CREATIVE QUESTION

The very act of asking a question contains an element of creativity in its implied desire to extend your knowledge from the known to the unknown. The great breeding ground for questions involves reaching the limits of knowledge and a desire to know more. To cite a simple example, we know how to drive to Cleveland but not how to find Euclid Avenue, and so we ask.

The same principle guides our thinking in journalistic interviewing. A building catches on fire—that much we know. We don't know what caused it, so we ask. We don't know if anyone was hurt or how much damage resulted, so we ask. We interview a celebrity whom we've seen constantly on TV. We don't know what she's really like in a personal way, so we ask questions. Curiosity prompts us, for example, to wonder what it's like to be mobbed by adoring fans wherever you go, so we ask.

We ask assuming that we can't find out through pre-interview research. We conduct such research so that as we approach a respondent we know what has appeared before. The more we prepare, the more we can extend our knowns. If we discover that Ms. Celebrity hates those fans, then we wonder about other unknowns. What does she do to avoid them? When we obtain the answers to those questions, we'll have others, many of them prompted by her answers. A creative interviewer, guided by lively curiosity, never runs out of questions.

Questions, then, help you extend your knowledge into the unknown. It's a little like stepping off the firm diving board into the unknown depths of the swimming pool. Some find it frightening. Others find it exhilarating to let their questions draw them into evermore exotic unknowns and to learn from the answers. The more daring your approach, the more you will learn.

TYPES OF INTERVIEWS:
DIRECTIVE AND NONDIRECTIVE

One basic division of the journalistic interview distinguishes the *directive* from the *nondirective* interview. The terms come from the psychological counseling field. The directive interview calls for lots of questions and short answers.

Q. Did you see the robbery?

A. Yes.

Q. Where were you located when you saw it?

A. Just inside the front door.

Q. Was the robbery done by one person or more than one?

A. Far as I could tell, there was just one.

Q. Male or female?

A. Female, I think . . . it's hard to tell with the mask on, but she had a distinctly female voice.

Q. Did she come through the front door? [And so on.]

The nondirective interview lets the other person do the talking. Thus:

Q. Did you see the robbery?

A. Yes.

Q. OK, would you please start at the beginning and tell me what you saw?

A. Well, I was standing just inside the front door, and suddenly this weird character wearing a mask and sort of a clown's suit comes bursting through the front door and starts yelling "This is a stickup—everybody lie on the floor and you won't get hurt!" [And so on.]

In the second case the interviewer allowed the respondent to tell the story, whatever can be remembered. The account may be quite colorful and dramatic and, for a newswriter, quotable. At the end, the interviewer may ask some specific questions for expansion or clarification. In the situation depicted here, the nondirective interview works better. It saves a lot of questions and elicits a more accurate and colorful account. In other instances, when you're seeking specific information, the directive interview eliminates useless diversions. Often reporters will range back and forth between both forms in a single interview.

Both have a place in your interviewing technique, the directive for specific information, the nondirective for more wide-ranging conversations as in a personality interview. A variation of the directive interview is the "scheduled" interview—the type normally used for opinion polls. Here the interviewer operates from a script to interview the variety of people who have been selected to represent the general population. The interviewer asks each respondent the same questions in precisely the same way so that the responses can be tabulated.

▶ 3

The Ten Stages of the Interview

Q. General, how long have you been in military life?

A. If you don't know anything about me, why do you want to interview me?

What should you expect of a journalistic interview? Typical interviews vary widely, from quick phone calls for news briefs to marathon sessions for book-length biographies. Face-to-face interviews usually, though not always, run through ten stages. Four stages occur before you even meet your respondent. The success of the six subsequent ones depends largely on how well you accomplish the first four. The ten are:

1. Defining the purpose of the interview
2. Conducting background research
3. Requesting an interview appointment
4. Planning the interview
5. Meeting your respondent: breaking the ice
6. Asking your first questions
7. Establishing an easy rapport
8. Asking the bomb
9. Recovering from the bomb
10. Concluding the interview

Subsequent chapters will explore these elements in detail. This brief preview will help you get started.

DEFINING THE PURPOSE OF THE INTERVIEW

The two most important questions in any interview are those you ask yourself at the beginning. What information do I want? Who can best provide it? You want information about today's jail break (let's say that seven prisoners escaped this morning). Sheriff Jonathan T. Constable can provide it, and he probably will do so willingly. Interviews go especially well when both parties understand and agree to the purpose. Your desire to write a news story and the sheriff's desire for publicity that might lead to recapture form a perfect match. Sometimes it's not so easy. Suppose you want to interview Sheriff Constable about his failed marriage. He might not readily agree: "Why me?" he asks. "Why this topic? What has this to do with law enforcement?" Good questions. You'd better have some answers.

Generally, the better your answers—that is, the more precisely you define your purpose—the better your interview will go. Your candor about your purpose will sweep away barriers of distrust. Some people shy away from talking with reporters. It helps them to know precisely what you want and to learn that you've come to listen and understand, not confront or accuse. Purposes vary. Interviews with the sheriff could range beyond routine crime reports. Topics could extend from trends in crime to overcrowding in the jail. Or you could conduct a personality interview.

Or ask about the failed marriage. But why that topic? Why would a news organization or the public care about an officer's failed marriage? Let's suppose that psychological counselors have told you that men and women in high-stress occupations—police work is one of them—often develop personal problems, including failed marriages. The divorce rate among police officers is higher than that of the population as a whole. You learn about the formation of a new support group, "Stressed-Out Cops Anonymous." Now we have a potential news story. The interview wouldn't focus just on one man's failed marriage but would explore the relationship between occupational stress and domestic problems. Specifically, did job stress lead to a failed marriage? Would Sheriff Constable agree to talk? We will see.

A final note on purpose: Sometimes the procedure—need for information first, identity of the right respondent second—works in reverse. Ross Perot, the Texas billionaire and one-time presidential candidate, plans to visit your city tomorrow and will make himself available for an exclusive interview. What will you interview him *about?* The more you can narrow down the purpose to a specific topic or set of related topics, the more interesting information you will receive.

CONDUCTING BACKGROUND RESEARCH

If you're interviewing Ross Perot tomorrow, then start work today. Read everything you can about him—clips or database files, magazine articles, anything that will acquaint you with the issues and events that have touched his life. Only by research—reviewing what's gone before—can you grasp what questions may lead you into new territory. *New* is the key word. Without the background you might repeat the same questions already asked a hundred times and end up presenting material already reported.

The nature of the story dictates the kind of research needed. The reporter conducting interviews on how work-related stress leads to marital problems will benefit from reading books and articles on marriage and family topics and from interviewing family counselors—some of this even before approaching Sheriff Constable. The reporter writing the personality profile about the sheriff should interview others who know him—colleagues, enemies, friends, family, ex-wife—anyone who can provide insight into his character.

Not every interview requires massive research, however. The veteran sportswriter interviewing a college quarterback may rely mostly on memory or clips of similar stories done in the past. Reporters in a hurry, as often happens in busy news offices, may find that other reporters or editors can offer suggestions about the respondent or about the topic under discussion. Suppose you've been assigned to interview the undersecretary of agriculture during a stopover at the airport. You have only twenty minutes to prepare. A quick call to the agricultural extension agent or the president of your local Wheat Grower's League can yield enough information on farm issues to permit an interview. Reporters often conduct research in two steps: preliminary research to help them secure an interview appointment, the rest afterwards.

REQUESTING AN INTERVIEW APPOINTMENT

No one is obligated to grant you an interview. Keep that in mind as you call for an appointment. The process seems simple—you identify yourself, explain what you want, ask for an appointment, and settle on time and place. But if you have not met the person before, and if the topic seems out of the ordinary, then you may have to sell yourself much as a salesperson would. Your own enthusiasm can help. The task of persuading Sheriff Constable to talk about job stress and marriage problems, for instance, may start like this, after you've identified yourself:

"I've begun research on an interesting topic, and I'm quite excited about it. It's about the relationship between high-stress jobs and domestic problems. I've talked with a marriage counselor and have read some articles, and I find that one spinoff from high-stress careers is marital conflicts. I've been talking with some police officers about what they've learned from their experiences that may help other people cope with similar problems. Can we talk about what *you've* learned from your experience—what you'd tell other police officers about the problem?"

Your arguments pull the proposed report out of the juicy gossip arena and into something potentially enlightening. Such proposals may require negotiation, however. Sheriff Constable may reply that he'd be glad to talk if you don't use his name. Or that if you use his name, he'd talk less candidly. Or that he'll talk about how officers cope with stress but feels unqualified to discuss its effect on their families. Or that he'll talk candidly about most things but not about his son, the one who died of a drug overdose.

Do you prefer less candor in exchange for identification? Do you have counter proposals? Here's one possible response: "I don't want to embarrass anyone. I'm planning to write a feature story for the *Times*. I'll interview about fifteen people in high-stress occupations, and if I could get each one to tell me just one important *lesson* learned from their experience I'd be delighted. For example, one officer took a counselor's suggestion that he call his wife occasionally and leave a verbal "candy kiss" on her answering machine—a brief love message that she could play when she returned home. She was thrilled with the first one—played it back fifteen times. So he learned something important, and they're still married. Those are the kinds of lessons I'll be seeking in my interviews."

Experienced journalists have an advantage in the negotiations if their previous reports have gained a favorable reputation in the community. It helps to show clips or videotapes from similar projects in the past. An unfavorable reputation in the community makes your task harder, to say the least.

Suppose the sheriff agrees to discuss occupational stress and its effect on domestic life with at least one example of a lesson learned from his own experience. Should you write up a contract? Of course not. As an interview progresses, attitudes change. Twenty minutes into the interview the sheriff may come to trust you more (or less), his candor may increase (or decrease), and the conversation will rise to higher levels of candor than ever imagined, or fall to lower. The direction up or down depends maybe 5 percent on luck and the rest on your conversational skills, especially nonjudgmental listening and your own (preferably enthusiastic) response to what you're hearing.

PLANNING THE INTERVIEW

The more you plan your interview, the more you can make it into a seemingly unplanned and casual discussion that your respondent will enjoy and from which you will learn much. Here are some planning principles:

First, plan to explain again the interview purpose when you meet your respondent. Don't neglect to make clear your goals (especially if they've changed since you first talked) so that the conversation can proceed directly toward the goals. Some reporters have found that the statement of goals is the only "question" required. A good respondent merely lays out the details that fulfill the goals.

Second, plan how you'll greet a person you've never seen before. Plan some seemingly trivial icebreaker comments to get things started. Sheriff Constable is an avid fly fisherman, so if you know the difference between a dragonfly nymph and a Baetis mayfly, you'll feel right at home. If you're no expert, plan at least to ask about his fishing luck and let him wax eloquent for a few moments.

Third, jot down the topics you'll want to cover with your questions. Make sure they're consistent with your purpose. Perhaps write out some questions, particularly the first serious one beyond icebreaker stage.

Fourth, plan to ask for examples and illustrative anecdotes and summarizing comments. Above all, plan to listen. Plan to respond to the answers you get with new questions, probes that focus on important points even though you don't know what those questions will be.

Build into your plans the likelihood of unexpected answers and surprising turns in the conversation. Indeed, the better planned your interview, the greater the chances that it will not go according to plan. That's good. The well-prepared interviewer does not seek answers that merely confirm what is already known. The interviewer seeks to venture into new territory. The sudden fresh insight, the new twists, the new pathways explored, the unexpected turns, the recalling of new illustrative anecdotes—all these are the golden nuggets of interviewing. They come more easily to the interviewer who has planned for them and who can recognize them when they drop out of the conversation.

MEETING YOUR RESPONDENT: BREAKING THE ICE

Strangers meeting for the first time normally test the conversational waters with icebreaking techniques born of social convention. "Hello, how are you? Nasty weather outside. Have you ever seen such cold weather? By the way, we have a mutual friend—your college buddy, Charlie Frazer, says hello." And so forth. This is the time to bring out your remarks about fly fishing or other icebreakers uniquely suited to your respondent. Keen observation of the respondent's surroundings will yield on-the-spot possibilities. ("I love the view from your window. . . . Your wall posters of outdoor scenes remind me of my vacation in Colorado . . . .")

Use of small talk identifies the conversation as a human one, not a mechanical Q–A format. But some busy respondents want to get right down to business and resent wasting time on trivia. Others seem to need the sense of trust and security that builds through small talk. Be prepared to go either way.

The other person will use these moments to size you up, too, deciding whether you're sincere and trustworthy. One authority suggests that what

Breaking the ice

happens in the first four minutes of a meeting between strangers largely determines what happens thereafter, so starting on the right foot is important. (Zunin 1972.) This early conversation should exude a friendly, amiable tone. Humor can lubricate the conversation with most people.

ASKING YOUR FIRST QUESTIONS

The best interviewers will guide the opening small talk into the first serious questions so smoothly that the transition is barely noticed. They gently steer the small talk to business talk. One moment you were talking about fly fishing and suddenly along come your first "business" questions—is fishing a good way to cope with stress? Does he recommend that more officers take up fishing or similar hobbies? Should they take their spouses and kids along? Would that help stabilize their marriages? What other ways could officers cope with stress and save their marriages? What about your own marriage? Your interview is off and running. Don't forget to outline the purpose of your interview if you haven't done so by this stage ("Let me pause a moment to tell you what I'm looking for, and then I want to get back to fishing. . .").

ESTABLISHING AN EASY RAPPORT

This is the heart of your interview, the part where the exchange of information flows freely and candidly. If you've done the first six stages properly, this one should follow naturally. The conversation should settle into an easy rapport, something akin to the two barefooted women talking, as noted in Chapter 1. The more informal the conversation, the more you will learn. The more you listen and respond enthusiastically to what the source says, the more you will learn. And the more you show your curiosity and your preparation by the questions you ask, the more you will learn.

When things go wrong, you may have neglected an earlier stage. Perhaps you didn't explain your purpose sufficiently or you failed, despite your best intentions, to convince your respondent of the importance of your mission. Perhaps in the first four minutes, the respondent has judged you untrustworthy.

But you may find it amazing, as I have occasionally, how a bad start can still reach this mellow stage of easy rapport. I can cite an example from experience. I'd been interviewing public officials about their relationships with the news media. I had an appointment with a city manager. I called his community relations assistant, identified myself, said I was working on a research project to determine public officials' attitudes toward the news media. Could I talk with her about Mr. So-and-so's experiences with the media?

She replied testily that she'd never heard of anything so outrageous in her life. Who was I to be asking those kinds of questions? She hinted darkly that I must have some ulterior motive—just what kind of dirt was I looking for?

Such a response from a public relations person bewildered and angered me. I tried to explain further, and I recall my use of the term "interview" set off another tirade. I toyed with hanging up but couldn't think of a devastating final remark. But after much peevish discussion I realized I had not really explained the details of my mission and how she fit in. Finally I did, in the halting, wayward manner typical of a slow-witted guy on the ropes.

Then something remarkable happened. I can't explain it except to say she mellowed out. So did I. The conversation began anew. She made suggestions for my interview with her boss. We made a date for coffee a day or two hence. We had a friendly conversation, talking and laughing about the episode. I'm surprised we didn't fall in love. Lessons:

1. Begin by explaining—fully, in detail—who you are, what you want, and why.
2. People are unpredictable, paradoxical, mysterious. Marvelously so. As a result, conversational rapport between two persons can emerge under the worst of circumstances.
3. Rapport—based on mutual interest and mutual trust—forms the essence of the interview. With it you can fumble like the fictional TV detective Columbo and still receive candid answers. Without it you can ask superb questions and receive little or nothing.

ASKING THE BOMB

If you have potentially sensitive or embarrassing questions to ask, do so late in the interview, expecting that the rapport you've established will carry the conversation through dangerous minefields. The term *bomb* doesn't imply aggression. Rather it means that caution in handling sensitive questions will prevent an emotional reaction.

As you plan an interview, you'll realize that some questions will be easy and pleasant to answer and others will not. The county sheriff who speaks so openly about stress in the men and women he oversees may balk at talking about his own stress, maybe his own problems with drinking, depression, or whatever. Yet he may tell *you*—if rapport has been established in Stage 7— because you're the sensitive interviewer who has come to understand, not the mean-spirited journalist out to impale a victim.

Do not assume that all interviews contain a bomb stage and accompanying uneasy rapport. Most do not. But remember that seemingly innocent questions can produce emotional reactions, too. You asked a naive question about childhood memories and you received a tearful response. How could you have known that you were stepping on an emotional landmine?

RECOVERING FROM THE BOMB

Sensitively handled, Stage 8 merges into Stage 9 with little loss of rapport. Sometimes a little human reassurance can help at this point ("I'm sorry to hear about those problems. . . . They could have happened to anyone"). Rarely do embarrassing questions kill an interview if the original rapport has been good. If rapport has been shaky in the first place, you'll appreciate the fact that these were among the last questions you planned to ask.

CONCLUDING THE INTERVIEW

Some interviewers find it hard to break away gracefully from conversations that have gone well. Try following these steps:

1. Offer to stop the interview on time but carry on if the respondent seems eager and gives useful information. Or make another appointment.
2. Signal your intent to close, perhaps by reexamining your notes to see if you've covered everything ("I see time is just about out; may I take a moment to review my notes?").
3. Ask if the respondent has any "final thoughts," anything to add to what has been said. You may get answers to questions you didn't think to ask.
4. Leave a business card. "Call me if you have any further thoughts."

5. Ask for any documents mentioned in the interview; sources often mention reports, letters, and other materials they're willing to let you see.
6. Leave the door open by asking if you may call back if further questions come up.
7. Say good-bye—"and thanks a lot for your help."
8. Watch for the afterglow, an extension of the rapport. Some of the best comments come as you are standing at the door saying good-bye. Now the respondent, relaxing after the "ordeal," will offer some of the most refreshing insights and most quotable summarizing remarks. Listen carefully.
9. Write a thank-you note for interview response and cooperation above and beyond the norm. It will work wonders for obtaining future interviews with the sheriff and for using him as a reference to secure interviews with other sources.

▶ 4

Elements of
the Interview:
A Case History

Q. Judge Hammond, you've served forty years on the Superior Court
Bench, and today you're retiring. How do you feel?

A. With my hands.

What's a typical, routine news interview like? Consider a hypothetical example, one based on actual news reports, to illustrate those interview stages.
Let's say the *News–Tribune* city editor summons reporter Betty Paterson one
afternoon and asks her to write a "dull, routine story, a 200-word advance"
about a retired teacher giving a lecture tomorrow night about the history of
lighthouses in the United States.

"*What?!* You know how I hate dull, routine stories!"

"Just kidding," says Betty's boss, acknowledging that she often chafes at
the term routine. In her mind, *routine news story* is a contradiction in terms. If
it's news, it ought to be new, or at least different, not routine.

Shall we eavesdrop on the interview? Yes. Many journalists say they
learned interviewing largely by listening to telephone conversations of experienced reporters at nearby desks. This interviewing case history may offer
the closest thing to eavesdropping possible in a text. The model interview illustrates several principles already discussed:

1. *Structure.* This example contains most of an interview's ten stages. But
   this brief conversation takes some shortcuts typical of telephone interviews.

2. *Rapport.* The principle of working toward a harmonious personal relationship shows up in the dialogue, largely through the reporter's preparation, her enthusiasm for the topic, her informal telephone demeanor, and her encouraging responses such as "that's interesting."
3. *Creativity.* The principle of "creative" interviewing shows in the reporter's attempt to bring something fresh to her story.

DEFINING THE PURPOSE

Starting this project, reporter Betty Paterson knows only that historian Clarissa McGee will speak tomorrow night at the monthly meeting of a civic organization. She will obtain additional information via the interview so that tomorrow morning's *News–Tribune* can inform readers of an upcoming public event.

Reporters more or less automatically define a purpose for their interviews, one largely governed by the kind of story planned. Clearly a 200-word advance requires less information than, say, a major personality feature or an ambitious documentary about lighthouses. The reporter will need the speech's title, its time and place, the identity of the agency sponsoring the talk, some background on the speaker, and perhaps an example or two of the content of the speech—just enough to give a clear preview so that people can decide if they'd like to attend. A simple mission. Betty adds another purpose to most of her interviews, however: *find something interesting.* Find a *RAFF*, as Betty calls it: a *Remarkable And Fascinating Fact.*

BACKGROUND RESEARCH

Betty counts among her worst faults the fact that she loves learning new things and meeting new people. That's why she became a reporter—to become a lifelong learner and get paid for it. With her imagination Betty pictures lonely outposts solidly embedded on rocky headlands or offshore islands, stormy nights, angry seas, lost ships, ships dramatically saved from doom, lonely lighthouse keepers desperately trying to avoid going insane, maybe even a Gothic-style murder mystery.

But on to reality. Betty consults the newspaper library, which contains reports of previously published items indexed by name and topic. First question: Who is Clarissa McGee? Many newspapers use computerized files, so Betty can obtain information on previous stories almost at the touch of a button. She asks the computer to search for stories containing "Clarissa McGee" and finds fourteen "hits," stories about her in the past two years. Betty learns that she is a retired high school history teacher who has won numerous teaching awards, that she has traveled widely to visit lighthouses, that she has written a book, *Lore of the Sea*, and that she's a popular lecturer, often addressing groups around the country. Audiences loved her in Kansas City where she spoke last March about the many ghosts that haunt seacoasts around the world. Slides and videotapes often augment her lectures and her appearances on television talk shows.

By asking the computer to search for "Lighthouses," Betty finds three more articles worthy of note. From them she learns that the United States once had as many as 1,400 lighthouses serving as navigational beacons for seafarers. Now the number has dwindled to a mere 750, of which fewer than 400 still operate.

PLANNING THE INTERVIEW

Perhaps the ghost stories stir Betty's enthusiasm. Or perhaps Betty believes that few topics have the potential for producing so many RAFFs as lighthouse history. She even envisions writing a major feature story about McGee because the file contains no such story from the recent past. Perhaps later. Today's story is simple. Betty will ask the questions necessary to establish the who, what, where, and when of the forthcoming event, as well as the how (will she show slides? videotapes?) and the why. Curiosity prompts the reporter to wonder why a local teacher should devote her life to studying the sea.

True to her creative nature, Betty toys with questions that might ferret out those RAFFs. She runs through what she already knows from her background research and tries to develop questions that project from the known to the unknown. To do so, Betty lets her professional imagination wander.

Known: Lighthouses are declining in number. Unknown: Will they eventually all disappear? Is anything being done to save them? What's replacing them—electronic innovations, perhaps?

Known: McGee has spoken about ghosts of the sea. Unknown: Do ghosts frequent lighthouses, too?

Known: She's visited lighthouses. Unknown: Has she developed favorites among them? What's the best, the worst, the loneliest, the most precariously perched lighthouse she's visited?

Known: She's devoted much time and effort studying the sea. Unknown: Why? During the interview, the answers themselves will turn unknowns into knowns—which in turn prompts further unknowns. Suppose, for example, that the question, "What's the most precariously perched lighthouse you've visited?" leads to an answer: "Thunderation Point" (not a real name). Now a new unknown: Where's that? Why is it your choice for most precarious? And so on, one answer leading to another question until the reporter determines that she has the information she needs for a remarkable and fascinating story.

Betty envisions the kind of story she might write. She will avoid, if possible, the routine story, one that begins, "Clarissa McGee, noted historian and authority on lore of the sea, will speak on [insert topic or title] tomorrow night at 7. . . . " In her mind Betty develops a crude sketch of the story she'd like to write:

> *You probably didn't know [Remarkable And Fascinating Fact] about the na-
> tion's 750 standing lighthouses. You might not even know [RAFF #2].*
>
> *Tonight at 7 Clarissa McGee, local authority on lighthouses and sea
> lore, will discuss why [RAFF #1] is among the strangest mysteries of
> the lighthouses that guide seafarers along [insert number] miles of U.S.
> seacoast. . . .*

The preliminary research and planning help guide reporters' curiosity and imagination. Because Betty eagerly seeks RAFFs in every interview, she usually finds them—a self-fulfilling prophecy. Betty has developed ways to find them. For example, consider another known: lighthouses are lonely sentinels. Seek a related unknown: have lighthouse keepers ever gone crazy because of the loneliness of their task? (Wouldn't it be fascinating to find examples of those who did?) If "yes," plan to probe further: "Can you cite an example?" If "no" or "rarely," plan to ask, "How do they keep from going crazy?" (Maybe a RAFF emerges in the unique ways they cope.)

Betty seldom writes out her questions, but prefers to jot down a few words to remind her of items she plans to cover. Thus a word like "decline" will remind her to ask about the dwindling numbers of lighthouses; "save" reminds her to ask about attempts to preserve them; "ghosts" reminds her to ask about haunted lighthouses; "lonesome–crazy" will guide her into questions about lighthouse keepers. Betty notes eight elements:

1. Details [who, what, where, etc.]
2. Decline?
3. Save?
4. Replace?
5. Ghosts?
6. Loneliest/most precarious?
7. Lonesome–crazy?
8. McGee's start—why?

Some reporters write more elaborate questions, but Betty prefers to improvise on the spot. She likes to keep the conversation informal and perhaps even a little rambling—just like real people talking. Betty knows that she may not cover all of those topics in detail. She may not cover some at all. She likely will cover topics she could not envision at this preliminary stage. She will remain alert for whole new lines of inquiry based on what happens in the interview itself—topics that just drop out of the conversation. The best reporters adapt quickly to new information, and they don't mind improvising their questions on the spot, even at the risk of sounding clumsy. In short, a creative interview does not follow a straight line of Qs and As but a winding conversational pathway in which a professional observer and a knowledgeable source compare ideas.

ON THE PHONE

Phone interviews contain fewer icebreaking social amenities than do personal ones. They are more businesslike. They require a reporter to state promptly the purpose of the call. People resent "junk" sales calls. Note how Betty strives to make clear immediately that her proposed article will serve the respondent's purpose as well as her own. Eager verbal responses—"Uh-huh. . . . That's interesting. . . . Mmmmm"—lubricate conversations where nonverbal signs are absent. Through the interview, the reporter will take notes, perhaps on a computer, perhaps by hand, depending on personal preference.

A. Hello?

Q. Hi. May I speak to Clarissa McGee, please?

A. This is she.

Q. Well, good afternoon! My name is Betty Paterson, and I've just been reading about you and your work with lighthouses and the lore of the sea. I'm a reporter for the *News–Tribune.* I've just learned of the talk you're giving tomorrow night, and I'm planning to write a short article for tomorrow's paper about it that I hope will enlarge your audience. Before I can write that article, though, I have a few questions—would you mind talking with me for a few minutes on the phone so that I can get the information I need? [Note the ego reinforcement: I've been reading about *you* . . . hope to enlarge *your* audience. . . . Who can resist such an approach?]

A. I'd be glad to help you any way I can.

Q. Thank you. I trust I'm not interrupting anything?

A. No, go right ahead.

Q. Good. This will be a brief story citing the time and place and topic of your speech, and I also hope to include some little touch of fascinating folklore about lighthouses—maybe something about ghosts in the lighthouses or lighthouse keepers gone crazy or something. . . . Is it true that some of them are haunted?

A. Just about all of them are.

Q. Really? How interesting! [Bingo! This could be RAFF #1.]

A. Well, I won't swear to it, but I've visited a lot of them and I usually could find a local person to tell me some fanciful story about a ghost that frequents the place. Lighthouses are such legendary and romantic places, you know, so picturesque and all. Well, it's hard to imagine such a legendary scene and not find a ghost story attached to it.

Q. That's interesting. I read that there are about 750 lighthouses still standing in the United States—how many of those have you visited?

A. Close to 300.

Q. I want to get back to ask you about some of those 300 and especially about the ones that are haunted, but I do have a few elementary questions to ask, especially about your speech.

A. OK.

Q. First I need to know the title of your talk, when and where it will take place, and also the name of the civic group that is sponsoring it.

A. I'm calling it "The Case of the Disappearing Lighthouse and Other Tragedies of the Sea," and it will be illustrated by slides. [Gives further details.]

Q. Sounds like interesting material . . . give me just a moment to get all this in my notes . . . the clacking you may hear in the background is my taking notes on my computer. . . . OK, let's see, uh, is this a case history of a particular lighthouse disappearing?

A. Well, the talk is about the sad state of our lighthouses, how they're falling into disrepair. We have only half as many as we once had, and we are losing lighthouses at the rate of several a year.

Q. What's happening to them?

A. They're being decommissioned and left to disintegrate. I do have several specific examples that I will be talking about.

Q. Well, I think it would be fun to include a tantalizing tidbit about a specific lighthouse in my story. For example, what's America's most precariously perched lighthouse that you've seen?

A. That's easy—Tillamook Rock.

Q. Really? Where is it? And what's precarious about it?

A. The lighthouse stands perched on a tiny, rocky island in the Pacific Ocean a mile off the Oregon coast. "Terrible Tilly," they used to call it. It's still there but no longer in use. Ferocious winter storms often stranded the lighthouse crew for weeks at a time.

Q. Wow! The loneliness—it must have driven the keepers crazy. Or did they have ways of coping?

A. One lonely lighthouse keeper at Terrible Tilly amused himself by writing notes about the idyllic life on his little island. He put them in bottles and cast them into the sea, hoping that they'd be discovered by beautiful Polynesian maidens who would return his greeting.

Q. Did he hear from any Polynesian maidens?

A. No, but he did receive a note from a woman who lived on the Oregon coast just a few miles from the lighthouse. It said her husband found his note inside a dead sea lion. She said, "My husband thinks you're nuts—Tillamook Rock is the most godforsaken place he knows of!"

Q. Great story! [A RAFF suitable for the opening of her story, Betty thinks.] You seem to have a lot of enthusiasm for the topic—I'm curious to know how you undertook lighthouses as an area of interest.

A. I think it's because of a deprived childhood.

Q. Deprived childhood?

A. It's human nature to spend one's adult years making up for some child-hood deprivation. The hungry kid dreams of big meals and eventually takes up gourmet cooking. The scrawny kid too small for athletics becomes a sportswriter. I grew up on the plains of Kansas and never saw the sea until I was twenty-three. So naturally I thrived on sea lore as a child, read every book on the sea, *Moby-Dick* thirteen times, saw every sea movie. I remember the first time I saw the ocean. It was on a trip to California and we went to the beach at Santa Monica. What a disappointment!

Q. Disappointment? Why?

A. The Pacific Ocean just didn't look that big. It didn't look any bigger or rougher than Lake Michigan! I don't know what I expected—mountainous waves crashing against the shore I guess; I expected to be thrilled—terrified, even.

Q. And you weren't?

A. Not at Santa Monica. There were times, however, when I was working on a fishing boat in the Gulf of Alaska. . . .

Q. You worked on a *fishing boat*?

A. I was young and single then, and as a teacher I had my summers free, and. . . .

Perhaps we can leave the interview at this point. The interview will proceed through the planned topics (rearranging and skipping and adding as the con-versation progresses). We have thus seen the interview through seven stages: defining purpose, background research, planning, meeting/request for inter-view (combined on phone), first questions, and rapport stages. The bomb and recovery stages don't apply to this kind of interview. That leaves the problem of concluding the interview.

Q. Clarissa, I think I have enough for my story—may I take a moment to check a few things with you? [As often happens, reporter and source are on a first-name basis now.] First, am I correct in assuming that the main thrust of your speech is the decline and deterioration of lighthouses around the country?

A. Yes, together with the attempts of citizens and groups to restore and preserve them.

Q. I see. You'll talk about what's happening to the survivors?

A. Yes, some have been taken over by civic groups for restoration, some have been purchased by private citizens—a few have even been converted into small inns.

Q. How interesting! I'll make a note of that. Can you think of anything else that belongs in the story?

A. I suspect you have more than enough.

Q. OK. I do want to check some minor details—I have your name spelled [spells out name], and I plan to identify you as an "author and historian, retired from East Jefferson High"—is that correct? [The details may seem minor but they're essential to avoid error; it takes only a moment to double check names, ages, addresses, titles, and similar details.] And one final point—may I call you back if, in the middle of writing this, a question occurs to me that I should have asked but forgot?

A. Of course.

Q. Great! Good-bye, and thanks a lot.

SOME POINTS TO REMEMBER

Here are some points illustrated by the case history in this chapter:

1. Interviews work best when the reporter has prepared through research and has thought through some areas of inquiry.
2. You'll secure a more productive interview when you envision the ideal form a story might take and look for the kind of information that will help to produce that story. Make sure, though, that you do this objectively—do it in terms of story technique rather than content.
3. Interviewers should communicate fully. Tell your source the kind of story you envision, one filled with fascinating facts. Don't keep secrets.
4. Accuracy is vital. Double check your understanding of concepts such as the central theme of the forthcoming speech.
5. Small details are important such as double checking names and titles.
6. Ideas for future stories often emerge from these conversations. Perhaps the speech should be covered or a story written about Clarissa McGee and her lifelong romance with the sea.
7. Note-taking is important. In telephone conversations it helps to report that you are taking notes, which will explain any delays in responding or asking another question.

8. Repeating a few words from something a speaker said earlier can encourage further discussion, as in the reporter's comment, "deprived childhood?" and "disappointment?"
9. If Betty writes a story bursting with RAFFs, her editors may agree to give her work greater length and better page positioning than originally intended. It's just one of the rewards of creative interviewing technique.

▶ 5

Asking Questions

Q. Princess, if it's not too personal, can you tell me why you never married? Are you just not interested in men, or what?

A. Not interested? I'll have you know that I've had no fewer than thirty-three lovers in the past twenty years!

Q. Ah. . . . [blushes]

A. So! You didn't expect such candor, I see. It seems they didn't teach you in journalism school to cope with real life!

Students frequently complain that they "never know what to ask" in an interview. The irreverent reply: "Whatever you ask, make sure it's a question." Judge a man by his questions, said Voltaire, not his answers.

How do you decide what to ask? Simple—use your human curiosity. Sources tend to respond to what they perceive as the underlying curiosity more than to the questions themselves. The questions are merely conduits fueled from the reservoir of curiosity. Can you watch a great teacher in action—call him Larry Lecture, a teacher who holds students spellbound—and not wonder about him? How did he become so smooth and beguiling? What's he like in ordinary life? Does he ever get stage fright? Was he bashful as a kid? Did a lecture ever go bad? By contrast, how about Professor Barry Boring, the dullest lecturer in the business? Do you not wonder about him, too? Does he realize how dull he is? Has he tried to do anything about it? What kinds of thoughts flash through the minds of his students midway through Boring's treatise on Joycean epiphanies? Ask, and they may tell stories vastly more interesting than the lecture.

What a wonderful key the question becomes. It unlocks hidden treasures. You gain entry to all the little human ironies that make life interesting for a journalist. Wouldn't it be interesting to learn that Larry Lecture was so bashful as a kid that he once feigned illness to avoid giving a scheduled five-minute speech to a high school class? Don't laugh—it happens. People disclose unexpected events, even embarrassments, if you ask. One of my students, Dwight Schuh, interviewed a history professor known for interesting lectures. Curious, Schuh asked whether a lecture had ever gone astray. The professor said he had an iron-clad rule of lecturing—if he encountered among his students three yawns in unison, he'd immediately drop in midsentence whatever he was saying and spin an illustrative and entertaining anecdote. That worked for years—until one of his students caught on to the technique. She arranged with two friends who, on a given signal, would join her in yawning. "The first time that happened, I fell for it like a ton of bricks," the professor confessed. "By the third time, with the same three women involved, I knew I'd been had. Then I thought to myself, what an extraordinarily clever young woman!"

Given, then, that curiosity remains the force behind the questions, let us turn to the questions themselves.

"I understand that you, and/or, your organization, are directly responsible for the recent upsurge (or as some would have it, incline) in the current situation facing the global, economic environment; or, at the very least, partially in favor of inverted trade sanctions against all, or most, of the European Common Market, at least according to my most reliable sources. Would you care to comment?"

PHRASE YOUR QUESTIONS SIMPLY AND CLEARLY

Even simple questions can be troublesome, such as the "blind-man's bluff" series of questions illustrated here in a dialogue with a weather forecaster.

Q. Is it going to rain tomorrow?

A. No.

Q. So we'll have good weather?

A. Depends on what you mean by "good."

Q. Sunny?

A. No.

Q. What, then?

A. Snow.

Q. Why didn't you say so?

A. You didn't ask.

A clumsy dialogue. By asking about rain the reporter blindly closed out all other possibilities. Had the reporter asked, "What's your prediction for tomorrow's weather?" the answer would have been easy: snow. True, the forecaster was playing games, but the lesson remains clear: Ask what you really mean. Many bureaucrats take advantage of verbal fuzziness to evade your questions.

Make them clear and direct, as well as unbiased. Note how people display personal biases through questions. "I don't feel well," says Jim. His friend, Bill, asks, "Is that because you drank too much last night?" Bill is not asking a question; he's expressing an opinion about Jim's drinking. A cleaner question would have been, "Why don't you feel well?"

Avoid also the overdefined question. A student once asked this question of a police officer who visited our class:

Q. Sergeant, have you ever had to use your gun, I mean, more than just target practice, like, for example, shooting at a fleeing robber, or maybe a hostage situation, or maybe like so many police officers I've read about, you've never actually used your gun in anger, so to speak—

A. Yes, I—

Q. —and then again maybe. . . .

The student just couldn't let loose of the question. What's wrong with making it simple? Use follow-up questions if the answer doesn't provide detail.

Q. Sergeant, have you ever had to fire your gun in the line of duty? [Note the change from *use* to *fire* to avoid ambiguity.]

A. Yes, just one time!

Q. Would you tell us about it?

OPEN VERSUS CLOSED QUESTIONS

Questions come in two broad categories: open and closed. Open questions are general and allow leeway for the answer. Closed questions are specific and call for a specific answer. Examples of the open question:

"What can you tell me about yourself?"

"Mr. Kennerly, after seven broken marriages, what have you concluded about the institution of marriage?"

"Governor Caxton, what are your views on the legislature's tax-reduction package?"

Examples of closed questions:

"Governor Caxton, do you plan to veto the legislature's tax-reduction package?"

"Sergeant, what type of weapon was used to kill the victim?"

"Admiral, where will the battle fleet be sent next?"

As the examples suggest, both types have their place in the journalistic interview. Sometimes inexperienced interviewers jump too quickly into the closed question. A reporter approaches a witness to an auto accident and asks, "Was the driver of the green car drunk?" The question not only suggests a bias, but it calls for a conclusion that the witness is not able to draw. Even if the driver were staggering as though drunk, other explanations are possible, an injury perhaps. A more objective question would be, "What did you see?"

Some questions straddle the two categories: "Senator Fogg, I understand you had an argument last night with the President over foreign aid. What happened?" Is that open or closed? Perhaps more closed than open, but a little of both because it allows the senator wide latitude in commenting on foreign affairs.

SEQUENCING OF QUESTIONS: THE FUNNEL

Journalistic questions typically come in sequence, either from specific to general or from general to specific. Comments that emerge from general questions will logically lead to a request for details. The reverse is also true. Here are hypothetical examples of both. First the general to specific, sometimes called the *funnel*. Note how closed questions follow the open.

Q. Coach Meyers, as your football team moves into the first game of the season, do you see any major problems ahead?

A. I'd say injuries are gonna slow us down quite a bit in the first week or two.

Q. Oh, you've had some injuries among your players?

A. You bet.

Q. Who?

A. Well, Charlie Rice for one. He's the guy we originally planned to start at quarterback.

Q. Rice is out? What happened to him?

A. Sprained an ankle in practice yesterday. . . .

The reporter will ferret out the additional specifics about what happened to this and other players. A specific-to-general sequence ("reverse funnel") looks like this:

Q. Coach Meyers, I notice Charlie Rice is on crutches—what happened?

A. [Gives details.]

Q. How is his absence going to affect your opening game next week?

A. It's gonna slow us down quite a bit the first week or two. . . [and so forth].

OPENING QUESTIONS

Many journalists consider an interview's first questions "throwaways" intended merely to get the interview under way. Yet they do help to start the interview on the right track. Imagine the television interview where an articulate but nervous guest stumbles over the first question, something unexpected. This proves so embarrassing that the guest never recovers. Better to throw away an initial innocuous question or two than to throw away an entire interview. Opening questions come in two categories, icebreakers and first moves.

An earlier chapter suggested some icebreaking comments on first meeting your respondent: remarking on personal effects or the office scene or reviewing mutual acquaintances or topics in which you share an interest, such as fishing or art. Icebreakers can also serve as introduction to your first moves—your first business questions. "How about them Dallas Cowboys— did you see last night's game?" you ask Governor Caxton, an enthusiastic football fan. After ecstatic moments of football talk you move deftly onto the business at hand with a transition: "Speaking of the Cowboys, I wonder if you consider your speech to the legislature last night a first down and three yards to the goal line kind of scenario?" (Ask a metaphorical question, maybe get a metaphorical answer.)

Whatever those first serious questions, they should contain four qualities:

1. They should be easy to answer, particularly for a broadcast interview.
2. They should reinforce the respondent's self-esteem. Save touchy questions for later.
3. They should demonstrate that the interviewer has prepared for the conversation.
4. They should follow logically from the interviewer's announced statement of purpose.

FILTER QUESTIONS

Filter questions establish a respondent's qualifications to answer subsequent questions. You arrive at the scene of a tragedy and ask, "What happened?" You're told lots of details, only to learn that the respondent didn't really see it. A simple filter question—"Where were you when the building exploded?"—would have avoided the wasted effort.

A filter question proves useful whenever you're interviewing a person with unknown credentials. For a story about runaway children, you approach a police officer you don't know personally, and you ask a filter question: "Sergeant, how much experience have you had dealing with runaway kids?"

Filter questions enhance conversational rapport with highly qualified sources and weaken it with those poorly qualified. Questions that qualify you as an authority reinforce your ego. Remember, though, that celebrated people resent questions that advance preparation could answer. Don't ask Sally Field the extent of her acting experience.

PROBE (FOLLOW-UP) QUESTIONS

The probe represents the heart of the interview. It encourages the source to explain or elaborate on something already said. Imagine the response to the hypothetical dialogue at the head of this chapter. The reporter has asked about the princess's unmarried status, and she replies that she's had thirty-three lovers in twenty years. Here are typical kinds of probes designed to encourage elaboration:

1. *Passive probe.* "Hmmmm. . . . I see. . . . " It's probably accompanied by a deadpan expression. This kind of passiveness suggests that the interviewer

wants to hear more, though respondents sometimes take it to mean lack of interest.

2. *Responsive.* "Really! . . . . How interesting!" Accompanied by more animated facial expression.

3. *Mirroring.* Mirroring means repeating pertinent examples of the source's own words: "thirty-three lovers. . . ." It's used effectively by counseling interviewers working with psychologically troubled patients.

4. *Silent.* An expectant kind of silence, accompanied by the appropriate nonverbal signals, asks the speaker to continue. Often silence helps the speaker to collect her thoughts.

5. *Developing.* "Tell me more about the men in your life. . . . Why so many? . . . Are you bragging or complaining? . . . Tell me about the best and worst of them. . . . Whom do you have in mind for number thirty-four?"

6. *Clarifying.* "That's one and a half lovers a year, on the average; do you have affairs in sequence or concurrently? . . . Do these men know about each other?"

7. *Diverging.* "And yet you claim to be in the forefront of the feminist movement—do you see any conflict in that?"

8. *Changing.* "I'd like to move along now to another topic if you don't mind—tell me about your interest in Renoir paintings." (This assumes you have no interest in pursuing the topic.)

9. *Judgmental* (to be avoided usually). "Oh, boy, are you a fickle woman or what?"

Perhaps it's less important to learn the various types of probes than to let your curiosity guide you toward the heart of the subject. The best probe may be the question, "Why?" It's also the best question to ask when you can't think of any other. "Why do you say that?"

FACTUAL QUESTIONS: THE FIVE W'S

Use of who, what, where, when, why, and how has already been described as a means of obtaining information for the event-oriented news story. Who? (the governor), What? (vetoed the tax bill), and so on. The five W's and H are particularly valuable to lay a foundation of knowledge before you can proceed with more complex questions. You encounter a group of people picketing at City Hall. The event seems worthy of an item on the six o'clock news, but you haven't the faintest idea what it's all about. What now? You put your five W's to work. Who's in charge? When you find this person you ask foundation-laying questions. What's going on? Who are these people, and why are they here? And so on.

CONCEPTUALLY DEFINING QUESTIONS

You use a conceptually defining question to seek out the underlying causes or principles behind any event or situation. Sometimes it is a one-word question: Why? A simple question; however, it implies willingness to understand the answer and that can be complex indeed. Not only is the answer possibly complicated, but you're never sure it's true. Truth comes at many levels. So do "cover-ups." The real reason behind any commentary may lie deep below successive layers of political, sociological, economic, or even psychological complexities. You are tinkering with the fundamentals of human motivation, the stuff novelists and therapists deal with every day. Who can say the real reason behind the prison riot or the deterioration of a city's downtown core?

To understand the problem, consider a personal example. You ask your neighbor, Mr. Jones, why he bought a new Oldsmobile. "Because I like Oldsmobiles better than Buicks," he replies. True enough. You can settle for that superficial answer, or you can peel away successive psychological layers to get somewhere close to reality. Perhaps he is a timid man who hopes through the purchase of a powerful and expensive car to gain self-confidence, the admiration of friends and neighbors, and the respect of his family. Jones may deny such a motivation should you ask, and who's to say he's wrong? He was merely trying to keep up with the neighbors.

Understanding the conceptual underpinnings beneath the superficial events is less a matter of questioning technique than a complex pattern of learning and understanding. Tracking down concepts sometimes requires dogged pursuit:

Q. Governor, why did you veto the capital punishment bill?

A. Because it was a bad bill.

Q. What was bad about it?

A. Everything!

Q. Well, what would be an example of one bad element?

A. In the first place, it's in conflict with the state constitution.

Q. How so? [And so on, until you get to the heart of the governor's attitudes about capital punishment and her reasons for the veto.]

Professor LaRue Gilleland has suggested a pattern for conceptual interviewing (1971). It's called *GOSS*, an acronym for four stages of questioning.

    Goals
    Obstacles
    Solutions
    Start

GOSS draws on the principle that most of life—that of bureaucratic agencies as well as humans—involves reaching for goals, not all of them within grasp. If you ask about goals and get realistic answers, then you will begin to learn the concepts. Why did the governor veto the bill? Because her goal is (whatever). You invariably find obstacles blocking access to those goals. But possible solutions exist, either in fact or in theory. The final S suggests that understanding concepts comes more easily if you return to the beginning of an event or situation. How (and why) did it all begin?

You can apply GOSS to interviews ranging from simple news-event queries to full-fledged biographical profiles. You can discuss the governor's goals at any stage. "Governor, what are you trying to accomplish in the field of prison reform? What kinds of problems or obstacles stand in the way? How have you—or will you—worked to remove those obstacles? How did your interest in prison reform begin?"

You can add two letters to GOSS for interviews requiring conceptual depth:

E for Evaluation
Y for "Why"

That makes it *GOSSEY*, still an easily remembered pattern. Evaluation means asking for a historical overview of the subject under discussion: "Governor, please tell me how you evaluate the controversy between you and the legislature over prison reform." And the Y for *why* reminds you to press for a complete understanding: Why does the governor feel so strongly about prison reform?

NUMBER QUESTIONS

How many? By what percentage has population increased over the last decade? Answers to number questions give a sense of definition and precision to the topic under discussion. Vague is dull; specifics can be interesting, even dramatic when used properly. Numbers and statistics seem to dominate sports reporting—the .314 batting average, the coach's won-lost-tied record. Other people accumulate statistical records, too, though the numbers may not be so easily accessible as they are in sports, business, the economy, and the census. Yet a mountain climber could tally his lifetime record of 122 peaks climbed, 383 glacier traverses, or whatever. The questions used to discover such dramas are simple. How many? How many miles did the retiring postman walk during his forty-year career? To make it dramatic, use comparisons. He walked 120,000 miles, a distance equal to almost five times around the world at the equator.

REFLECTIVE QUESTIONS

Reflective questions are not really questions but comments on some point the interviewer would like to hear addressed. They are largely conjectural comments, usually delivered in a casual, ego-reinforcing manner: "You seem to enjoy teaching, Ms. Johnston," and "I notice, Senator, that you chuckle every time I bring up the subject of the federal deficit."

Such comments are more conversational and less threatening. They allow the respondent to choose the direction of the reply, which frequently leads to a surprising counterpoint:

Q. You seem to enjoy teaching, Ms. Johnston.

A. Oh, I do—at least 89.3 percent of the time.

Q. I see—the other, uh, 10.7 percent sounds troublesome.

A. It's just that when you try harder to make sure your students learn what they ought to know, you put more pressure both on your students and on yourself. You run the risk of misunderstanding, and pretty soon delegations of parents come to see the principal. That part I don't enjoy.

Q. But apparently those delegations have not weakened your resolve [and so on].

Not all such comments must massage the ego, of course. Negative comments, preferably attributed to someone else, can encourage lively responses.

Q. Some students tell me that they avoid your classes because you're so demanding.

A. Yes, and some teachers resent the fact that the very best students register for my advanced English classes, but I want to point out that I also teach remedial English.

CREATIVE QUESTIONS

By definition, the creative question emerges when you venture beyond the limits of present knowledge. You see the star quarterback on crutches (the known aspect), and so you call the football coach to find out what happened and what implications it might have for future games (the unknown).

That definition confirmed, let us acknowledge that some reporters are more creative than others. Their minds sift through conversational minutiae for bits of information that seem to combine into new and novel revelations. Some of the pieces are not even verbal.

Why, for example, does the senator avoid your eyes whenever you ask her about foreign policy? She won't talk about military problems and revolutionary hot spots except to ramble on about "fire-engine diplomacy." Last week a newspaper quoted her as saying, "I have more questions than answers about American foreign policy." How does that fit in? As these and similar items accumulate in an interviewer's mind, they seem to form a pattern, a possible meaning to explain the fragments. You form a hypothesis— a possible explanation—and drop it into the conversation.

Q. Senator, several things you've said today suggest that you may be considering a sharp departure from your support of the President's foreign policy, particularly with regard to intervention in localized conflict.

A. Good heavens! How did you reach that conclusion? [A typical reaction.]

Q. Just things you said.

A. Well, you're right! How perceptive! Yes, it's true; I feel the President is deviating from his previously announced policy. . . .

If she denies your hypothesis, you've lost nothing. Perhaps she'll offer some other explanation for the pattern that puzzles you. When a respondent confirms such a creative hypothesis, however, the conversation spirals upward with renewed energy. That's because the respondent views you with new respect, seeing you as the brilliant and perceptive observer that you truly are.

LEADING, LOADED, AND JUNKPILE QUESTIONS

Finally, here are three question-types with tarnished reputations and questionable validity.

Leading Questions. The leading question telegraphs its expected answer: "You really do love sunsets, don't you?" Should such a question be used in a journalistic interview? Generally no, unless you want to shake up a lethargic respondent. Imagine this question asked of a city official who has dedicated his life to developing parks and playgrounds: "Mr. Mayor, don't you really think the city would benefit if some of those parks were converted into business properties? I mean, think of the tax income and the economic benefits to the city." The interviewer, exhibiting a jovial tone, doesn't think for a minute that the provocative question will mislead the mayor into saying yes. It may, however, stimulate a lively response.

Loaded Questions. If the leading question can stimulate spirited response, the loaded question poses even greater provocation. "Mr. Mayor, isn't there something almost criminally wrong with city government when police officers harass citizens almost to the point of brutality?" Or, "Isn't it true that in your ultimate avaricious greed, your company has raped the land and polluted the air with absolutely no concern for the health and welfare of your workers and the general populace?" Such questions and responses represent "news theater" more than information gathering.

Junkpile Questions.   This is an obstacle-course question. Interviewers shovel piles of rhetorical junk onto the roadway, trying to force respondents to pick their way through them en route to the answer. Not easy, even for sources trying to give an honest reply. Sample question: "Governor, given the fact that two of your top aides have resigned, that state spending is several million over budget, that tax collections are down at least 11 percent according to the latest accountings, that there's a certain flip-flop quality to your decision-making, that the opposition party is calling for your resignation, and that the polls show your popularity is down to a meager 37 percent—how can you possibly put an optimistic face on your chances for reelection next fall?" This kind of question should be banned. It forces the governor to pick her way through the scattered debris. She probably won't bother. The question is so unfocused that she'll merely deliver a rehearsed campaign speech. Who can blame her?

▶ 6

The Conversational Dynamics of Interviewing

Q. Okay, Dogbreath, up against the wall—come clean with me or I'll break your arm!

A. Gee, I love it when you reporters talk tough like that!

In this chapter you will learn that men and women are different. For one thing, the genders talk differently, listen differently, and mean different things by what they say. For the journalistic interviewer, the implications are enormous.

The 1990s have brought new and popular literature on gender differences in conversation. Deborah Tannen, professor of linguistics at George Washington University, has called attention to gender differences through two books, *You Just Don't Understand* (1990) and *Talking from 9 to 5* (1994). We learn that, according to anthropologists, women are more naturally inclined to ask questions than to utter assertive or challenging statements. They respond more easily to show they are listening ("Uhm . . . Uh-huh," agreeable laughter, etc.). People therefore perceive women to be better listeners. (Tannen 1990.)

For interviewers these traits mean that sources may respond more candidly to questions asked by women than by men. Ever the competitors, men tend to see conversation as gamesmanship. The game puts them "one up" or "one down." To respond candidly to a male reporter's question may mean

"Is there anything particularly fascinating about you, Mr. Aldridge?"

one down. That sometimes leads to defensive responses or facades less likely with a female reporter.

Other gender differences cited by Tannen and others (especially Mayo and Henley 1981) affect journalistic interviewing. Here are six examples:

1. While women have few qualms about stopping their cars to ask directions, men hate to do so. It puts them one down. (So asking questions seems less embarrassing to women than to men.)
2. Men speak as though teaching; women listen as though learning. (The listening–learning mode enhances reporters' interviews.)
3. Men are more direct in their speech, women more circumspect. (Both traits help interviews, depending on circumstances—direct for interviewing a hostile or evasive bureaucrat, circumspect with a beleaguered crime victim.)
4. Women exhibit a more "affiliative" demeanor (getting to know and appreciate the other person); men exhibit more independent and aloof mannerisms. (Affiliative behavior may draw more candid personal responses, but the implied liaison can be dangerous when dealing with controversial topics—sources may perceive an "ally" in the friendly reporter.)

5. Women more than men accept blame for miscommunication. (Male: "You misunderstood my point." Female: "I didn't make myself clear." The female approach, less egotistical, helps build rapport.)
6. Men joke and tease conversational partners more than women do, the playful insult being among their favorites. (The teasing can raise or lower the rapport, depending on how deftly it's done and how the respondent reacts—does he/she tease back?)

Because building good rapport is important to interviewing, the women's approach seems to make women the more natural interviewers. Men have to learn many of the traits that come naturally to women. Yet sometimes the games men play produce livelier responses, more witty repartee, and more colorful quotations.

Tannen recalls a dramatic experience in gender differences in journalistic interviewing. On one occasion, a male reporter's adversarial methods of questioning seemed to border on belligerence. He challenged almost everything she said. In another interview, a female reporter seemed friendly and agreeable to Tannen's every statement. Tannen says she expected to see a critical article by the man and a positive one by the woman. Precisely the opposite happened. "To my amazement he wrote a flattering portrait with no hint of the belligerence he had used to get information from me." But the woman reporter's story "cast me in an unflattering light. . . . Whereas I was pleasantly relieved to see that the first article was more favorable than I expected, I felt betrayed and tricked by the second." (Tannen 1994.)

The experience, running counter to conventional wisdom, prompts questions. Is her experience the exception, or does the male tendency toward adversarial interviewing produce more benign outcomes than expected? Do the smiles and nods of the female interviewer belie a mean-spirited interior? To cite an academic cliché, more research is needed.

THE VALUE OF RESEARCH

Journalism has produced few studies that document what techniques work best for interviewers. What evidence, for instance, supports the claim that gentle conversational methods, empathic listening, and nonjudgmental demeanor draw out sources more effectively than a demanding interrogative technique full of "tough questions" and deceitful tactics? Do we really disarm sources by attributing dirty allegations to third parties, as in, "Senator, your opponents claim that you're a philanderer and a scoundrel—how do you respond?"

Rarely do researchers explore journalistic interviewing methods, so we turn to other sources such as anthropologists, psychologists, sociologists, and linguists. They have uncovered information that seems helpful to journalists, though we must make a leap of faith to believe their findings apply to journalistic interviews. Consider an example:

In a psychology experiment in California, researchers advertised for volunteers to participate in a four-week weight-loss project. (Chang 1994.) Of the 127 people responding, 67 were selected, all women who averaged 28 years and 147 pounds and who hoped to slim down to about 125 pounds. So few men applied that the project proceeded with women only.

The counselors offered a legitimate weight-loss program, but the study's real purpose was to ascertain the effect of positive versus negative interviewing techniques. Suppose, the researchers conjectured, the interview questions were put in a positive light, "Has anyone ever complimented you on the way you look? In what ways do you like yourself the most?"

Or suppose the questions were negative: "Do you recall anyone ever teasing you or making fun of the way you looked? In what ways do you dislike yourself the most?"

Group One received the negative questions, and Group Two the positive. The researchers suspected that those hearing negative questions would lose their motivation to continue their weight-loss regimen. Not so, as it turned out. The nature of the questions made no difference. The surprise in this project came when the researchers studied how interviewers responded to the participants' answers.

Some participants, call them Group Three, received positive responses to their answers—comments that showed appreciation for their disclosures, praise for their honesty, and encouragement for their efforts to lose weight. They also received warm nonverbal responses: smiles, nods, and lots of "uh-huhs."

Group Four received "neutral" responses—no smiles, no nods, no encouraging remarks. The male interviewers even held a clipboard directly between them and the respondents.

So which interview technique worked best? The results clearly showed that those who received warm responses to their answers (Group Three) did the best, as measured by their willingness to comply with the recommended weight-loss regimen and to continue the program.

Success also was measured by this group's loss of weight. The warm-response group lost four pounds apiece. The neutral-response group lost less than a pound apiece, and most did not even finish the program.

What can journalists learn from such an example? It suggests that questions are less important than listening to and responding to the answers. A sincere compliment opens the gates to ever more candid communication. Researcher Peter Chang, who described the project in the *Journal of Counseling Psychology*, speculates that the female respondents may have been uneasy about talking to male counselors about something so personal as weight problems. But those who received the positive feedback felt particularly inspired by the praise.

Other studies do indeed suggest that men are less likely to use the smiles and nods and responsive laughter that women provide naturally in conversations. They also suggest that men and women mean different things by positive response. Men tend to use it to suggest that they agree with the speaker's view; women use it to say only, "I'm listening; please continue." (Tannen 1990.)

A study of newspaper interviewers in Oregon offers further support for the positive-response idea. Videotapes of reporters in action showed that those considered by their supervisors to be "above average" in interviewing skills responded with smiles, nods of the head, and eye contact more than those considered merely "average." They also dressed better. (Cerotsky 1989.)

SCANNING THE LITERATURE OF INTERVIEWING

This suggestion that social science research can offer insight into journalistic interviewing is not new. The first effort to draw on research data from other areas to fill the void in journalism is that of professors Eugene J. Webb and Jerry R. Salancik. In 1966 they published a literature survey entitled *The Interview, or The Only Wheel in Town*. The title suggests one conclusion drawn from studies in sociology, psychology, and other disciplines applicable to journalistic interviewing. "The only wheel in town" refers to a gambler's lament that a roulette wheel is crooked. Then why play it? "Because it's the only wheel in town."

Journalistic interviewing, the authors concluded, is equally warped, but it's the only game in town. They cite numerous confirming studies from survey research interviewing—the kind intended to determine people's opinions on issues. One pioneering example (Rice 1929) compared the findings of two interviewers who were attempting to learn why a group of welfare applicants had ended up as skid road derelicts.

What had caused their downfall? Overindulgence in liquor, according to one interviewer. Social conditions over which they had little control, concluded the other. How strange. Why would two interviewers come up with such divergent results? Rice identified the problem as "contagious bias." The first interviewer was a prohibitionist. The other was a socialist. Their interviews produced an uncanny reflection of their own beliefs. They got the answers they wanted by subtly telegraphing their own views.

This and similar studies suggest that attitudes of interviewers can influence answers. Most of us unconsciously transmit our attitudes about certain questions, particularly those about which we feel strongly, via the nonverbal smiles and affirmations described earlier. Nonverbal communication serves as part of the *exchange* of information that helps to form the definition of the creative interview. Say Webb and Salancik:

> For our purposes, "exchanging information" is an essential notion. An interview is not just a set of questions and answers. By the character of his question, accompanying gestures, the clothes he wears, and a thousand

*other elements, the reporter communicates to his source clues as to what
kind of man the reporter is, how he views his source, and what he thinks
about the source's replies. A titanic amount of information pours toward the
source, and it heavily influences both the amount and tenor of the information he sends back.*

Webb and Salancik also report that varying circumstances tend to cast interviewers into different roles—therapists to the beleaguered, saviors to the
downcast, pipelines to power and influence for social climbers. Their evidence also suggests that journalistic interviewers should avoid arrogance or
hostility. The authors refute a reporting textbook that says reporters should
"inspire confidence and even awe by directness in speech."

"It might do the reporter's ego a great deal of good to have someone
stand in awe before him," they write, "but what confident, direct speech does
for the completeness and accuracy of the information this cocky interviewer
extracts is open to question. The evidence and idea of role suggest less attention to creating an impression of omnipotence would be advisable."

Considerable literature has accumulated in the decades since *The Only
Wheel* emerged. A more recent compendium of research literature (Dillon
1990) confirms most of what *Wheel* proclaimed earlier. Professor J. T. Dillon of
the University of California–Riverside consulted the literature on "questioning" from teacher–student dialogue, police interrogation, medical and thera-
peutic interviews, and many others, including journalism. Dillon found still
more studies that dramatize the fragile nature of the interview as an instrument of truth-seeking.

Synthesizing the literature on questioning, Dillon identifies three elements to the questioning process: (1) assumptions, (2) the questions themselves, and (3) the answers. All three contain the risk of interviewer bias and
inaccuracy.

The assumptions typically include the belief that the respondent has the
answers and that any factual basis for the question is accurate. Such is not always the case. For example, the proverbial question, "Have you stopped
beating your spouse?" assumes that such beatings have occurred in the past.
Unless that assumption is correct, it's merely a loaded or trick question,
unanswerable except to deny the assumption. More subtle assumptions
creep into the work of reporters every day and can color both the questions
asked and the thrust of the subsequent report. Among them are:

1. That the person interviewed is qualified to answer—did the witness *see*
   the accident or did she merely hear about it secondhand?
2. That words have the same meaning to all parties. Does "excessive speed"
   mean the same to a police officer as to a race car driver?
3. That reputations are true. "She hates reporters and won't talk to you." Being told that could color your approach and your questions. Perhaps she
   hates only the reporters who bring false assumptions into the interview.

4. That background information is always correct.
5. That things are what reporters imagine: "Where were you standing when the plane blew up?" Why do you assume the respondent was *standing*? "Where were you?" involves a safer assumption.

Studies of questions have tended to confirm the Webb-Salancik thesis of the crooked wheel of interviewer bias. One report (Loftus 1987) suggests care in word choices. Interviewers asked accident witnesses, "How fast were the cars going when they *contacted/hit/smashed*?" The estimates averaged thirty-one mph when they "contacted," but forty-one mph when they "smashed."

Literature dealing with answers is even more revealing. The term "response" better describes what happens after a question is asked because many of the reactions are not answers at all. The nonanswers range from evasions to "stonewalling." A report entitled "How not to answer a question" (Weiser 1975) suggests that responses to so simple a question as "How old are you?" can extend from "selective ambiguity" ("Don't worry, they'll let me into the bar") to direct refusal ("I'd rather not answer that") and may even include sly diversions ("Oh, no! I think I left my headlights on").

Responses can change with circumstances, as suggested in a study (Getzels 1954) that envisioned three different situations calling for answers to the question, "How do you like meeting strangers?" A person nervous with strangers answers, "I enjoy meeting them" to an employment interviewer, "depends on the stranger" to an opinion pollster, and "strangers make me feel nervous and inferior" to a therapist.

The solution to such nonanswer responses and the associated problems? Listen to and respond to answers, suggests Dillon. "The practical importance of listening to answers should be obvious, yet practitioners seem to be preoccupied with asking their questions and thinking up the next one to ask."

THE PLACE OF THE GENTLE QUESTION

Additional searches through the literature of interviewing affirms that the gentle, listening, empathic style of interviewing works best. Not much evidence supports the idea that arrogance somehow helps interviewers discover truth. Most evidence suggests the contrary. Even the literature of law enforcement interviewing eschews rough techniques, emphasizing kindness, tact, empathy, and honesty. (Buckwalter 1983). One book on police methods bears the title, *The Gentle Art of Interviewing and Interrogation.* (Royal and Schutt 1976.) "Gentle" art? The impact of court cases has accounted for the change, especially the Miranda case, which resulted in the requirement that officers warn suspects that they have a right to have a lawyer present during questioning and that they need not answer any questions. How does an officer interview a suspect after such a warning? Gently, tactfully, empathically, and logically, because courts have overturned convictions based on evidence or confessions obtained through deceit, coercion, or strong-arm methods. "Any interviewers who have need of such methods are certainly sadistic, uninformed, and incompetent," say Royal and Schutt.

"Taking an adversarial stance," says Buckwalter, "is inviting the suspect to hurl defiance at your attempts to overcome him. . . . The 'hatchet-man' interrogator is a failure. He has never learned how to gently but persistently probe for the facts, or how to lead the suspect to reveal himself and his doings. Any suspect will resent an abusive or antagonistic approach."

NONVERBAL COMMUNICATION

All of us read people. Research suggests that we read others' actions as more accurate than their words whenever the two come into conflict. An obvious case would be sarcasm. "I had a *wonderful* time on my blind date," says a college woman. Do you believe that? You'd realize the falsity of the words if said in person and accompanied by appropriate sneer, rolling of the eyes, and inflections in the words.

Interviewers use nonverbal communication in two ways. First, they make sure their own dress, mannerisms, body posture, eye contact, and similar behavior communicate sincere interest and careful listening. Second, they observe respondents' nonverbal behaviors. These behaviors provide clues— often subtle, sometimes dramatic—to what respondents are thinking. The perceptive interviewer can find meaning in a subtle frown, a shrug of the shoulder, a wisp of a smile, or the raising or lowering of the voice. Given a choice between following up a sly chuckle in response to a question or the long-winded verbal comment, the interviewer may pursue the chuckle.

Q. That was an interesting comment, Ms. Celebrity, but I couldn't help noticing the sly little chuckle that preceded it. So naturally I'm wondering what the chuckle means.

Nonverbal communication comes in several categories:

Paralanguage

The grunts and noises we make in response to comments—the "umms," "uh-huhs," and "mmmmms"—are called *paralanguage*, and the numerous studies of their effects leave no doubt that they contribute to the rapport. People speak longer when they hear those kinds of responses, as they do in response to smiles and nods of the head.

Voice

Our tone of voice carries subtle but effective meanings, including the sarcasm mentioned earlier. Albert Mehrabian (1981) performed experiments concluding that when words clash with the tone of voice and facial expression, people tend to believe the nonverbal aspects.

Eyes

That eyes speak volumes is suggested by the folklore on the subject, ranging from language terms ("shifty eyes") to proverbs ("reproof on her lips but a smile in her eyes"). Various studies suggest that eye contact enhances response and that people tend to look at the other person more while listening than while talking. One study used film clips and asked viewers to evaluate the people who looked at them while speaking compared with those who seldom looked at them. Viewers judged the lookers as friendly, self-confident, natural, mature, and sincere. They judged the nonlookers as cold, pessimistic, defensive, evasive, and immature. (Klick 1968.)

Kinesics

Numerous research studies have suggested that we communicate with our bodies—from a speaker's pounding the table to subtle changes in facial expression. The signs do not always contain clear meanings, however. A study once asked people to act out six emotional messages through nonverbal methods. As a video camera rolled, the amateur actors tried to project anger, fear, seductiveness, indifference, happiness, and sadness. When audiences viewing the tapes tried to determine which emotion was which, they usually misperceived four of the six. They perceived one young woman as "seductive" in every one of her six mood transmissions and another woman as "angry" in all six of hers. (Beier 1974.) So much for decoding nonverbal signals. For the interviewer they merely provide hints to be probed for detail.

Proxemics

Edward T. Hall, an anthropologist, defined four levels of distance between human pairs as they converse in everyday life: intimate, personal, social, and public distances. They range from touching at the intimate distance to about twelve feet and beyond for public distance. (Hall 1966.) The typical interview tends to range from the far side of personal distance (eighteen inches to four feet) to the near side of social distance (four to twelve feet).

People put up barriers when others approach to an uncomfortable distance, Hall says. We all retain a bubble of private space to be invaded only by selected intimates, and we move to preserve that bubble with others. People indulge in various "barrier behaviors" when others approach too close, either by moving back to preserve the bubble or by putting up barrier objects, a

Some interviewees try to put obstacles between you and themselves.

book or purse on the table between the two parties, for example. Or they may fold their arms in front of their chest, clutch a book to their chest, or cough, scratch, or avoid eye contact.

You can use this kind of research as a means of perceiving touches of character. Does the bureaucrat hide behind a fortress of a desk with the visitors' chairs strategically placed directly across from him? This person demands a large space bubble and probably has the status to enforce it. One of my students encountered not only the fortress of a desk but noticed to his discomfort that the legs of the guests' chairs had been shortened so that visitors sat slightly lower than the host. Enlightened design has called for offices that resemble living rooms, a desk at one side, a sofa and coffee table arrangement on the other side. Some democratically inclined executives use an office with a circular table so that no one sits at the head of the table.

Visiting interviewers cannot always dictate the interview arrangements. Given a choice, you should opt for the most informal arrangement—the coffee table or the round table instead of the big desk, or around the corner of the desk instead of across, or possibly moving to a conference room devoid of defensive paraphernalia. It's equally important to avoid bringing defense symbols of your own. Taking notes on a big tablet or clipboard—and holding it directly between yourself and the respondent—is a defense symbol, like a shield and sword. Keep the notepad off to one side.

Avoid microphone swordplay in broadcast interviews. A student once witnessed a TV reporter doing a standup interview with a U.S. senator. Most of the time the interviewer kept the microphone in a neutral position between them. But when the senator evaded her question, she thrust the microphone in his face, even forcing him to step back on one occasion. Neither party seemed conscious of these microphone dynamics.

ESSENTIALS OF PERSONAL COMMUNICATION

From the studies of interviewing, three conclusions emerge:

1. Almost all evidence about interviewing—and most notably from sources dealing with police investigative techniques—suggests that communication flows most freely in an atmosphere of sincerity, trust, and informality.
2. Communication works best when reporters strive not to win a victory but to create and maintain a conversational atmosphere that fosters a high degree of candor.
3. The interview is a fragile and wayward means of learning factual reality.

Of course, journalistic interviewing does not follow the rigidly controlled nature of social science interviewing for presidential popularity ratings or favored detergents. Author Lewis A. Dexter in a book called *Elite and Specialized Interviewing* (1970) proposes a "transactional theory of interviewing," which means each interview encompasses a unique set of questions and answers. That's how new ideas emerge—creative interviewing, indeed. Too much structuring of interviews can dampen dialogue and new ideas. Let the conversation proceed to new horizons guided by altruistic journalists who can put aside personal biases and listen carefully while keeping an open mind.

▶ 7

Being Interviewed

Q. What is your preferred color?
A. Yellow journalism written in purple.

What's it like to be interviewed? "It's like playing Russian roulette," says a journalist from Oregon, Melody Ward Leslie. "You never know which question's going to kill you." She gained moments of fame as the subject of feature interviews after her surprise discovery that her birth thirty-three years earlier had been the result of donor insemination. She became the subject of media scrutiny for several months as she undertook to investigate the subject and write a book. Suddenly lots of fellow journalists, including NBC and the BBC, wanted a piece of her time. Every interview unnerved her, she said.

But she's a journalist herself. When the tables are turned and *they're* the respondents, strange things happen. They often show discomfort in interviews. They worry about what they said. They seem more unnerved by interviews than ordinary sources do. Some refuse to be interviewed. Oriana Fallaci, the feisty, in-your-face Italian journalist who has interviewed many world leaders, refuses most interview requests. "I don't give interviews. . . . Once I accepted an interview by phone with a Dutchman. 'What is your preferred color?' I said, 'Sir, the rainbow!' and, pooh! I put the phone down. So they want to interview me, and I don't want to see them." (Huber and Diggins 1992.) Even Mike Wallace, the prosecutorial interviewer of CBS *60 Minutes* fame, has shown strain when the tables were turned. By one account, Wallace acted "guarded" during a series of newspaper interviews—"during one recent session he snapped off the reporter's tape recorder every time the conversation edged into what he deemed sensitive territory." (Lesher 1982.)

Such comments prompt one to wonder why anyone would agree to an interview with a news reporter. Considerable evidence suggests, however,

"Being interviewed is like playing Russian Roulette." Label your own question-bullets, or try these. Round One: "People say you're a scoundrel—how do you respond?" Two: "How do you feel about the mess you've gotten yourself into?" Three: "If all hell breaks loose, how will you react?"

that most Americans who have experienced a news interview found the experience worthwhile, even enjoyable, and often useful for their purposes.

Such was one conclusion reached in a research study conducted by Abilene Christian University professor Merlin Mann. Then a doctoral student at the University of Missouri, he surveyed both reporters and sources involved in 315 news articles selected from 42 daily newspapers in Missouri. Of the 171 sources returning questionnaires, most agreed with the statement, "I enjoy being interviewed." And most thought the reporter who interviewed them enjoyed it, too. The typical news interview started a little awkwardly but soon warmed into a suitable rapport. (Mann 1991.)

The sources generally approved of the way newspaper reporters conducted their interviews and the stories they produced. They found reporters adequately prepared to ask questions—they listened well, they didn't talk too much, and they showed concern for the sources' viewpoints. They wrote articles the sources judged to be essentially accurate.

The reporters themselves tended to share the generally favorable view of their work, differing occasionally in degree. Reporters had a more positive view of telephone interviews than the sources did. They thought themselves better prepared, less aggressive, and more conversationally on-target than sources perceived them to be.

As a group, the sources were older and better educated than the reporters. They were predominately male, as were the reporters. Allowed their preferences, the sources favored in-person over telephone interviews and longer interviews over shorter ones. Most interviews in the survey ran fewer than twenty minutes. The longer the interview, the more sources perceived it as having reached a stage of "conversational warmth." Longer interviews, respondents said, also produced a higher level of candor in their answers and greater accuracy in the published reports. Asked to identify characteristics of a good interviewer, they named preparation, an open-minded attitude, willingness to listen, enthusiasm for the topic, and "interpersonal skills" such as a friendly attitude and empathy.

Were there no problems? Occasionally, yes, though only nine respondents (5 percent) cited such lapses as biases, failure to honor off-the-record requests, or failure to make the point of the interview clear. Some said a few reporters seemed dogmatic—they knew beforehand what the story should say and wanted from the interview only a few confirming quotes.

The most serious ethical lapse Professor Mann encountered concerned an organ transplant procedure at a Kansas City hospital. In the operating room as organs were being removed, two nurses unguardedly spoke with someone they thought was an "inquisitive medical student" dressed in surgical garb. Two hours later they discovered that he was a reporter writing an article on organ transplants. He had attended the procedure at the invitation of a surgeon but had not made his identity clear to the nurses, who found his story essentially accurate but sensationalized by such touches as "blood dripping on the floor" and "the sour odor of the heating scalpel." The nurses felt betrayed. (Mann 1991, Hoffman and Voda interviews 1991.)

PLIGHT OF THE SUDDEN CELEBRITY

Ethical lapses are clearly the exception to what seems a reasonably good report card for newspaper reporters in Missouri. My own conversations with news sources over the past twenty years—some 300 conversations specifically focused on "the joys and problems of being interviewed"—largely confirm the findings: give the mainstream news media a B or B-plus grade and quite a few conscientious reporters deserve an A.

Most of these conversations, 200 of them since 1990, dealt with a new and growing phenomenon—the emergence of the "temporary celebrity," a person rising from obscurity to fame. An assailant slashes a model's face in New York, and suddenly victim Marla Hanson emerges as an international celebrity. They make a movie about her life. A baby falls into a well in Midland, Texas in 1987 and suddenly paramedic Steve Forbes bursts onto the six o'clock news—it was he who etched an unforgettable image when he emerged from the rescue hole and delivered a live baby. In the ensuing months, more than 100 journalists wanted one-on-one interviews with Forbes.

Sometimes it doesn't take much to elevate an ordinary citizen to celebrity status. Just go to the wrong bathroom. Denise Wells did that at a stadium in Houston, Texas during a country music concert in 1990. Feeling an urgent need, she discovered an impossibly long line outside the women's room. The nearby men's room had no line, and she saw a man escorting his girlfriend into it. She slipped in behind them. A police officer cited both women for a city ordinance violation and ordered them out of the concert. The *Houston Post* wrote a news article—and Denise Wells became another household name, fielding calls from news media all over the world, pictured in *People* magazine, even appearing as a guest on the Joan Rivers and Johnny Carson shows, all expenses paid. Wells's greatest moment of fame, she claims, was cracking a "potty parity" joke that caused Johnny Carson to laugh. (Wells later fought the citation in court and won.)

How do these kinds of sources react to media interviews? Pretty much the same as those surveyed by Professor Mann. They found most reporters sincere, conscientious, and essentially accurate. They enjoyed being interviewed—at least the first few times. But being an international celebrity takes time and robs them of privacy. They obtained unlisted numbers or used answering machines to screen calls. Big-time calls—*Life* magazine or network news—often meant expending huge chunks of time: five hours in the case of *Life* for photos of a Provo, Utah policewoman, Jackie Guibord, who became a pinup celebrity during the Persian Gulf War. Because the war ended quickly, the photos were never used. These sources also learned that network TV takes both time and emotional energy responding to tactics calculated to elicit emotional responses on camera— "verbal hand grenades you're constantly trying to defuse," as one expressed it.

The celebrities quickly tired of the same old questions, particularly the ones calculated to elicit an emotional response. "How did you *feel* when you carried the baby out of the well?" is one that paramedic Steve Forbes particularly detested. It was his most frequently asked question, particularly by TV reporters. He had a second complaint: being "trapped" by reporters who come personally to his home or work and won't leave until he's agreed to do an interview. They won't take no for an answer and won't reschedule it for a more convenient time. (Forbes interview 1990.)

Some celebrities soon escaped back to obscurity; others continued to live a celebrated life. Some turned their status into causes, such as a rape survivor on a lecture circuit as spokeswoman for crime victims.

WHY BE INTERVIEWED?

There's only one thing worse than being interviewed and that's not being interviewed. Consider why people will agree—or won't agree—to media interviews. Keep the reasons at your fingertips so that when you encounter reluctant sources, you can develop persuasive arguments. Here are the most common reasons for agreeing to media interviews:

1. An opportunity to obtain recognition and publicity.
2. An opportunity to tell your side of an issue or controversy.
3. An opportunity to educate the public on some issue about which you feel strongly: There's a little educator (or propagandist) in all of us.
4. An opportunity to promote, such as an actress pushing her latest movie.
5. An opportunity to clarify a position or eliminate misunderstanding.
6. An opportunity to influence or impress others.
7. A novel experience, ego inflating.
8. A touch of immortality, words frozen into print to be seen by future historians.
9. Sympathy with a purpose or cause—enough to override the pain. The 1990s brought examples of rape survivors willing to go public with painful stories of their attacks and the often greater pain of coping with the legal system's wayward machinations.
10. Sympathy with a new or novel topic or approach—the promise by the interviewer to cover new ground, not just a rehash.

Here are some standard reasons *not* to grant interviews:

1. Distrust of interviewer's motives: "He's just looking for dirt."
2. Aversion to specific interviewers, the ones who have gained unsavory reputations for aggressive or deceitful tactics.
3. Lack of time.
4. Lack of interest in subject.
5. Lack of knowledge of subject.
6. Lack of sympathy with interview purpose.
7. Lack of confidence in interviewer's ability to handle complex subject.
8. Desire to avoid publicity or minimize it, such as a bureaucrat under fire for malfeasance.
9. Wanting not to stand out: for example, a "team member" trying to avoid a publicity-hog reputation.
10. Reluctance to be thrust into role of spokesperson for a group.
11. Snobbery—interviewer's paper or station lacks prestige.
12. Broadcast stage fright.
13. Vague unease caused by less-than-candid explanations of purpose.
14. Resentment of past media injustices such as a media hatchet job, misquotations, or critical newspaper editorial.
15. Wariness of theatrical tactics that one erstwhile celebrity calls the "Sam Donaldson hit-'em-in-the-face-with-a-wet-rag-and-see-how-they-respond technique."
16. Interview burnout. Established celebrities often say "enough." New celebrities soon learn the value of that embargo.

Even after granting interviews, established celebrities often set ground rules. Actress Jodie Foster won't discuss John Hinkley's assassination attempt on Ronald Reagan. Eric Roberts won't talk about his sister, Julia Roberts.

A NATIONAL ORGANIZATION FOR NEWS SOURCES?

Given the plethora of organizations, why not one for news sources, complete with an annual national convention? Narrowly focused groups, such as police information officers and business communicators, do meet regularly, but no organization allows actresses and crime victims—or even notorious criminals—to trade ideas on media relations with police sergeants and business executives. Yet it's such serious business that elaborate and expensive workshops have become popular for executives and bureaucrats who face the media—intense sessions that simulate the most arrogant, insensitive style of interviewing that television can muster.

In a convention setting, you can mingle with the crowd, rubbing elbows with people who have one thing in common—at some point in their lives, news media sought them out for interviews. With some, the requests never cease. Let your imagination wander. Isn't that Ken Kesey, the author of *One Flew Over the Cuckoo's Nest*, talking with a group? Perhaps he's discussing how to handle interview requests by college students. He's besieged by them, so he has a rule: Ask him two quick questions, and if he finds them interesting he'll grant the interview. One young woman, flustered by his challenge, blurted out, "What role has Christianity played in your life and work?"

"That's very good—I like that," Kesey said. He called for question number two. The student mumbled something about the "effect of drugs on your imagination and your work." No, replied Kesey, that doesn't do it. Maybe if question number two were more closely integrated with number one, it might have worked—but as it is, "You just missed it." The student, admitting in retrospect that number two was a boring cliché, vowed she'd never again ask for a celebrity interview without proper preparation. (These comments attributed to the hypothetical convention are not imaginary but are based on interviews with the participants by the author.)

You see others milling about convention headquarters. Some are household names. Dr. Jack Kevorkian says he's alternately appalled and intrigued by the media stakeout, the wolfpack that sometimes hangs around his residence whenever he's in the news. Captain Steve Millikin may not be a household name, but he was chief spokesman for the Tailhook Association after the infamous Las Vegas party in 1991, not an easy position for a retired officer whose primary job is editing the association's glossy magazine, *The Hook*. One thing he learned from the experience, he says, is never try to stonewall the media, but talk about the lessons learned from the bad experience and about future reforms.

Author–historian Shelby Foote, who gained national attention as a commentator on Ken Burns's Civil War TV series, says he enjoyed the media attention, especially at the point when the last few seconds of his fifteen minutes of fame began ticking away. Authors must write, he says, and must not let media attention go to their head.

Even celebrity criminals attend this imaginary meeting, for they, too, are besieged by media attention. Diane Downs, convicted of killing one of her own children, expresses huge dissatisfaction with the media, including the off-the-wall kinds of questions reporters ask ("Are you as good in bed as they say?" is one example) and the false assumptions she says underlie some of their questions, such as her alleged obsession with a particular lover.

The agenda for the national convention of news sources will no doubt include major speakers with wide experience facing the media—Robert Shapiro, the O. J. Simpson defense lawyer, comes to mind—and then break into smaller, more specialized caucuses. Shapiro gave just such an address in 1993, prior to the Simpson connection.

"It is never a good idea to lie to the press," he said. He spoke about lawyer–press relations at a meeting of the National Association of Criminal Defense Lawyers at Lake Tahoe. "To simply make up facts in the hope that they will later prove correct is too big a risk. To allude to defenses that are unrealistic or unlikely, again, leads to a potential backlash later in the case. Remember that everything you say will be recorded on videotape and in voluminous handwritten notes."

Nor is stonewalling the press a good idea. "A simple *no comment* is the least appropriate and least productive response," said Shapiro. "Coming at the end of a lengthy story, it adds absolutely nothing and leaves the public with a negative impression." (*San Jose Mercury News*, 7–10–94.)

Imagine another speaker discussing the "most dangerous questions" likely to be posed by interviewers. The *speculative* question, or hypothetical premise, stands as *number one* danger, the speaker suggests. Think twice about any question that begins with *if*: "Governor, if your daughter were raped and murdered, would you still stand against the death penalty?" Close behind comes the verbal hand grenade, one cold-bloodedly calculated to elicit an emotional response for the camera. "What will you say to little Johnny to tell him why Mommie's never coming home again?"

Respondents soon learn other tricks of the trade. They sense that interviewer silence can be a dangerous lubricant that causes one to babble on to fill the void. Some also recognize the "afterglow effect"—the sudden candor that unwary sources exhibit at the end of a successful interview. They quickly catch on to the deceitful tactics of some reporters, such as tossing out false-data questions in the hope that a source, in correcting false information, will reveal true data. A police spokesman calls that a "slash and burn" technique by reporters who assume they'll never have to deal with that source again.

They also identify the "chummy" technique ("Just between you and me—whisper the answer to me") and the typical media practice of putting a label on people and events: "Governor, given all the political setbacks you've suffered in recent months, would it be fair to characterize your administration as a *total failure?*" The term, with its skinny letters, fits headlines well, and the reporter hopes the governor will say, "It's *not* a total failure," thus repeating a catchy and headlineable label.

INTERVIEWEE PREPARATION

Your convention notes will reveal that respondents prepare for interviews, too, probably more than reporters do. A reporter for a farm paper stopped a farmer midway through an obviously rehearsed mini-speech and said, "Wait, I want to ask some questions." The farmer held up the palm of his hand on which he'd penned the outline of his agenda. "I thought that's what you wanted—a speech!" he said. That's typical of sources. They've learned never to go into an interview cold, even a benign interview. Especially for TV they rehearse twenty- or thirty-second mini-speeches and use them whenever they can. They also rehearse quotable sound bites—whittling those down to ten seconds as required by current practices. They find that local broadcast news personnel usually appreciate sources who shape responses to fit their needs. Some interviewers even ask, "What shall I ask you?" and sources should come prepared with suggestions.

INTERVIEW GAMESMANSHIP

Whatever the issue, some perceptive sources discover a certain gamesmanship in the news media interviews—a superficiality that seeps through much of the Q–A dialogue with routine questions that lead to expected answers. Former New York model Marla Hanson is a case in point. Early in her interviews she said she didn't blame New York for the razor attack on her face. "I love New York—I wouldn't think of leaving," she said, an offhand comment that made headlines and set a theme for subsequent interviews. She became the plucky kid from the Midwest, undaunted by adversity. That's what the media wanted and expected, she believed.

One time it was different. In one of those long, intimate conversations typical of the magazine interview, she made a confession to a writer from *Vogue* magazine. She was falling apart, she said. She was often depressed. She put on a brave face for the media, she told him, but sometimes she was so depressed she could not get out of bed the whole day. "So in other words, you were being dishonest," he replied, according to her account. "Don't you think you were doing a disservice to other crime victims who are going through a bad time and they think you were so brave and in reality you were a mess?"

"But what other choice did I have?" she asked, recounting the incident later. The exchange was not printed in the article, but could she have met the media with anything but a brave face? How would it sound confessing the depressing truth to the milling reporters and camera operators? Would they respect her candor and human vulnerability, or would they merely shove her into the whiners and complainers category? (Hanson interview 1991.)

She is not alone among sources in raising such questions. Some ask, "What does the typical reporter want out of the typical interview?" Some suspect that reporters prefer lots of blacks and whites with few intermediate grays—cardboard cutouts rather than real people.

That is why many would agree with San Francisco attorney Melvin Belli who has defended many high-profile criminal cases. When meeting the media, trim your points down to a precious few and present them, one-two-three, in order of importance. Don't be surprised if points two and three get left out. Use your own labels to identify people and circumstances, and speak in clear, simple language. Seeding legalese or bureaucratic jargon into the interview only leads to misunderstanding. Belli says that if reporters misunderstand something, the blame rests not with the reporters but with him for not having made himself clear. (Belli interview 1991.)

Other veteran sources speaking at our conference will suggest avoiding "off-the-record" statements altogether. Anything said, if sufficiently newsworthy, will be published sooner or later. Also, never guess when you don't know the answer; just say, "I don't know but I'll find out for you."

No doubt someone in the convention, probably a politician, will suggest a curious irony: "If you want lots of publicity, bar reporters from your meetings. If you want little or no publicity, particularly when something bad has happened, call a press conference and confess everything in excruciating detail. It will be a one-day story and quickly forgotten."

Some speakers will cite lessons from experience, what they'd do differently next time. Marla Hanson would be far less open and candid. So would paramedic Steve Forbes. Geologist Anita Grunder, who fielded questions about volcanoes after the 1980 eruption of Mount Saint Helens, says she'll try to think up colorful analogies. One would dramatize the long passage of geologic time before the dawn of recorded history. Think of time as a roll of toilet paper. If the roll contains a thousand sheets, *recorded* history would occupy only half of the last sheet.

Some speakers will suggest avoiding interview promiscuity. Carefully select your interview partners. "Being interviewed is the quickest damned way to go broke," says a farmer. Another farmer says that "if a journalist called and said, 'Do you have a message about farm life you'd like to get out to the community, and if so, may I come out at *your* convenience and talk to you about it?' I'd jump at the chance." But, alas, reporters think only of themselves and their own interests and time constraints, he says.

Business leaders will advise talking in terms of the public's interest, not the company's. If the issue is a labor demand, don't discuss your opposition as "the company can't afford it," but rather as "we'd have to raise prices for the goods we sell to the American public."

And many will recommend use of the corporate press kit for anyone frequently interviewed. It contains names and identifications of persons, the history or background of any topic expected to come under discussion, and sometimes even a list of frequently asked questions about those topics, along with the answers. If the interview will deal with a specific issue on which the source has taken sides, a statement of position and arguments on its behalf will prove helpful. For authors, a synopsis of the book's story line can ensure accuracy.

FINAL POINTS

Finally, some minor points from those small-group sessions. While respondents consider the work of reporters *essentially* accurate, there remain some minor irritations that reporters—if only they knew—could easily correct.

Accuracy in Details.   Names and personal details often come out wrong. Writer Gretchen Olson became the subject of a twenty-minute telephone interview after she finished a novel and submitted it to a competition. The title of the book: *The Pleasure Is Mine*. The article erroneously reported the title in capital letters as "EL GUSTO ES MIO." How did that happen? Because the author told the interviewer that the book's title is the English translation of a Spanish idiom, *el gusto es mío*.

For sources, the lesson is *keep your comments simple*. For reporters, it's double checking details. Such errors frequently come from sketchy note-taking or allowing notes to grow cold if the writer doesn't produce the story immediately. Wary sources find unnerving any reporter who fails to take lots of notes or use a recording device.

Officer Guibord, the Persian Gulf pinup, says reporters constantly erred in her age (invariably twenty-eight when she was then thirty) and how many children she had (two instead of the actual one). Why do reporters repeat such simple mistakes? Because they examine database files of previous stories and perpetuate an original error. They should run those details by the source every time they do an interview, says Guibord. Never assume that an earlier story is accurate—best to assume it's *not* accurate because the earliest stories are often based on hasty reporting. "I love it," says one source, "when a reporter says, 'just give me a moment to go back over my notes and check a few things.' "

Runaway Trivia.   In big stories done under frenzied conditions, sources find it scary to think that a single slip of the tongue can make them an international laughing stock. They think of Jimmy Carter's "lusting in my heart" for other women, Bill Clinton's "but I didn't inhale," and Dan Quayle's misspelling of potato—fodder for David Letterman jokes and never to be lived down. Sources joke about it and express the wish that reporters would reassure them that they don't play "Gotcha!" type journalistic games. Or if they do, they should present a Miranda warning: *One verbal slip and it's curtains for you!*

In the same vein, sources wonder why it's so important that their answers be spontaneous and unrehearsed. Why do reporters think the superficial, off-the-top-of-the-head answer is closer to truth or more quotable than the well-thought-out one? Given time to think, some suggest they could not only find better, more truthful answers, but could package them in quotable quotes and sound bites honed perfectly for media distribution.

Some sources feel uneasy about telephone calls after-hours to their homes—away from records, computer databases, and precise answers. The impromptu answers lack the precision some sources would prefer.

Here's another puzzle to sources: Why is something said early in an interview always etched in stone even though subsequent discussion causes a change of mind? A good interview often plows new ground in which early answers are tenuous and subject to further consideration. Some reporters prefer to cling to an ill-considered preliminary remark than to learn a source's true conclusions after discussion and thought. The headline will likely read, MAYOR FLIP-FLOPS ON ISSUE. So the joke goes. Sources often find reporters' stories accurate but headlines misleading.

Sensationalism.   Reporters constantly seek out the extremes—the best, the worst, the most bizarre. Sources tend to understand that this is the nature of the news business, but they often resent the fact that reporters make no attempt to identify the "mode," which is the circumstance that happens most often. Reporters ask about and write about exceptions rather than rules with a resultant distortion. While sources understand the need for reporting the sensational incidents, the thoughtful ones yearn for more stories that give a statistically accurate picture of trends.

Sensationalism is not always negative. A farmer suggests that urban reporters can't resist the notion of an idyllic life on the farm. They want to describe it in glowing terms, and can't be dissuaded by the realities of farm life: the price for farm produce is down, equipment and supply expenses are up, and government regulations are oppressive. Tell them that and the published result *still* clings to the notion of bucolic paradise.

Checking You Out.   Just as reporters have favorite sources, the reverse is true. Some sources may want to know whom you've interviewed in the past and will check out those references before agreeing to talk.

What kinds of reporters are these sources looking for? "Reporters who are as open, honest, and direct as they expect everyone else to be," says a former school administrator, Robert Peterkin, who was superintendent of schools at Milwaukee, Wisconsin before taking a position at Harvard University. Generally sources prefer a thorough, accurate reporter who is prepared to ask good ("creative") questions and to listen open-mindedly to the answers. Many say they will confess things to such a reporter not always in their own best interests. They do so in the belief that the reporter will use that information in a meaningful context—that is, will present the total picture. They relish the reporter who asks, "Who else knows about this that I can talk to?"

And sources do have their little tricks to retaliate against dangerously blind reporters. One district attorney told student interviewer Natasha Shepard that he always returns reporters' calls. But he knows the deadlines for all the media in his community. One disfavored reporter sometimes receives his callback at 11:59 A.M. to meet the reporter's noon deadline.

▶ 8

Planning Your Interview

Q. Senator, if you were conducting this interview, what questions would you ask?

A. I'd ask myself, "Why am I so poorly prepared as to make an idiot of myself before thousands of viewers?"

A well-planned interview contains an organizational pattern similar to that of a news or feature story. In newswriting you usually write from the bottom line forward—that is, the most important element first and secondary details later: the inverted pyramid. That the king died ranks higher than funeral arrangements or quotes from heads of state. So it is with the interview. News interviews open with attempts to discover the bottom line, the essence of a situation or event: What happened to whom, and when, where, how, and why? Other interviews unfold like a feature story: an opening anecdote (ice-breaking conversation), a statement of theme (describing the interview's purpose), and then point-by-point elaboration of the theme (questions that cover the points that interest you). Finally, some interviews work best in chronology. You ask a person who has witnessed a street shooting to "start at the beginning and tell me what happened."

Three basic organizational patterns, then, emerge: (1) inverted pyramid—important matters first, (2) thematic organization, and (3) chronology. Avoid the hit-and-miss style of interviewing that often characterizes the work of amateurs. Any interview fits at least one of the three patterns; complicated ones may combine all three. Planning for the interview typically proceeds through seven steps:

1. Defining your purpose
2. Requesting the interview

3. Conducting pre-interview research
4. Assessing your source's character and interests
5. Developing specific areas of inquiry
6. Anticipating answers
7. Developing a game plan

PLANNING STARTS WITH PURPOSE

As noted earlier, a strong sense of purpose serves as the key to planning. How do you arrive at purpose? Start by knowing precisely what you're looking for. An account of a news event? Employ the bottom-line methods. A feature story with action or dialogue? Use a thematic plan with emphasis on observation and questions of the what-happened-next variety. Some action may depict melodramatic happenings such as a firefighter rescuing a child. Equally dramatic narratives can show something internal, such as a business leader making a difficult decision.

For the sake of discussion, let's plan a hypothetical interview with such an executive—Elizabeth Morgan, chief executive officer of XYZ Corporation, an electronics manufacturing firm that employs 6,000. Purpose starts with asking yourself, why do you want to interview Elizabeth Morgan? Consider some possibilities.

- A newspaper business editor wants to assess the growth of electronics manufacturing in your locality. Morgan is one of several executives contacted.
- A feature writer for the "People" section wants to explore how Morgan, a single parent, combines family responsibilities with a career.
- A TV reporter wants to check rumors of workforce reductions in the wake of an economic recession.
- A writer for *Executive Woman*, a hypothetical magazine edited for women in management, wants to write about Morgan's struggle against the odds to reach the top of the corporate ladder in essentially a man's world.

Such reasons seldom come from nowhere. They grow from small seeds, sometimes a chance remark. The editor of *Executive Woman* attends a meeting of business leaders and hears talk about the "remarkable turnaround" of XYZ Corporation, once headed for bankruptcy "until they got that woman in there." Because the editor seeks inspirational case-history articles useful to women in management, she takes an immediate interest. "Who is that woman?" she asks, and the editorial game is afoot.

Magazines cover beats and maintain contacts much the same as newspapers cover the courts and city hall. Through business contacts—mostly executives and consultants familiar with XYZ and the new Morgan management—the editor learns that Morgan coped with alcoholism, vicious company politics, and bad managerial decisions ("made every mistake in the book"), but somehow learned from her mistakes to become a successful candidate for chief executive officer in a directors' meeting three years ago. She straightened out both the company and her personal life. So goes the talk. And just how did she accomplish this turnaround at XYZ? A little downsizing, a little streamlining, but mostly she did it by listening—listening to the customers. "She reads the market," your business contacts tell you, "she really helped XYZ get the voice of the customer into the company. . . . She has a sixth sense about marketing, and she translated that savvy into new product lines and new markets nobody there ever dreamed of."

Magazine articles emerge from such tenuous beginnings. What kind of article? You must find a purpose that will directly serve your readers and that Morgan would possibly agree to. The more specific the purpose, the better. An article entitled "Everything You Wanted to Know about Elizabeth Morgan" has the appeal of a dishrag. "Elizabeth Morgan's Struggle to Reach the Corporate Top Against Great Odds in a Male-Dominated Field" has more possibilities. You could redefine it even further. Could we develop a "learning from mistakes" theme? What has Elizabeth Morgan learned about management from those mistakes that will help other women? Tentative title: A Corporate CEO's Ten Worst Mistakes and How to Avoid Them. Magazine articles tend to focus sharply on narrow topics, and the best ones contain irony or paradox by depicting events that defy commonsense expectations. You don't expect an executive to reach the top after all those mistakes, yet here she is, the voice of experience sharing insights from which others might learn.

REQUESTING THE APPOINTMENT

Will Elizabeth Morgan buy such a purpose? Why would she confess all those mistakes? Don't make your own mistake of self-censorship. More good ideas are killed by timid journalists afraid to propose a provocative project than by uncooperative respondents. Consider a classic example.

In 1986 Washington reporter Lisa McCormack proposed an idea that few colleagues thought would fly—interviewing famous people about their "Walter Mitty fantasies." Why would Gerald Ford, G. Gordon Liddy, Richard Nixon, and others confess anything so personal as a fantasy? But to the surprise of everyone except McCormack, they talked freely. Ford imagined himself a famous baseball player, Liddy a World War II fighter pilot, Nixon a musician conducting a symphony orchestra. McCormack thinks the project succeeded because secretaries and aides—the gatekeepers reporters must get past to reach important people—found the question so provocative that they themselves wanted to learn the answers. (*Washington Times*, April 16, 1986.)

So journalists should not hesitate to try. Requesting an interview appointment requires preparation. Background reading and discussions with other business executives can help identify the typical mistakes of managers. In this instance—because we are writing for a magazine specifically aimed at executive women—our interests focus primarily on those unique to women.

Our mission is not merely to ask Morgan to list ten mistakes—rather, it is to come prepared with our own notions and *exchange* ideas. A busy executive will not appreciate our approaching her with a journalistic tin cup to beg for morsels. We should come as intellectual partners expecting that the conversation will produce the aforementioned higher level of enlightenment. If nothing more, our preparation will allow us to discard the clichés of women in management and let Morgan lead us to new horizons.

When you call Morgan for an appointment, you must be prepared to talk knowledgeably about the subject. Consider the request from her perspective. Why would Elizabeth Morgan make public her mistakes? It could get her in trouble with her board of directors, maybe even lead to declining values in XYZ stock. When she receives your request, she will, if she's smart, have the company's public affairs office check you out, both the interviewer and the magazine. From her perspective, it's wise to be wary.

A complex set of perceptions runs through the mind of the typical respondent. Foremost is the prestige of the magazine. If Morgan and her advisors hold *EW* in high regard—and if she identifies with the woman managers portrayed in previous issues—she may find the prospect exciting. She'd be in excellent company, with such executives as Sherry Lansing, Elizabeth Dole, Donna Shalala, and Helen Gurley Brown already portrayed in the magazine. Second, the editors speak her language. They are "students of management." Their kinds of interviews give as much as they get. And how does *EW* handle delicate information should alcoholism emerge as a topic of inquiry? The public affairs advisors say that the editors demand a lot of intimate information, but they handle it discreetly. The magazine is upbeat. It stands on her side—it sincerely wants women to succeed in management. The prestige of being featured in a reputable magazine could do more good than harm to her career and make a major contribution to understanding management problems. It could put XYZ on the map. Of course, some of her mistakes were pretty dumb—maybe they could be presented humorously. Anyhow, they're in the past, and if she hadn't learned some important lessons from them she'd never have succeeded as CEO. Being interviewed is always risky—but risk taking helped put her where she is now.

That would be the ideal reaction from the journalist's perspective. Clearly, success in securing such an interview depends on the reputation of the medium and of the writer as much or more than the focus of the interview. Your request involves six steps.

1. By phone, letter, or personal visit, you outline your project and tell why you think it's worthwhile. You may need to make your pitch first to subordinates, perhaps the public affairs people. You supply past issues of the magazine containing similar articles about prominent executives.

2. You suggest reasons why she should agree to it—educating the public, helping people achieve, helping women avoid mistakes. You "sell" your magazine's ideals: to help women succeed. Ego strokes can help. Many important people are talking about XYZ's remarkable recovery. Managers desperately need her visionary ideas. Other executives have singled her out as uniquely qualified to discuss the points you have in mind, especially the success in marketing.

3. You anticipate objections and develop arguments to overcome them. Yes, you'll want to talk about past alcoholism, but overcoming that demon puts you in the company of important people such as former Texas governor Ann Richards—"Our magazine has written about her and handled it decorously; would you like to see a copy of that story?" You negotiate any objections you can't overcome. "Can we put a more positive spin on this?" she asks. "More emphasis on *overcoming* mistakes, maybe, less on making mistakes?" (Of course. Tentative new title: A Corporate Executive Tells How to Overcome Ten Pitfalls of Management.)

4. You're prepared to engage in preliminary discussion. "What kinds of pitfalls are you talking about?" she asks. You offer suggestions. "Because our magazine speaks to women, I'm looking for ideas that directly affect our lives and our work," you say. "I can tell you from previous conversations with managers some areas where pitfalls commonly lurk. Risk taking, financial and otherwise, is one. Also skills in conducting negotiations with all their curve balls and sliders and end runs—our letters from readers suggest that they have concerns about that. How shall we behave in order to be taken seriously? Do we smile less, tell more jokes, pound the table—what? Even the jargon of business concerns us. Remember the Harragan book, *Games Mother Never Taught You*, about women not knowing a Hail Mary pass from Four Yards and a Cloud of Dust? Let's hope *those* days are past! So these are some areas where problems exist, and I hope they'll stimulate your thinking."

Such provocations often prompt respondents to debate points right on the phone. "Smiling will get you just so far," says Morgan. "I think one of the biggest mistakes women make is not getting angry on demand. I've learned to yell at meetings—a cold-blooded kind of anger. It's something I would not normally do, but it has a significant impact when used sparingly, and—" and suddenly you both realize that the interview is a go, with only the details to be worked out.

5. You arrange time and place.

6. You suggest points that you'd like her to think about before the interview. "I hope the article will contain anecdotal examples from your own experience, so I'll be looking for those as we talk."

DO YOUR HOMEWORK

A good rule of thumb: five hours of preparation for each hour of interview. For Richard Meryman, a former *Life* magazine writer, the preparation also includes avoiding alcohol, starch, and sugar for several days before an important interview, staying in bed most of the day before the interview, and eating a high-protein breakfast that morning. The purpose: clearing one's mind to listen carefully and prepare good follow-up questions. (*Life*, July 7, 1972.) Prepping for an interview has two major elements.

Documents. You're looking for information that will help you plan the interview, develop your questions, and better inform yourself about the issues. Consult a news library and databases for past articles on Elizabeth Morgan and XYZ, especially its flirtations with bankruptcy and the steps taken to make it solvent. Also look for general articles dealing with women in management. Consult national newspaper and magazine databases. Go to your local library; books such as *Wall Street Women* and *Feminine Leadership* can help you form your own list of typical managerial mistakes and how to overcome them. The XYZ public affairs department will provide information on both Morgan and XYZ.

Meanwhile, you can produce your own documents. You are lecturing to a group of management women—not an uncommon experience for an editor of a magazine. Passing out slips of blank paper on which you ask each member of the audience to list anonymously her "worst managerial mistake" can yield surprisingly effective responses.

Talking to Others.   You'll find valuable help via preliminary interviews with those acquainted with your person or with the issues. You may gain good advice on how to approach her, what subjects she might prefer to talk about or to avoid, her leisure interests, the books she enjoys, and so on. Consult an expert such as a professor of management for suggestions. Business competitors can provide worthwhile insights. Colleagues and family members can provide personal asides if needed. Exercise caution in approaching them, for their loyalty is to her, not you. Talk to them after she has agreed to the interview. They will check with her before they agree to talk with you. If she has come to trust you, so will they.

ASSESSING CHARACTER AND INTERESTS

History shows that Theodore Roosevelt shone as a brilliant conversationalist, equally at home with cowboys and diplomats. How did he do it? Simple. Roosevelt sat up late the night before reading up on subjects he knew would interest his visitor. (Carnegie 1936.) If you've done an adequate job of research, you'll know what those interests are. All people worth interviewing have an interest such as art, great books, mountain climbing, military history, river rafting. Knowing of that interest will allow you to prepare for the small talk that typically precedes an important interview. Knowing that Morgan adores the work of impressionist artists and steers rafts down treacherous whitewater rivers from the Chattooga to the Salmon can assist your preparation. Spend an evening reading about Van Gogh or about John Wesley Powell's 1869 exploration of the Colorado River. The knowledge you gain from the evening will not only open conversational pathways but the discussion may yield fragments of character that you can work into your article. Does risk taking on raging rivers equate with risk taking in business? A question worth asking.

PREPARING AREAS OF INQUIRY

Precisely what do you want to ask? In part the answer lies with your writing style and the kind of article you plan. Some magazine writers might envision a case-history narrative that sees our heroine through a series of critical mistakes and solutions that lead dramatically to snatching XYZ from the jaws of bankruptcy. The article will read like a short story complete with the proverbial "darkest hour" and the "dramatic resolution" common to fiction writing. The interview approach and the questions themselves will reflect this goal and will therefore contain lots of "what happened next?" questions.

By contrast, an article that merely identifies ten mistakes and their solutions would have a simple numerical structure with a lead-in that identifies Morgan and her role in saving XYZ, along with some conclusions at the end about the nature of corporate management. Here you have but one basic question: "How do we overcome or avoid those ten worst pitfalls?" You have a focus so precise that both interviewer and source can follow it easily. But your article will benefit from an interview that contains lively and wide-ranging discussion about problems and mistakes, particularly as they involve women. So you'll prepare questions, or topics of inquiry, to help identify those problem areas. Based on books by women for women in management (see Bibliography), here are some of the often-cited problem areas where pitfalls may reside. They should go into your interview schedule as questions or points of discussion.

1. Power. (How do women get it and use it?)
2. Risk taking. (How to avoid timidity?)
3. Listening, paying attention to customers. (If, as your contacts suggest, she succeeded by getting "close to the customer," she'll have useful comments here.)
4. Negotiating ability, especially in securing financing or dealing with creditors. (Are women at a disadvantage? Can we turn our better listening ability into an advantage?)
5. Insufficient assertiveness. (How do we toot our own horn?)
6. Harassment, hostility, lack of acceptance in men's groups, and so on. (Plenty of room for miscalculation here—how to handle?)
7. Humor. (Men use it effectively in business, why not women?)

The list could go on. It is possible that not one of these points relates to what Elizabeth Morgan considers mistakes needing to be overcome. If so, you're lucky. Your interview may forge into new ground. That, after all, is what you've come for: something new. Or, if not exactly new, at least a new perspective on the old. Or a set of illustrative stories depicting a unique experience. That's why you plan and prepare, so you can identify what is new.

ANTICIPATING ANSWERS

Suppose you plan to ask Morgan a question on the subject of corporate structure. Literature suggests that women are more comfortable with a flatter organizational hierarchy that allows ideas to emerge from the lower echelons rather than a narrow military structure with orders filtering down through many layers of command. The flatter structure means that a manager will have more people reporting to her; the reward comes from good ideas bubbling up from below with fewer gatekeepers in the way. You can anticipate Morgan's answers to a question like "What are your thoughts on flat management structure versus hierarchical?" By anticipating her answers, you can think ahead to follow-up questions.

1. She might suggest that flatter is better for women and for her method of operation. (Probes: Why? What are the benefits? What problems does it contain? What mistakes are possible? Did *you* overcome any mistakes in this area? Can you cite an example?)
2. She might reply that flatter doesn't work as well as she first thought. (In that event, you'd ask essentially the same probes, especially "Why not?")
3. She might say some modified system works for her. (Probe for details and for accounts of earlier trials and errors that led to her conclusion.)
4. She might suggest some point you did not anticipate. How fortunate! You cannot anticipate every answer. The ultimate follow-up question is the one that you didn't know you were going to ask because of answers you could *not* anticipate. Something's desperately wrong with an interview that contains no unexpected answers.

It's useful, in any event, to put yourself in the other person's place. Think how you might answer some of your own questions, the one about drinking, for example. Suppose you'd had a bout with alcoholism in your past. You'd talk about it—you may decide—only if you're convinced that an article describing recovering from alcoholism will help others solve or avoid the same problem. So if you plan to ask about drinking, you must prepare a reassuring sales pitch: "The article will talk about alcoholism in a way that avoids sensationalism—we'll write it in the context of how you think others can avoid that pitfall."

Plan how to approach a sensitive subject. You may decide to approach drinking indirectly. You quote from literature: "On the subject of drinking, Betty Harragan's book discusses the differences in expectations between male and female executives. She says men can get smashed at the office party and people hardly notice, but if a woman does the same thing, it's a corporate scandal. Have you noticed these kinds of expectations through the years? Have things changed?" What you ask next depends on her response; she may volunteer to talk of past problems if she has come to trust your sincerity and judgment in handling sensitive topics.

THE GAME PLAN

Eventually the elements of the interview will settle into a master plan, such as this thematic organization:

1. Start with icebreaking conversation about art or rafting the Colorado River.

2. When the time seems right, move to the theme of the interview, starting with a reiteration of purpose.

3. Discuss the issue conceptually. Why do women executives need this advice? Why is Morgan the key source in providing it? (Your article will use the comments as a lead-in to the ten pitfalls to be avoided.)

4. If appropriate, open with some of your own suggestions about managerial pitfalls to prime the pump. Or suggest areas where problems are likely to occur. Or ask if she has ten pitfalls already in mind; she may have prepared for the interview, too.

5. Continue your agenda, point by point.

6. Discuss anecdotal experiences in relation to each major problem; come prepared with your own stories about executives as pump primers.

7. Stress the need to cite a "lesson" from each pitfall.

8. Save any sensitive questions such as drinking problems (the bomb) for late in the session.

9. Ask any questions you haven't already covered, and offer her a chance to comment on anything not already covered or to rethink earlier commentary.

10. Ask your final questions. Once you have jointly settled on the final ten pitfalls, those final questions will seek some overall conceptual statement, perhaps a quotable comment that sums it all up now that you've identified the points.

11. As always, be prepared for the "afterglow" effect—the personal candor that often follows a successful interview.

KEEP YOUR PLANS FLEXIBLE

Interviewers can benefit from the advice that philosopher–educator William James gave to teachers: Know your subject thoroughly and then trust to luck. Knowing your subject permits you to follow down new conversational pathways you could not have envisioned in the planning stage. A certain spontaneity—the off-the-wall answer, the unexpected response—contributes to a more robust and insightful interview.

But it means frequent departures from your game plan. Suppose you have ten basic questions, and the answer to Question 1 happens to include a partial answer to Question 4. Do you insist on returning to Question 1 or do you follow through with Question 4? There's no good answer other than to suggest that the more the interview follows the pattern of normal human conversation—with all its stops and turns and erratic patterns—the better. If your source is enthusiastically discussing Question 4, why not let her continue rather than dampen the enthusiasm? You can return to Question 1 later. Your organizational pattern will make it easier to keep track.

In such wayward conversations you must serve as guide. Use of transitional phrases helps keep the organizational pattern on track. "I think we've covered the problems of management structure sufficiently, so why don't we move along to the subject of power? . . ." Transitions flow more smoothly when you utilize the respondent's words. "Something you said earlier—about your having to learn to be less thin-skinned in response to criticism—reminds me that I want to talk about that." Flexibility also means changing your article focus if necessary or maybe settling on only eight points—or twelve—rather than clinging tenaciously to ten.

A PLANNING FOOTNOTE

The potentially uncomfortable element called the "bomb" works both ways. Your respondent may have a bomb in her briefcase, too—a startling revelation that may change your story line. As you're at the door saying your last good-bye, Morgan says, "Oh, by the way, I'm resigning, effective tomorrow, as CEO for XYZ. I meant to tell you this earlier, but it slipped my mind. Well, thanks for a wonderful conversation. . . ."

What now? Will it change your article? Probably. Make it better? Maybe, especially if you ask a few probes. "Why? Was there a problem with XYZ? What will you do now?"

So much for planning.

An interviewer should always ask how a series of events turns out. Let's imagine that Morgan says her biggest mistake as CEO has been listening to her board of directors, most of them men, telling her how to run the company. "I've decided to start making my own mistakes instead of making *their* mistakes." Now there's a fine quote for your article.

She will start her own manufacturing company, Morgan Products Development, Inc. Financed by venture capital and employing forty, it will manufacture liquid crystal display (LCD) screens to be used in miniature computers and tiny television sets, the type commonly used in airplanes, rail cars, and mobile homes. "LCD panels will grow to a $20 billion market worldwide in the next five or ten years," Morgan says, "and I thought I would spend a few years trying to secure a slice of it."

What a lovely ending for your article. Plan for the unexpected—it's what makes journalism fun.

▶ 9

Lessons from Failure

Q. ?
A. !

Frankly, I love failure. Failure contains the seeds of learning. Most college students find it less painful to learn from other people's mistakes than from their own. So here, for your edification, comes an example of failure.

First, the setting—a seminar room with fifteen students seated around a big table. We selected one student, Margaret Laine, for a grand experiment: We will interview her in front of the class. We sent her out of the room so that we could discuss interviewing strategy out of her hearing. Laine, a graduate student, once worked as a venereal disease investigator for the health department in Oklahoma City. The job required extensive interviewing under difficult circumstances to determine the identity of sexual contacts. The job also required visiting some of the worst districts of the city to locate some vaguely described person who had been identified as the sexual contact. She then encouraged the person to visit a clinic for examination and possible treatment.

Our interview, we decided, should deal with interviewing itself. We'd ask her to describe how she used interviewing in her work, with special emphasis on difficult interviews. What tips and ideas and experiences could she describe to help us deal with persons who may not want to talk about their intimate experiences?

A young man in the class volunteered to start the interview. When Laine reentered the room, she did not know the purpose we'd established. She sat in a chair across a conference table from the interviewer. We turned on a tape recorder.

Here is the verbatim transcript. The Q-numbers serve as reference points for the interview analysis that follows.

Q-1. I'd like to ask you some questions about your job as a VD investigator in Oklahoma City.

A. Okay.

Q-2. Okay, I think I'd like to start out not by trying necessarily to pin you down in your own experience but in some of your impressions of the most successful techniques you used for getting the information you wanted—

A. You mean—

Q-3. Ah, your contacts that, ah, or other contacts that you found that were the, ah [4–5 seconds of silence] . . . when you go out and meet someone, you ran into someone we'll say was kind of hard to talk to—

A. Uh-huh—

Q-4. —what did you find worked most successfully in getting through to them—

A. Okay, I—

Q-5. —in terms of loosening them up to the point where they'd, you know, be willing to go along with whatever it is you wanted them to do?

A. Are you talking about the regular interviews with someone who has venereal disease, or are you talking about—

Q-6. Right.

A. —trying to find someone in the field?

Q-7. Well, we understood that you went out and contacted people . . . or did you have a number coming in—

A. Uh—

Q-8. —volunteers—

A. Okay. Well, it's a combination of both, and two highly different situations. Some people came into the clinic with VD, and anybody who came into the clinic, we talked to them while they were at the clinic. That was the formal interviewing situation. Going out in the field was to find people who had been exposed to VD and to get them into the clinic. It was not an interviewing situation, more a finding situation.

Q-9. How did you get word on them?

A. From the people that came into the clinic or from private hospitals or private doctors or from laboratories.

Q-10. When you went out, would you pick a particular time of day you thought would be most successful—I mean, you probably wouldn't go out at night—

A. Yeah, you'd go at night sometimes. Of course lots of people would be home at night that weren't home during the day.

Q-11. Uh-huh.

A. Ah. . . . [silence]

Q-12. So the time of day wouldn't have much to do with it—when you were going out?

A. Well, it had a lot to do with it when you're going out. It varied with each case.

Q-13. Did you work all hours?

A. Yeah, you pretty much had your own hours. Your job was to do the job, and sometimes it was done before five, and sometimes you just went swimming and you did it at night. It just depends on who you were looking for and when. We worked every morning.

Q-14. Can you give me some idea of what would happen during an initial contact, say, someone who's not particularly glad to see you?

A. [Chuckles.] That's kind of a hard question to answer because, ah, many, many different things would happen. If you kind of narrow it down to—

Q-15. Sort of type of person?

A. Yeah, type of person, or someone who's angry or someone who's crying or someone who is belligerent, you know; I don't know exactly what you're looking for.

Q-16. Let's say someone who is belligerent . . . older than you, who is belligerent. Male.

A. Okay, that I've gone out to look for?

Q-17. Uh-huh.

A. And . . . okay, let me think if I can remember an instance like that. . . . there were lots of them, of course, ah. . . . the way you handle it, of course, just depends on the situation. . . . okay. . . . in this one particular instance, I went out in the country. . . . [She tells, with great animation and gesturing, how she'd visited a woman on the front porch of a dilapidated shack in rural Oklahoma. The husband was there, too, so she couldn't discuss the possibility of VD infection in his presence, so she alluded vaguely to the need for an "examination." The husband rose up and said threateningly, "Best be gittin' off my land before I get my gun." As Margaret beat a hasty retreat, she heard three shots, one of which shattered a window of her car. "I don't know if he was shooting to hit me or just to scare me, but I wasn't gonna hang around to find out." Clearly a most entertaining story that elicited much laughter and response from the students around the table. At this point, Margaret was no longer talking with the interviewer; she was playing to the crowd from which she received such gratifying response.]

Q-18. Have any of you ever been shot?

A. And killed, you mean?

Q-19. Well, I'd just settle for wounded.

A. Not in Oklahoma. One guy got beat up but nobody actually got wounded.

Q-20. . . . [Silence]

The interview ended at that point. Margaret Laine seemed willing to entertain the class with further accounts of her adventures, but it was time for analysis. Everyone present agreed that it was a fumbling, unsuccessful venture—in short, a splendid learning experience. What lessons can we draw here?

1. The interviewer never made the purpose clear. Laine confirmed that she really hadn't understood what we wanted. She said she could easily have provided the *interviewing* experiences and advice we sought had we made those interests clear. How could we have explained the purpose? Imagine this replay of the interview's beginning:

> *Q.* I'd like to ask you some questions about your job as a VD investigator in Oklahoma City.
>
> *A.* Okay.
>
> *Q.* Let me explain what we're looking for. I know from the discussion we had in your absence that you used interviewing quite a bit in your job, even took intensive training in interviewing. I think you'd have a lot of ideas and experiences that would prove helpful in our own interviews—particularly the kinds of interviews where people might not want to talk with you or might not want to reveal intimate details of their sexual experiences. Perhaps you could tell us a few of the basic problems, particularly the ones you think are pertinent to journalistic interviewing, and explain how they're handled. And, of course, I'd be delighted if you could illustrate the problems with examples from your experiences. Do you understand what I want, and do you have any questions before we start?

Absence of a clearly stated purpose heads the list of errors in just about every failed interview, and this was no exception. In contrast, the other problems seemed less severe, though they represent a certain contributory negligence:

2. Absence of icebreakers.

3. Absence of careful listening. Question 12 suggests lack of listening, possibly a desperation remark to keep the conversation going. Question 13 seems equally irrelevant. Both parties continue to misread each other through the dialogue.

4. Absence of ego reinforcement. The "best be gettin' off my land" story calls for response—"Wow, great story!" (True, the story was off-target. This would have been a time to rescue the interview by citing its purpose. The next story she told might have hit the target once she understood what we wanted.)

5. Lack of interviewer enthusiasm for the subject. It was unflattering and discouraging that he ran out of questions at Question-20. People tend to clam up when they're not appreciated.

6. Lack of organization, a problem brought on by the unclear purpose. Some questions are random shots in the dark. We as readers know what should have been the purpose and can therefore see a slight relevance, but Laine was entirely in the dark. As a result we, and even you as readers, were deprived of Margaret Laine's wisdom—her potentially useful ideas about interviewing under difficult conditions.

This kind of exploratory interviewing resembles walking into a black cave with an armload of unlighted candles. Each candle represents a question to be ignited by the answer. The lighted candle illuminates a tiny part of the cave. One question leads to another, and eventually a whole section of the cave becomes visible. A well-organized set of questions, especially the ones prompted by earlier answers, will systematically lead to a visible reality, to truth. Too often interviewers light random candles so that only random fragments of reality show up. Most times fragmented reality is no better than the proverbial blind men describing the elephant, if you'll pardon the mixed metaphor. It serves humanity no better than abject darkness. Too many reporters end up with ear stories or trunk stories rather than whole-elephant stories, and the fragmented interview is to blame.

▶ 10

Learning to Listen

Q. Tell me about listening.

A. Ah, listening. Listening is the one area of human activity where it makes sense to be selfish. Imagine! The more you take from a speaker through listening, the more that speaker will give. (Paraphrasing Nichols and Stevens 1957.)

Q. Huh?

Journalistic interviewers are not equal: Some get more than others. They do it not by clever questions or intimidating tactics. Quite the opposite. They get more by asking fewer questions, listening more intensely, and responding to what they've heard. Imagine that you're in an unfamiliar neighborhood and you're lost. You "interview" a passerby. You're not looking for a dramatic outburst or a sensational news lead; you simply want to get to the corner of Elm and Main Streets. What counts is listening. You may even repeat back the instructions to make sure you understand. That kind of listening—where you can accurately repeat the essence of what someone said—belongs in the journalistic interview.

Journalistic listening occurs when you know precisely what kinds of details you want out of an interview. If you want quotable quotes or anecdotes, you must listen for them and recognize them when they occur—and react so as to encourage more of them. Sources don't say, "Here's an anecdote for your lead"; they just talk. It's up to you to distinguish the quotable kernels from the chaff. Yet you must not listen so narrowly that you fail to perceive the essence of what a source is saying. That could be the definition of journalistic listening: to hear and to understand, so that you are able to present the respondent's essential message, even if you disagree with that message. Call it "paying attention."

AGGRESSIVE LISTENING

Listening is not a passive activity. "Aggressive listening" may seem a contradiction in terms. But you have to work hard to catch the meaning of what the other person is saying, and you have to encourage that person by the way you react, both verbally and nonverbally.

Research evidence suggests that adults spend more time in listening than in any other communications activity. An early study (Rankin 1926) calculated that people spend 42 percent of their communications time listening (versus 32 percent speaking, 15 percent reading, 11 percent writing). By 1975, when another researcher updated the study, the time spent listening had risen to 55 percent. (Werner 1975; reported in Wolvin and Coakley 1985.) Yet schools pay scant attention to listening as an academic topic, and even academic research on the subject remains sparse.

The key to listening appears to be the speed at which the human mind processes information. We speak at roughly 125 words a minute, but the mind can absorb material at three or four times that rate. But you have a one-track mind—we all do. It can do only one thing at a time. So you dart into and out of the conversation, and use the extra time to take notes, to retrieve pertinent pieces of previous conversations, to compare a speaker's ideas with other ideas, and to contemplate follow-up questions. Or you can use that time to take totally irrelevant excursions.

How people use the gap between the mind's activity and the speaker's pace distinguishes the listeners from the nonlisteners. The best listeners, according to one authority (Nichols and Stevens 1957), tend to think ahead of the speaker, sometimes arriving at the point before the speaker does.

The best listeners hold other attributes in common, according to studies that compared the listening habits of the best and worst listeners, as measured by tests of their ability to remember material presented to them orally. The best listeners used the extra mental processing time to think about what was said. They periodically reviewed what the speaker had said and what they imagined would be said next. They weighed the speaker's comments against other evidence. And they listened "between the lines" for ideas and attitudes hinted at but not expressed directly.

The worst listeners tended to listen for facts, sometimes trying to memorize them without much regard to their meaning. They were often distracted by little things, the noise of a passing vehicle, perhaps, or by some personal quality possessed by the speaker—too ugly, too attractive, squeaky voice, or whatever. Often the poor listeners were distracted by a single emotion-laden word that derailed their attentiveness onto an irrelevant line of thought. The worst listeners often dismissed the topic or the speaker as boring.

The pioneering work by Nichols and Stevens defined listening by the ability to recall information from oral messages. More recent literature casts doubt on that definition. (What's the prime factor in the ability to recall—listening or intelligence? Studies have shown significant correlations with intelligence.) One report on the literature of listening lists no fewer than seventeen definitions for listening and concludes that we're still developing the definitive thinking on the subject. (Wolvin and Coakley 1985.) Perhaps a good listener is essentially a "caring, other-oriented person." (Bostrom 1990.) The journalistic interviewer who cares about the source—at least to the extent of listening to and representing the source's views—will gain more candid responses than the insincere reporter.

Meanwhile, the work of journalistic listening goes on with or without an appropriate definition. Because most journalistic interviews focus on gathering information for presentation to an audience, the task of defining becomes simpler. Listening means paying attention to the respondent's message. It means asking questions that will ensure that you understand the message. It means mentally juggling the many aspects of the interview in short-term memory so that your questions uniquely reflect what you've been hearing during the conversation (as opposed to canned questions prepared before the interview). And it means coming away with a record of what has been revealed, be it through notes, recording device, or memory.

Memory is the least dependable record, as studies of witness reliability have documented. (Loftus and Doyle 1987.) The process involves three elements of memory: short-term memory (STM), rehearsal, and long-term memory. (Bostrom 1990.) Memory disintegrates rapidly, often within seconds, unless rehearsed, meaning you have thought about what you have seen or heard, talked about it, or recorded it in your notes. If comments in an interview have no meaning for you, they will disappear quickly from memory. That suggests one fault of reportorial listening. Reporters often do not pay attention to comments made early in an interview, comments that assume meaning only in the context of subsequent revelations. Unless recorded, valuable comments become lost as a result.

Short-term memory becomes especially valuable in conducting the interview itself. An alert mind, paying close attention to the conversation, will integrate remembered fragments of conversation and allow you to form new questions based on those fragments. It's the kind of question that starts, "Something you said a few minutes ago seems to bear on what we're talking about now," and goes on to mix and match fragments with an eye toward providing new insights. The more you use your mind to evaluate, compare, and contrast the source's comments, the more you'll ask those kinds of creative questions.

Exercising your memory during interviews helps in another way. Both Carl Rogers and Irving Lee (both 1952) have proposed an experiment in which (at a meeting, say) no one can speak unless he or she has summarized the previous speaker's thoughts to that person's satisfaction. "If you try you will discover it is one of the most difficult things you have ever tried to do," said Rogers. Lee found that in meetings where it was tried utter confusion reigned for a time. Then something remarkable happened. Garrulous people tried to make their points more succinct, and timid people found the courage to speak up when they found others were actually listening. Equally remarkable things happen when reporters repeat back their understanding from time to time during an interview.

Listening also takes courage, according to the experts. It extracts at least two prices. The first price is the risk of having your ideas changed. What you learn by listening to others can change your life. "Such listening requires a kind of courage that few of us have ever mustered," suggest Nichols and Stevens. "Whenever we listen thoroughly to another person's ideas, we open ourselves up to the possibility that some of our ideas are wrong."

It's hard to be a good listener and to be narrowly self-righteous at the same time. Good listeners, as evidenced by the reaction of students who have taken interviewing classes, find a whole new world opening up to them: The timid find the courage to go out and meet new people, the arrogant find the courage to venture out from their fortresses to learn and appreciate other points of view.

The second price is the risk of involvement. So powerful a tool is listening that we find ourselves getting involved with the people to whom we listen. Author Studs Terkel explained that in the haste of interviewing the working people who populated his best-selling *Working* he sometimes neglected certain social amenities. A Brooklyn fireman invited him for dinner, and Terkel mumbled something about having to hustle to another appointment. "You runnin' off like that?" the fireman said. "Here we been talkin' all afternoon. It won't sound nice. This guy, Studs, comes to the house, gets my life on tape, and says 'I gotta go.' " Terkel stayed. "Looking back," he wrote, "how could I have been so insensitive?" (Terkel 1974.)

HOW TO BECOME A PROFESSIONAL LISTENER

The following suggestions will help you develop listening skills. Part of the skills development comes in recognizing common pitfalls. Another part comes with knowing what you want.

Get Ready to Listen.   What, precisely, do you listen for? Planning your interview will help you identify the points and supporting evidence for which you should listen. Like an editor, you will discard much, retaining those items that fall within your planned zone of interest. But don't cast your plans in stone; leave room for unexpected turns of conversation that may yield unusual insights still largely within that zone.

Getting ready also means being physically and mentally fit. It means discarding certain kinds of "emotional filters," that clog the listening channels. Such filters include the relative attractiveness of the speaker. She's fat, he's ugly, she smiles a lot, he stutters—all these reactions can interfere with listening. Certain words contain emotional dynamite for some: *home, mother, patriotism, abortion, right wing, liberalism, sex, AIDS, blood, naked*—an endless list. Mention of "home" triggers such strong emotions that instead of listening we are suddenly picturing a beloved or hated childhood experience. If you recognized these emotional land mines—perhaps by writing them down and studying them until the emotion has drained away—you'd not let them interfere.

Listen for Major Points.   Listening to conversation is not like listening to a prepared speech. A good speaker generally presents a theme supported by two or more major points, with each point supported by facts, illustrative examples, and anecdotes. Good speakers often identify their main points, alerting their audience by such remarks as, "My next point is . . ." Interviews, however, often ramble the way conversations do. That's not necessarily bad as a means of achieving conversational rapport, but along the way both parties to the conversation must identify the conceptual elements—the points—of the source's comments. The thematic style of interview that focuses on points will have an easier time of it because both parties have set out to identify those points. In a less specific interview, the points might not emerge so readily. Sometimes it helps to ask a garrulous talker what's the point. Do it in a nonthreatening way: "As I understand it, your point is . . ." or "Are you saying that. . . ?" Sometimes you will discover that the speaker has no point. Or you yourself may ultimately define the points, either during the interview or later when writing an article based on the interview. Some interviews, such as a witness telling you what she saw at a house fire, may have no particular point other than the eyewitness chronology. Sometimes an interview pair can arrive at a point together, through such questions as "Did you learn anything from your experience?" or "What's the moral of the story?"

Listen for Supporting Evidence. Once you understand the point and how it connects with the main theme of a person's conversation, you can seek supporting evidence. Suppose, as an example, you are interviewing a VIP about the hidden perils of celebrity status. Sally Celebrity says, "The worst part is venturing out in public." That's one of her points, now what evidence can she produce to support it? If she doesn't volunteer it, you ask for it. How many autographs has she signed? ("Approximately four and one-half million!") What happens when she goes to the grocery store? Or to lunch at a major restaurant? Listen carefully and maybe she'll tell you about drunks accosting her at the table or women staring at her in the ladies' room or requests for Polaroid pictures with Aunt Suzie—maybe even the time she was sued by a guy who wrecked his car because he was staring at her walking down the sidewalk instead of attending to his driving. He blamed her for the accident, and her insurance company settled. Supporting evidence, then, consists of anecdotes and examples such as those cited, even the hyperbole about the millions of autographs.

Listen for Counterpoints. When Ms. Celebrity says she hates her fans, she may not mean it as firmly as it sounds. Listen carefully for (or ask about) the other side of the issue or belief, and you'll find attitudes tend to be percentages of gray rather than pure blacks and whites. Was there never a time, Ms. Celebrity, when you felt a little unnerved when venturing into the grocery store and no one even seemed to notice?

Evaluate What Is Being Said. Open-minded tolerance and nonjudgmental listening do not mean unquestioning naiveté. If you have prepared for the interview, you'll know when something said in the conversation doesn't equate with what you have learned elsewhere. Asking about the possible discrepancy shows not only that you're listening but that you're thinking. Often you will think through several remarks, putting them together in novel ways, maybe even testing a hypothesis as defined in the creative question or merely clarifying comments that seem at odds.

Listen for What Is Not Said or What Is Only Half-Articulated. Listening with the third ear is the theme of a classic work by Theodor Reik who published a book by that name in 1952. People communicate in various ways, often nonverbal, as noted earlier. You ask a woman about her future and she blushes or smiles or raises an eyebrow ever so slightly. You suspect you may have hit upon a question that has more than routine significance to her. The signal doesn't tell you what the significance is, only that you might profitably ask further questions, even if only, "Why do you smile when I ask that?"

How to be too casual while interviewing

Similarly, people's word choices are clues to deeper meanings. An interviewer sensitive to words will pick up on a phrase such as, "As a public administrator, you are subjected to many questions that defy explanation. . . ." Or, "Our agency is currently in the clutches of the county commissioners. . . ." *Subjected? Clutches?* What interesting choices of words. What do they mean to the speaker? That's precisely what you must ask.

Offer Encouragement and Direction.   Interviewers should respond and should ask questions. If this oft-stated point seems obvious, apparently it isn't to many unskilled interviewers who tend to state agenda topics and then, with no further comment or follow-up questions, simply sit back deadpan and take notes, like a stenographer, on the response. When the monologue has ended on Topic #1, the interviewer announces Topic #2 and the monologue begins anew. Such interviews aren't much fun. A listening interviewer will not only smile, nod, frown, say "uh-huh," and so forth, but will direct the conversation with probe questions.

Show That You're Listening.   When people aren't listening, they're obvious about it, often through distracting mannerisms such as averted eye contact. Men often use body posture to demonstrate nonlistening attitudes. They slump down or twist into contorted shapes. The extreme instance in my experience came in a classroom exercise where students were paired off to interview one another. A young man interviewed a young woman while slumped down in his chair, his feet up on a window ledge. His head rested lower than his feet, and from this supine position he conducted the interview. When, in subsequent class discussion, she commented on his "strange posture" as being a little *too* informal, he confessed that he wasn't even aware that he was flat on his back. The problem is not confined to students. When I mentioned this bizarre posture in a workshop attended by newspaper professionals, a business writer confessed to the sudden realization that he, too, had indulged in sloppy posture almost as bad.

Dress for Listening.   What has dress to do with listening? People often dress to tell the world something about themselves. Other people perceive that message. Visiting the plush office of a bank president while wearing faded jeans and tattered sweatshirt will probably result in disaster. Your mode of dress suggests that you've come to make a statement, not to listen. True, that might not be your conscious intent, but that's the way the president perceives it—unless you can offer a reasonable explanation as Scott Martell did (Chapter 1) when he showed up for a black-tie store opening wearing blue jeans.

▶ 11

Journalistic Observation

Q. So, Champ, you've been in the boxing ring with the great prize-fighters of all time. What's it like to get creamed by someone like Sugar Ray Leonard?

A. Stand up, fella, and I'll show ya.

Some journalists will go an extra mile for a story. George Plimpton, a skinny guy who edits a literary magazine, practices what he calls "participatory journalism," which means getting his nose bloodied in a boxing match with the light-heavyweight champion of the world. Jann Mitchell, a reporter for *The Oregonian* in Portland, spent three days as a denizen of Skid Road, begging for handouts and even retrieving a half-eaten sandwich from a garbage can one time to assuage her hunger. It's tough on the streets—and in the boxing ring—and who can better describe the perils of either than reporters who have experienced them firsthand?

We come now to a different kind of journalism, one that requires information gathering beyond the interview. Here reporters not only witness events, in many instances they participate in them.

It is not new. Anthropologists have been doing it for years. It's not even new to journalism. A century ago Elizabeth Cochrane, writing under the pen name of Nellie Bly, feigned insanity to get herself admitted to a New York insane asylum so that she could write about it for Joseph Pulitzer's *New York World*. She became a legend in 1889 by circling the world in seventy-two days—eight fewer than the eighty envisioned by science-fiction writer Jules Verne. Some great literature has emerged from participatory journalism, including such classics as *Black Like Me* in which John Howard Griffin, a white man, darkened his skin so that he could pass as black. His moving account about travels through the South as a black man helped to usher in the Civil Rights movement of the 1960s. Feminist author Gloria Steinem provides another example. She secured a job as a Playboy bunny so that she could write a magazine article about the experience (*Show*, May–June 1963)—another landmark effort and a harbinger of the feminist movement.

Sports writing has long relied on observation. So has coverage of murder trials and legislative debates. Yet matters have changed. Increased attention centers on nonfiction that contains vivid detail, dramatic action, suspense, and irony. These elements give writing the emotional and sensory impact of good fiction while retaining the authenticity of fact. It goes by several names—literary journalism, creative nonfiction, new journalism. Its best-known practitioners include George Plimpton, John McPhee, Gay Talese, Tracy Kidder, Tom Wolfe, Hunter Thompson, and Joan Didion. Newspaper writers have earned plaudits as well, such as Pulitzer Prize winners Jon Franklin and Jacqui Banaszynski, who produced feature articles showing scenes gained through journalistic observation. They were there when events happened: Franklin in a tense hospital operating room witnessing brain surgery, Banaszynski on a Minnesota farm where two young men were dying of AIDS.

Observation techniques emerged from a simple truth about writing. If you want to describe vividly the activities of coal miners or hoboes, go into the mines or ride the rails yourself. Sociologist Nels Anderson did so in a pioneering study about hoboes in 1923. Perhaps the hoboes' days are past, but as late as 1983 a *Sacramento Bee* editor chanced to talk with an aging hobo who said the ancient art of hoboing had been taken over by a "bunch of greenhorns." The editor assigned reporter Dale Maharidge and photographer Michael Williamson to the story, and they promptly hopped a freight to Oregon. They became so enthralled with the project that they not only produced an award-winning series for the *Bee*, but they became "professional hobos" for a year, producing a book (*Journey to Nowhere* 1985). Almost ten years later, they documented the end of the hobo era with a second book (*The Last Great American Hobo* 1993).

THE NEW RESEARCH REQUIREMENTS OF "LITERARY JOURNALISM"

Print reporters have witnessed a nearly forty-year trend toward "literary journalism." To one observer it represents no less than the death of a contradiction in terms. "Literary newswriting," says R. Thomas Berner, "is the marriage of depth reporting and literary techniques in newspaper writing. Among those techniques are narration and scene, summary and process, point of view, drama, chronological organization, rhythm, imagery, foreshadowing, metaphor, irony, dialogue, overall organization (beginning, middle, end)—all girded by good reporting." (Berner 1986.) Theodore A. Rees Cheney (1991) calls it "creative nonfiction," and says it "requires the skill of the storyteller and the research ability of the reporter." Cheney says the new approaches to nonfiction set new standards for writers who must "not only understand all the facts, but also see beyond them to discover their underlying meaning. And they must dramatize that meaning in an interesting, evocative, informative way."

Examine the kinds of newspaper articles that win prizes, for instance. The Pulitzer Prize committee began awarding prizes for feature writing in 1979, giving the first to a *Baltimore Evening Sun* science writer, Jon Franklin. His "Terrifying journey through tunnels of the brain" was a suspenseful account of a brain operation. Details march relentlessly through complications toward the climactic resolution.

Among the details are tense scenes. One of them shows the surgeon's probe pressing through a tunnel in the brain, nudging up against an aneurysm, a ballooned-out section of artery resembling, in Franklin's words, "a balloon ready to burst, a time-bomb the size of a pea." The surgeon must defuse this time-bomb before the probe can pass on to reach a malformation farther along the tunnel. Franklin shows the probe nudging gently against the aneurysm and quotes a nurse: "Sometimes you touch one and blooey, the wolf's at the door."

The nurse's remark came as an aside to Franklin during the operation. In an interview years later, Franklin said the story involved many pre- and post-operation interviews as well as observation. Obtaining permission to witness the operation came readily because he'd gained the respect of doctors through six years of writing medical and science stories. He sought to witness and write about a surgical procedure, and on a "whim," he asked the surgeon to select one in which the outcome would be in doubt. Mrs. Kelly with a malformation in the brain known as an AVM (arteriovenous malformation) became the focus of the story. The surgery—complex, delicate, dangerous—revealed an inoperable formation. Mrs. Kelly died. Franklin left thinking that the tragic outcome left him with no story. But as he began drafting he realized the story was in the doctor's efforts, not in the patient's misfortune. (Franklin interview 1995.) Life goes on even after a tragic outcome, and that became the theme of the revised story, the one that made history as the first Pulitzer Prize awarded for feature writing.

The standards set by this and subsequent Pulitzer winners place ever more pressure on the information-gathering function. "You've got to do deep and thorough research," author Gay Talese told an audience at Yale University. "You've got to have an affair with your subject." He participated in a panel discussion with writers Joan Didion, John Dunne, Lewis Lapham, and George Plimpton. All agreed with Talese's assertion that "in creative nonfiction the rules of accuracy must not be violated. All that we write should be verifiable." (Cheney 1991.)

Inevitably, some will violate that rule. This led to one of the all-time great scandals involving the Pulitzer Prize. It occurred in 1981 when Janet Cooke, of the *Washington Post*, won a Pulitzer for an article titled "Jimmy's World," about an eight-year-old heroin addict. The intricate detail about him, even the "cherubic expression on his small, round face," seemed real enough. But the city's mayor ordered the police to find Jimmy and help him, and when they failed, doubt began to loom. Eventually the hoax was revealed. Everything, including the cherubic expression, came out of the writer's imagination. The 1981 Pulitzer was returned and awarded to another writer.

The moral? Don't try writing dramatic nonfiction until your ability to interview and observe catches up with your ambition to produce literary journalism. Hone your skills, meanwhile, as a careful observer.

You may want to start somewhere short of a book-length account. Observation will enhance most any news account from a sports event to a murder trial. Does the prosecuting attorney speak harshly in cross examination of the defendant? Then let part of your report show—complete with dialogue—such elements as the sarcastic questions, the obsequious responses, the hushed courtroom, the petulant judge.

Points made in previous chapters about interviewing—especially about having a well-defined purpose and knowing precisely what you want—apply to observation. If you are going to observe people in action as a means of developing narration, then you'd better recognize when pertinent activities occur and get them into your notes.

THREE TYPES OF JOURNALISTIC OBSERVATION

The interviewer's techniques normally involve three types of observation: nonparticipant observation, participant observation, and unobtrusive observation.

Nonparticipant Observation. This is the first level of observation, and it is something journalists do routinely. The sports writer covering a basketball game, the drama critic attending a play, the political reporter viewing a debate in Congress—all are examples of a "spectator" kind of reporting common to much news coverage.

Think of nonparticipant observation as "going along for the ride." It means sitting in on the action but not taking part. It can be more than a city council meeting, however. You ride with the teenagers in a car cruising Main Street on a Saturday night for a story on teen society. You stand by in the hospital emergency room to witness the handling of victims of Saturday night traffic accidents. You accompany a long-haul truck driver on a trip across America. You witness your favorite celebrity in action on the movie set.

Participant Observation. Posing as a Playboy bunny. Riding the rails with the hoboes. Begging for handouts on Skid Road. Entering the ring to take on prize-fighter Archie Moore and getting your nose bloodied. All are examples of participant observation. Author George Plimpton's literary adventures saw him in action in several venues in addition to the boxing match with Archie Moore. Plimpton pitched to some of professional baseball's great stars

"So, tell me, do you find this exhausting or what?"

(he almost beaned the Phillies' Richie Ashburn, and Willie Mays popped one of Plimpton's pitches to the infield for an easy out). (Plimpton 1961.) He played quarterback for the Detroit Lions, running five plays and telling the story in the book *Paper Lion* (1966).

Observation offers an opportunity to exercise all the senses—not only what you see, hear, touch, taste, and smell, but also what you feel inside. Your internal response—your own thoughts and emotions—can produce drama or irony. As George Plimpton was being pummeled by Archie Moore he heard a spectator yell, "Hey, George, hit him back"—and his thoughts turned immediately to how inappropriate was the name "George" for the ring—"rather like hearing 'Timothy' or 'Warren' or 'Christopher.' " (Plimpton 1977.) You can report somebody else's internal response, too, such as the thoughts of the champion athlete as she approaches the finish line to achieve a new record in the women's 10,000-meter run. (At least, whatever thoughts she relates to you in a post-victory interview.)

Sometimes reporters keep their identity secret, as in Gloria Steinem's Playboy bunny episodes or John Howard Griffin's travels as a black man in the South where it was important that people behave as they normally would. In other instances, such as George Plimpton's adventures as an athlete, the participants know of the reporter's identity. That knowledge gives the reporter certain advantages: With no deception involved, you're free to circulate and to ask questions. People often seek you out to offer suggestions when they know your identity.

The secret-identity type of project poses ethical questions. If you're posing as a panhandler and the mayor responds to your request for donation by saying "Go to hell!", what does your conscience tell you about quoting the mayor by name? Does the mayor have a right to know he's talking to a reporter who may quote him in the story or even make his remark a headline? Also, how do you feel about hidden camera interviews? See Chapter 20 for discussions of ethics.

Unobtrusive Observation.   This is a quiet mouse-in-the-corner type of observation, often accompanied by numerical tallies. College students do it frequently in their classes, it seems. When members of an interviewing class undertook to query students about what they thought about while sitting through "dull" classroom lectures at the University of Oregon, the answers astonished them. They expected to hear confessions of students daydreaming anything from erotic fantasies to vacation plans. They did find that. But they also found that students spent vast amounts of time engaging in precisely the same kind of unobtrusive observation that professionals use.

They tallied such things as the times various professors uttered clichés in their lectures. Each "viable alternative" and "in my judgment" found its way into one student's tally chart. The all-time winner was the phrase, "In the final analysis." Another student tallied no fewer than seventy "y'knows" in a teaching assistant's fifty-minute lecture. Professional observers use the same technique, known academically as "nonreactive measurement," so called because the observation does not affect the behavior of the people under observation.

So it is with social scientists. In a classic study in 1922, for example, researcher H. T. Moore spent several weeks strolling up New York's Broadway and recording any fragments of conversation he could overhear. Among 174 fragments, Moore found "talk of the opposite sex" in 8 percent of the man-to-man conversations and 44 percent of the woman-to-woman conversations.

The difference between the genders has been the subject of observation ever since. One study reported differences observed in speech patterns between the sexes: Women ask more questions, and men interrupt more often, particularly when talking with women. One observer found that when crossing the street, men strayed outside the painted crosswalk lines more than women did (23 percent versus 10 percent). (Webb 1981.)

WHAT TO OBSERVE

Authors' requirements vary in the need for detail gained through observation. Exciting writers require more detail than dull writers. A system of observation can help you decide what to look for. If you want to write something dramatic, use what the Greek philosopher Aristotle identified as the four elements of dramatic literature—tension, unity, action, and irony.

Tension means suspense, and unity means that your story ought to hang together on a theme—a central point you want to make. Action means showing characters doing something. And irony has two primary meanings: (1) an unanticipated and unpredictable outcome of events, and (2) a meaning opposite of the intended meaning, that is, a meaning humorously or poignantly reversed from the intended meaning. Review Chapter 1 for an example of the unanticipated outcome definition—falling down a flight of stairs or spilling your coffee and yet obtaining a better interview than expected.

The reversed-meaning version of irony has a classic example in fiction: In a play, a husband praises his wife's virtue even as we, the audience, know that the wife's lover hides beneath her bed. Nonfiction can also take advantage of audience omniscience. If your readers learn early in your article that a man has died racing automobiles, for example, writing a flashback about his childhood fascination with fast cars provides irony—readers will realize that the tragic outcome of this interest will be the opposite of the character's intent.

Those points in mind, what, precisely, do you look for in the three observation methods cited in this chapter? In a word, detail—massive amounts of it, preferably organized in a way that clarifies the overall meaning of the detail. As you gather details, you see patterns and trends emerging. You explore them further and develop a tentative hypothesis about their meaning. If, for example, you watch a classroom teacher berate a student for lateness on Monday, explode in response to a student's "stupid question" on Tuesday, and angrily fling an eraser at a sleeping student on Wednesday, you might wonder what Thursday will bring. When Thursday and Friday bring similar spats with students, you may have come upon a noteworthy character trait, one that deserves a hypothesis as to its meaning.

Observation comes in four categories that help to capture the essence of dramatic nonfiction writing. You can observe much of the tension, action, irony, and unity by using the acronym *SCAM*. If, as Shakespeare suggests, all the world is a stage and all the men and women merely players, it follows that writing about reality can benefit from the elements used in playwriting. Here they are:

Scene or setting
Character
Action
Meaning

These elements resemble the journalist's traditional news elements: Where and When (setting), Who (character), What and How (action), and Why (meaning).

Setting.   All but the most routine news stories benefit from descriptive touches that give your readers a firm sense of place. You may even seek out for your interviews (television especially) places that have special meaning. Backstage, perhaps, for your profile of the famous play director. On the Los

Angeles freeway for your documentary on traffic problems. You may switch scenes, on the freeway for one segment of your traffic story, at police head-quarters for another, even in a hospital emergency room or the morgue if the article pertains to traffic accidents. Whatever the scene, you should take systematic note of what you see, starting with the overall scene—like a crowd shot at the football stadium—then focusing on individual items, like a closeup shot of one or two spectators.

Sounds and smells also deserve your attention. As you observe the scene where brain surgery is about to begin, do you hear the laughter of children playing across the street? Life goes on outside the life-and-death setting of the operating room, and that eerie touch of symbolism will heighten the reader's experience.

Character.   Static descriptions of scenes are dull; they come to life only when characters enter. Your observations of character can come on several levels ranging from the superficial physical aspects to deeper values and motivation. A good writer depicts character through action, in any event, so it is hard to discuss character without also discussing action. Your observations will focus on activities, partly to understand character and partly to illustrate it. Often the understanding comes through interviews with friends and colleagues, people who can explain the phenomenon you are witnessing.

Imagine, for example, the fiery-tempered play director. People who know him say he gets outstanding results from mediocre actors because he alternately loves them and hates them. He knows precisely how much love and how much hate to expend on each performer, and some need more of one or the other. So you attend rehearsals and watch your director in action. You'll watch for examples—dramatic scenes—of that love–hate relationship. If it happens often enough, you will have confirmed and illustrated a significant character trait. Take complete notes so that you can recreate the best one of these scenes in your story.

Your observation of character should also focus on symbols. People are constantly telling the world about themselves and their opinions through possessions, mannerisms, clothes, even through such subtle signs as body posture and hair style. The observer who remains alert for symbols will not only learn a lot about the topic or person being observed, but will also use them as illustrations. You visit the home of your respondent, a stunningly beautiful fashion model. Her apartment is a mess—abject chaos. Keep an eye on her actions as you help clean up the place (participant observation) for the photographer soon to arrive. Try to determine through questions what this says about her character.

Action.   As noted, action illustrates character, though not always an individual person. Suppose you wanted to illustrate the character of the worst drivers on the Los Angeles freeways? You tally instances as a traffic officer drives you along the freeway at rush hour. How many sudden, unannounced lane changes do you count? How many slow, careless, or possibly intoxicated drivers can you spot? Show your police officer escort commenting on the near accidents and foolish activities of the motorists under observation.

Don't neglect the emotional trifles that make people laugh or cry. A magazine writer, Ken Moore of *Sports Illustrated*, calls this one of the most important parts of interviewing and observation. Anytime you hear people laugh, think back to what caused the laughter. Recreate the scene in your story. Allow your readers to laugh, too.

Meaning.   Scene, character, and action should come together to produce the ultimate synthesis—the meaning. You'll arrange the details gained through observation into an orderly presentation. It is here that you arrange the trifles gained through observation to illustrate major points.

Dale Maharidge provides an example in his book about modern-day hoboing, described as people on the move by train, bus, or car looking for work. He and his partner drive an old car with Ohio plates into Houston, Texas where they encounter a local police officer. He stops them with roof lights blazing and "sashays forward, hand on gun." A dialogue ensues:

> *"How long you staying?"*
> *About another week.*
> *"Okay. If we see this car here past one more week, I'm going to throw you in jail!"*
> *We ask, What for?*
> *The cop puts his hand on his chin and squints, examining the car for an excuse. After a minute he points to the worn wheels. "Tires."* (Maharidge 1985.)

This and similar scenes make the meaning clear: Unemployed migrants will not find the promised land in Texas. So Meaning as part of SCAM really refers to the central theme of what you're trying to project through a piece of writing. Points work off the central theme, illustrated by dramatic examples.

Observing for meaning, then, involves two elements. The first is observing to discover some kind of meaningful item—a point, a trend, a personality trait, a characteristic—or to confirm one obtained from another source. The second is to use one or more specific observations to illustrate the point, such as the hobo encounters with hostility.

If this seems vague and confusing, you are probably en route to becoming a splendid journalist. That remark is not intended in jest. It merely confirms that the world is complicated, and things happen that seem disorderly, totally meaningless, hopelessly chaotic. If any kind of central point exists, it will not announce itself in bold letters against a crimson sky. A central theme and the supporting points are what you, the journalist, decide upon, much as a reporter decides upon the most important element of a news event for the lead paragraph. It is never easy, and chances are that no two journalists would agree on the identity of those points.

▶ 12

Interviewing for Quotes and Anecdotes

Q. Can you give me a funny story, a true story drawn from your experiences in life, that illustrates your point?

A. No, nothing comes to mind.

Think of the *Wall Street Journal* and you probably think dignified, staid, absence of photographs, and acres of statistics, not to mention frequent use of arcane business jargon. Dull.

A careful reading of articles reveals something different, however: interesting anecdotal accounts that show how business decisions and policies affect the lives of ordinary people. The anecdotal accounts dramatize those actions and they quote the way real people talk.

So it was in 1994 when the *Journal* wrote about the problems of new-home warranties. The story showed a Texas couple frustrated by years of cracked walls, bad plumbing, and similar problems that were never fixed despite the warranty. So what's the value of the warranty?

"It's not worth the powder to blow it to hell," said Mrs. Roach, the homeowner, apologizing for her language. Nice touch, a crimson splotch in a serious report that suggests home warranties don't really protect the home buyer, particularly those who don't read the fine print. "You have more of a warranty on your toaster than on your house," said the president of a homeowners advocacy group. Another nice touch. (*Wall Street Journal*, 11–30–94.)

The anecdote and the quotations represent the ultimate humanizing device in nonfiction writing. They make nonfiction articles read more like short stories. They show action depicting what novelists call the "human condition": showing real people doing real things. Absence of anecdotes and quotations forms a common malaise in nonfiction writing called "flat writing." It lacks the color and drama that the human touch would provide.

In nonfiction you can avoid flat writing by searching out good anecdotes and quotations through your interviews. This chapter offers suggestions for doing so. Obtaining good quotes from an interview involves two tasks. First, you must recognize a good quote when you hear it. Second, you must carry on the kind of conversation that encourages quotable remarks.

LEARNING TO RECOGNIZE QUOTATIONS

Consider the recognition problem. In a newswriting class, I asked students to write a news story from a verbatim transcript of a hypothetical student council meeting. The transcript showed a lively debate on a controversial issue about a group called the People's Coalition. One student's story characterized as follows the comment of a participant in the debate.

> *She alluded to the fact that the People's Coalition was devoid of the feminine gender, and she chastised the chairman of the coalition for falsely claiming to represent the interests of all the people.*

The transcript shows that in addressing a fellow council member the woman said: "Harry, there isn't a single woman in your People's Coalition. You don't represent the people at all—you represent only male chauvinist people. Power to the people—hell!"

The quote, simple, dramatic, explodes off the page. It captures personality. It's specific. It's six words shorter. The student never considered it as a means of adding color to his story.

Some novice writers tend toward a far different problem—they put everything in quotes, even routine data. "I was born in Sandusky, Ohio in the summer of 1942." Imagine trying to illustrate the character of a grizzled mule skinner at the Grand Canyon. Do you quote him citing his birth date? No! You quote him cracking a wry joke with a group of tourists starting the precipitous trail to the bottom: "Be mighty careful, ladies—I can always get plenty of tourists but a trained mule is hard to replace."

Similarly, you can always get plenty of words, but a good quote is hard to find. You find them by recognizing them as they whiz by in conversations. To do that, consider some definitions.

Quotation simply means reporting what a person said. The *direct quotation* belongs in quotation marks and should run verbatim. *Paraphrased quotations* are what the person said but in somebody else's words, usually the writer's. Fragmented quotations are mere snippets of conversation. Thus when Jane Doe says, "Living in New York is like living in a cement mixer—it's tough and confusing," the direct quotation is what you see between those quote marks. A paraphrased quotation: Jane Doe says living in New York is difficult and confusing (no quote marks). The fragmented quote: Jane Doe finds living in New York confusing—"like living in a cement mixer." Here are some common ways to use such quotations in written material:

Use Quotes for Authority. Imagine yourself on a cruise ship and someone says, "This ship is in great peril." You'd pay closer attention if the comment came from the captain than a passenger sitting next to you. Authority quotes gain currency by the stature of the person saying them. "Ours is a singularly violent community," says the police chief. "Our foreign policy lies in a parlous and desperate state," says the secretary of state.

Quote for Human Color. Keep an ear attuned to the way people talk. Count your blessings if they proclaim a certain document "not worth the powder to blow it to hell." Idiosyncratic speech is a special treat. "The room was so small you couldn't cuss the cat without gettin' hair in your mouth!" (Old Tennessee saying.) "Down in Texas we say that under an attack like this you just act like a jackass in a hailstorm. You hunker down." (Attributed to Lyndon B. Johnson by columnist Carl Rowan, 8–13–93.)

Stay particularly alert for such personal asides because they differ sharply from the semiformal style of newswriters. Have you noticed that some newspaper stories offer direct quotations whose styles do not differ one from another nor from the style of the news account itself? They represent a blur of gray writing. You wonder why. Do sources talk the way reporters write? No. Reporters select quotes that fit the way they write. They don't listen keenly to the way people talk. Think how three different people say the same thing:

- Police officer: "At approximately zero four hundred hours, I observed the subject vehicle traveling at a high rate of speed."
- College professor: "It was four o'clock in the morning, and though bereft of any instrument to accurately ascertain the forward motion of the vehicle, I should tentatively suggest, in the absence of more systematic empirical data, that the motion was rather in an expeditious manner."
- A bystander: "Man, that puppy was flying like a bat outta hell!"

In short, your story's quotations should show individual character stamps. Do that and your writing becomes a rainbow of color, not a blur of gray.

Quote for Authenticity. A story that discusses a celebrity's shyness becomes more believable with a direct quote: "Yes," says Mr. Big, "I suffer agony in anticipation of meeting somebody for fear they won't like me."

In a similar vein, authenticity shows through quotes that reflect the jargon of the topic. You show the aging former hobo displaying the jargon of his past: "There we were, a couple of bindle stiffs off the red ball express, diming up on the stem." It sounds authentic, though you may have to translate the meaning—hoboes off the fast fruit train, panhandling on Main Street.

Quote Figures of Speech.   Some people normally talk in metaphorical ways. "Tomorrow's weather will be a real frog strangler," says a meteorologist. "When you think of a buffalo," says a biologist, "think of a two-thousand-pound steak." Some figures of speech have become clichés, "bat outta hell," for instance, or "not worth the powder to blow it up." You won't use them in your own writing, but they do convey colorful street jargon appropriate for quoting ordinary people.

Quote Summarizing Comments.   Experienced sources know how to use the capsule summary in speeches and interviews, often employing metaphorical devices. "The Legislature's action is nothing short of a war on children" or "Our children are being held hostage to the political machinations of the Legislature."

INTERVIEWING FOR QUOTATIONS

How in interview conversation do you encourage people to talk more quotably? Try talking more quotably yourself. You get out of an interview what you put into it—dull questions, dull answers. Here are some suggestions for encouraging quotable material in the interview.

Fish for Figures of Speech.   Certain questions stimulate imaginative answers, and one of the best is to ask for a simile or an analogy. The question is simple: "What's it like?" "What's it like to be looking for your first job?" a reporter asked a group of college seniors. "It's like sorority rush," a woman replied. "It's like asking your wife for money," said a man.

Use Metaphorical Questions.   If you want metaphorical answers, try using metaphorical questions or comments.

Q. Commissioner, a man in your precarious position, getting unmerciful criticism from all sides, must feel lonely, a man sitting on an iceberg in a storm-tossed sea.

A. No, it's more like lighting a cigar while sitting on a barrel of high-octane gasoline.

That sounds like a headline-grabbing quote, depending on the seriousness of the predicament. True, you colored the question. Had the commissioner replied, "Yes, that's a good way of putting it—sitting on an iceberg," then you'd better not use it. It's not authentically his. Keep priming the pump with metaphorical questions, and wait for the metaphors to flow. (Remember: It's a metaphor if he's sitting on a barrel, an analogy or simile if it's *like* sitting on a barrel.)

You can probe for colorful responses in other ways. "Is there an old Texas saying that covers this situation? . . . Can you put a label on this for me? . . . How would you explain this to your nine-year-old daughter? . . . The situation you describe sounds like a sophisticated Monopoly game—are you winning or losing?" Don't forget the sports metaphors so endearing to men in business: "Would you call this an end run play or a short pass? . . . What do you expect to happen your next time at bat?" Also military terms: "Are you suggesting damn the torpedoes—full speed ahead?"

Quote the Classics. An evening spent with Mark Twain or a book of quotations will produce examples of quotable remarks. They help you in two ways. First, they help you recognize a passing remark as something comparable to the classic quotations you've studied—and thus worthy of quotation in your article. Second, they allow you to salt your questions with classic comments that serve as the basis for quotable discussion. Thus:

Q. Senator, the news media controversies that focus on your work have a familiar ring. They bring to mind the quote from Oscar Wilde in *Dorian Gray*: "There's only one thing worse than being talked about, and that's not being talked about." What do you think?

A. Yes, the one great thing about being talked about is the opportunity to talk back. The chance to get your views across to the public can't be all bad.

I have used the Wilde quotation a hundred times, especially with people involved in sudden notoriety. It has fetched good responses at times, but it's even more useful in reminding respondents that sudden fame has its good side. Interviewers should stock up on other all-occasion classics, such as Shakespeare's "all the world is a stage," especially useful when approaching a question about certain political activities being largely theatrics.

Listen for Clues to Forthcoming Pearls. Veteran sources are seldom shy in pressing their views. In speeches and interviews they often telegraph a rehearsed quote. "In my view, it all adds up to this. . . ." or "Long years of experience in politics have prompted me to suggest. . . ." or "Here's my sound bite on this matter. . . ." Keep your pencil poised when those hints drop.

Use Silence.   This has been cited before as the interviewer's friend. Imagine this scene. The source has talked for several minutes about a complex issue. She finishes. You wait expectantly. She's not sure she's made a convincing point, so her mind runs through a more effective way of saying the same thing. More effective usually means shorter and more pointed. "In other words," she begins—and along comes the succinct summary or colorful metaphor.

Use Argumentation.   Do not carry to extremes the suggestion that interviewers maintain a low profile. A malignant dullness may creep into your dialogue, especially a broadcast interview. This does not mean picking a fight with your respondent. Interviewers commonly use counter arguments, usually attributing them to someone else. "Senator, your political opponents disagree sharply with what you say. Let me quote Congressman Claghorn from this morning's paper. . . ." You walk a fine line with this method; try to stop short of belligerence and news theatrics.

Show Your Appreciation for a Quotable Remark.   Show it dramatically: "Well said, Senator!" You'd think sources would tire of lavish praise, particularly those of high attainment that reporters normally interview. Not true. When you make a fuss over how much you enjoy a quotable remark, you open the floodgates. "So that's the kind of material she wants!" thinks your respondent. You'll probably get more.

Similarly, you must encourage people to use their normal manner of speaking, the more informal the better. People often try to clean up their conversation for your benefit—the ex-hobo doesn't talk about "diming up on the stem" for fear that you might not understand or appreciate the jargon. Show your enthusiasm for jargon and explain why you want to use it in your story. Try adopting the jargon in your own conversation. Your next question will seed the term "diming up" where you might have used "panhandling" before.

ELICITING THE ELUSIVE ANECDOTE

What is an anecdote? It's a factual storiette that illustrates a point. Ann Curry clumsily spilled her coffee during an interview (Chapter 1) and probably received more candid answers as a result. Nora Villagrán fell down the stairs en route to Joan Baez's house and probably got a better interview, too—two barefooted women talking. Writers find such stories useful to illustrate the hard-to-believe ironies of life. If someone tried to convince you that you could obtain more candor in an interview by falling down a flight of stairs, would you believe it? Not likely. Yet the factual story makes it believable. People can compare it to similar events in their own lives, and they may decide that, under the circumstances, it's not absurd after all.

Nonfiction writers who illustrate their points with interesting anecdotes accomplish three important goals.

1. Your writing is more believable.
2. Your writing is more fun to read; it entertains as well as informs.
3. Your writing is closer to people. Readers identify with characters and episodes in anecdotes, comparing them to their own experiences.

Student journalists find collecting anecdotes the most difficult aspect of interviewing. Often they expect them to come ready-made from their sources, all polished and ready to drop into a magazine piece. That seldom happens. People talk about their experiences; storytellers spin anecdotes. Most people are not storytellers. Writers are, or should be.

The story of Ann Curry's spilled coffee did not emerge as a full-blown anecdote. She merely remarked that the interview took a turn for the better shortly after she spilled her coffee. A storyteller asked for the details and shaped them into an anecdote. Here are some suggestions for improving your ability to obtain anecdotes from interviews.

Learn to Recognize an Anecdote in the Making. Most any human activity has potential for an anecdote in nonfiction writing. "Professor Blank entered the crowded classroom, walked to the lectern, and opened his file of notes for Thursday's lecture."

Is that an anecdote? Yes, of sorts. It shows a snippet of action. But what's the point? So far, none. It depends on what comes next. If Professor Blank falls mortally wounded moments later, a jeweled dagger in his heart, then the purpose becomes clear. The snippet shows an ordinary start to a bizarre classroom episode. The reporter who asks witnesses, "What did the professor do just before being stabbed?" will elicit such a description, and the writer thus adds a normal beginning to an episode of violence.

So it is you, the storyteller, who must assemble anecdotes from fragments of reality. Writing teachers are forever reading student-written articles that allude to a character trait—Professor Blank has a fiery temper and does not suffer fools gladly, we'll say—but never illustrate it. It doesn't help to include a supporting quote, either. What's the point of quoting someone saying, "Yes, he's explosive all right—many's the time I've seen him fly off the handle!" No, you have to show it with a "once upon a time" story like this:

> *One time Blank got so angry with a class that he shouted out the classroom window to startled passersby below, "Help! Help! I'm being held captive by a bunch of idiots!"*

What kind of question will elicit that information? Perhaps a simple one. "Can you give me an example?" Or a challenge: "I don't believe it—what's the angriest thing he's ever done?"

Tell Stories Yourself. You often obtain examples by priming the pump. "I remember a prof who used to display anger in the classroom. One time

Professor Jones got so peeved at his students that he kicked the waste basket clear across the room." That's a challenge to your source who will try to recall similar stories about Blank. The legendary shouting about idiots story will surely emerge sooner or later.

Simply asking for anecdotes seldom works. Try this experiment. Ask someone to tell you a humorous story from experience that illustrates how a human blunder brings candor to a conversation. The story won't come. First, the level of abstraction obscures your meaning. Second, the request for "a humorous story" intimidates people who are not accomplished storytellers.

Suppose you illustrate with one of the stories you've picked up in this book, the spilled coffee story. Tell such a story and your respondent's mind will search for similar experiences. The story so universally applies to human affairs that it can elicit similar tales. One student used it to land a story about a woman who had grown up on a farm. She met her husband of forty years by just such a gaffe. She'd been trying to impress a certain boy, she explained, but he paid her scant attention. Then one day he visited her house on an errand and encountered her just as she finished cleaning the stables and "smelled like horse manure." She was mortified. He was intrigued. The young man loved horses, and the chance encounter with the smelly young woman started their lifelong relationship.

What if you're not a good storyteller? So much the better. If you're too good, you'll intimidate sources. Where do you obtain your stories? Experienced journalists take them from previous interviews. Others clip and file stories from published sources.

Seek Examples.   When people talk in generalities, dull abstractions result. You need specific examples for your story. So you ask for them directly, as shown in this dialogue with a fire chief:

Q. You talk so matter-of-factly about your work—I wonder, have you ever been frightened when on the scene of a fire?

A. Lots of times.

Q. As you think back over those times, which one stands out in your mind?

A. I think it must have been the time someone said a child was trapped on the third floor of an apartment building, and we went in looking for her.

Q. I'd like to hear the details. . . .

A. You won't want this example because the child wasn't there—they found her later about a block away, wandering around.

Q. But at the time you didn't know that, right?

A. Right.

Q. So the fear was real?

A. Yes—ever more so as minutes passed and we groped through the smoke and we *still* couldn't find her.

Q. Then I definitely want the story. . . .

An ideal scenario—you ask for examples, find a particularly thrilling one, and out pour the details. Often it doesn't work that way. A respondent's memory often grows hazy at a request for examples. It's because of the peculiar way the mind retrieves events from memory. The information is there but sometimes we can't summon it immediately upon command. The mind needs cues such as key words that trigger memory. The interviewer can provide the cues.

A. I know I've had frightening experiences, but right now I can't think of any worth mentioning.

Q. I suppose they would come in certain situations, such as a building about to collapse, or maybe someone being trapped, or something involving imminent explosions—

A. Trapped! Yes, that reminds me of the time. . . .

Probe for Details. Even the simplest story needs descriptive detail and probably dialogue. Some sources can provide it handily because they've rehearsed anecdotes by telling them repeatedly over the years. They stretch the truth sometimes, however. Others have all but forgotten the incidents because they've never organized the experiences into anecdotal form. Memories fade. Often experienced interviewers can draw from their own memories or from pre-interview research. Clips will yield accounts of scary episodes you can ask about. Colleagues, family, and friends often mention events or details that the chief might not think to bring up. One way or another, you probe for whatever fragments of detail you can extract to portray the story more vividly.

Assembling the details requires patient probing. "What happened next? . . . What did she say? . . . What did you say? . . . Where did all this take place? . . . What was the weather as you were talking on the sidewalk—hot, rainy, snowy, what? . . . How were you dressed?" Clearly the more experienced you are as a writer, the more you'll know what to ask in these detail-seeking forays.

Some stories need only minimal detail, of course, to make their point. Others, such as the search through smoky corridors for a trapped child, require vivid detail to portray the tension.

Listen with the Third Ear. Catching half-articulated hints can provide a rich source of stories. Our strongest convictions are often born of dramatic experiences. Look for anecdotes in those experiences. You're interviewing a social worker about runaway children. "Sometimes," she says, "running away is the wisest and most mature thing a child can do." That's a startling and paradoxical observation. What basis does a social worker have for saying that? So you probe for the details. You learn that some children's home conditions—abusive parents, alcoholism, drugs, whatever—are so wretched that no right-thinking adult could reach any conclusion other than the one reached by the child. Now you begin to probe for the worst example the social worker can recall. You learn that a mother dies, and a ten-year-old girl takes on the full responsibility for running the household only to suffer constant physical abuse from a drunken father. Given a detailed account of such a scenario (a true story, incidentally), the reader will likely arrive at the same decision the child did.

Witness the Incidents Yourself.   As discussed in Chapter 11, personal observation provides a splendid way to discover anecdotes that illustrate points. Is the celebrated actor so insecure that he doesn't know what to order for lunch? Take him to lunch and find out for yourself. Do the military cadets on bivouac make little jokes about their officers? Sit with them at mess and listen.

Listen and Express Appreciation.   Same as with the quotes—know what to listen for and show your joy when you receive it. "What a great story!"

▶ 13

Telephoning, Note-Taking, and Taping

Q. Hello, I'm your friendly neighborhood computer conducting a survey of community attitudes. I would like to ask you some questions. . . .

A. Hello, this is your friendly answering machine substituting for Jim and Sally who can't come to the phone just now—if you'd like to leave a message, please wait for the tone. . . .

Interviewing by telephone. Using a tape recorder. Taking notes. These three areas account for more questions in college classes and workshops for professional journalists than any others, in my experience. Some student reporters claim a deathly fear of telephone interviews. Some print reporters are equally timid about using tape recorders. Note-taking continues to plague reporters.

INTERVIEWING BY TELEPHONE

Reporters prefer face-to-face interviews. So do respondents. That's what recent studies have suggested. (Mann 1991, Norris 1987.) Evidence even suggests that newspaper articles assembled from telephone interviews receive more thorough checking and rewriting from the editors than those written from face-to-face interviews. (Norris 1987.)

The telephone remains the most frequently used interviewing tool for most newspaper reporters. The study by Tim Norris at the University of Oregon covered 662 interviews done by nineteen reporters working for daily newspapers in Denver, Minneapolis, Omaha, and Milwaukee. They did two-thirds of them by phone. They'd have preferred in-person sessions, most said, but for various reasons—lack of time, mostly, or the wish to interview a wide range of respondents—they used the phone. Of four types of newspaper articles studied, only the personality profile relied mostly on face-to-face interviews. Telephones served the remaining three types: spot news coverage (phone used for 65 percent of those interviews), newsbeat reports (74 percent), and background or human interest stories (78 percent).

The phone interview has certain advantages, its short duration, for example (81 percent lasted fewer than 30 minutes). Reporters often found the phone useful when they preferred to maintain an emotional detachment from the topic or the respondent. They preferred the in-person interview, however, when they perceived the session might be hostile. Of 230 interviews studied in depth, only one in seven was potentially hostile. (Norris 1987.)

Clearly, reporters must learn phone interviewing techniques for maximum effectiveness. Phones may even offer an advantage in the power games bureaucrats so often play with the media. The telephone can be an equalizer in the intimidation game. Evidence suggests that the timid can find a stronger voice via the telephone; the aggressive and strong willed find it less effective than during in-person encounters. For one thing, the caller knows the purpose of the call; the person answering is more vulnerable picking up the phone with no idea of who's on the line for what purpose. (Robbins 1992.) Bureaucrats and other traditional sources have their calls screened, however, and may choose which media calls to accept.

How should a reporter proceed with a phone interview? Do so largely along the same lines suggested in earlier chapters. You form an interview purpose, conduct pre-interview research as necessary, and place the call. What happens in the first few seconds of that call largely previews the rest. It is within those seconds that you must, in an agreeable voice, identify yourself, state your purpose, and drop a hook that will capture the respondent's attention and interest. If all goes well, you proceed with your first questions. To cite a simple example, suppose you learn that Chester Bridlington witnessed an explosion at a chemical plant near his home. The plant burned to the ground. You've already talked to firefighters, but they offer only hazy notions of the fire's origin. You need Bridlington's account, so the purpose of your call is simple.

A. Hello?

Q. Mr. Bridlington?

A. Yes.

Q. Good evening, sir. My name is Larry Ashenbrenner, reporter for KMTR-Channel Sixteen News. We're doing a story on the big fire at the ABC Chemical plant tonight, and we understand you saw the explosion that started the fire. Is that correct?

A. Well, I seen quite a bit, all right.

Q. Well, Mr. Bridlington, I'm delighted to have you on the line. May I ask you for our story—and I'll be tape recording what you tell me—to describe what you saw?

A. Well, what I seen was just totally undescribable—it's like the gates of hell was unleashed and the next thing I knowed, that plant was a ball of flame.

Q. What was the first thing you noticed?

A. First there was this big boom! More like a whump, actually.

Q. An explosion?

A. Couple of 'em. I mean, I hear this big *whump, whump* and when I looked there was this lightening bolt of flame shooting skyward a hundred feet.

Q. Where were you at the time?

A. Well I was out walking the dog and I musta been standing maybe a block or two away. . . .

And so on. That would be the ideal phone interview, a forthcoming witness. Maybe his grammar is not the best. Maybe you'll clean up the grammar in your report—though maybe not; a recorded telephone actuality might serve well with the video of the fire.

Most inexperienced respondents enjoy being interviewed, so this example shows no need to draw on your charm or your stock of persuasive arguments to secure the interview. The most common complaint of the unsophisticated respondent is interview burnout—"Oh, no, not another one of them damned reporters!"—at which point charm or flattery will help: "Mr. Bridlington, you may not realize this, but you're the man of the hour here in River City—your prompt response in calling 911 probably saved a whole city from being burned down, and that is why we of the news media want to honor you. . . ." (All said in a jocular tone of voice. The flattery sounds gooey but is effective.)

For such routine news calls, nothing surpasses the telephone. Feature writers, too, find it useful when they want information from many sources. Sometimes a decision to use the telephone involves a tradeoff: Would you prefer to spend the morning fighting crosstown traffic to conduct one face-to-face interview, or would you rather interview a dozen different people by phone? Twelve phone interviews may yield more information than a single in-person conversation.

One celebrity interviewer, Nora Villagrán of the *San Jose Mercury News*, does three-quarters of her interviews by phone. "There's a shared intimacy on the phone, like making love, their lips right next to my ear, and I'm having an intimate conversation as though we are completely alone."

Busy public officials—though they claim to prefer face-to-face inter-views—also find the quick media phone call more efficient, less time con-suming. That's especially true once they've become acquainted with a journalist. For the reporter the phone allows you to work in casual clothes and to keep your notes, clippings, and other reference materials spread out on your desk. Some use headsets for telephone interviews to avoid the annoyance of shoulder clips. Headsets with big earphones also muffle nearby noise so you can listen better. Some reporters equip their desk phones with small tape recorders, using a Radio Shack device that splices the recorder onto the phone line.

Reporters for national magazines and newspapers have developed long-distance phone interviewing to a fine art. The long-distance phone has a high priority in the minds of many busy executives. A Washington reporter finds it effective to announce his location over the phone: "This is Jack Magarrell, *calling from Washington, D. C. . . . .*" The D.C. connection spurs calls promptly through secretaries to key executives.

But what about descriptive touches, you ask? Who says you can't obtain them via telephone? Michael Thoele, calling from his newspaper office in Oregon, asked an Alaska resident to "Look out your window and describe what you see," and obtained a fine description of a snowswept winter street scene in Kotzebue, Alaska. *USA Today* writer Carol Castenada suggests obtaining descriptions of interviewees by calling friends and close acquaintances and asking them to describe the person. "They'll tell you incredible things." (Crowe 1993.)

The telephone even works for sensitive questions. People often feel less threatened talking into an impersonal instrument precisely because it helps not to see a human reaction. The very weakness of the telephone, its impersonality, becomes a strength in some circumstances.

Support for that view comes from a bizarre source. In Honolulu a man telephoned dozens of women, identifying himself as a doctor engaged in research on sex patterns. He asked for and often received intimate details of their sexual experiences. Only in retrospect did some of them become suspicious enough to call the medical association, where they learned that the caller was a fraud. The women were charmed, they explained, by the "warm telephone personality" of a "skilled interviewer."

Just as evil-minded persons can use the telephone to exploit, so can altruistic journalists use it for the common good. Learning the following telephone courtesies will help:

1. Have a clear-cut, easily explained purpose and get to the point quickly. People seem increasingly wary of phone calls, the result of ever more sales calls, not to mention crank calls. Be prepared to make your first pitch to a machine or an aide.

2. Say something attention grabbing or flattering—the hook. Thus: "Hello, Ms. Costas, this is Mary Jones, a business-page writer from the *Star–Tribune*. I'm working on a story about women who have started small businesses, and your friend Shirley Lancaster gave me your name as one of the most successful examples in our community. She says you're a terrific innovator. Would you mind talking with me on the phone for a few minutes?"

3. Put a brisk but amiable and friendly quality into your voice; it's the only means you have to establish rapport.

4. Unless the call will be brief, give your estimate of the interview's duration—"perhaps fifteen or twenty minutes." After stating your business—and setting your interest-capturing hook—ask, "Is this a good time to talk?" You don't know what you're interrupting. Except in emergencies, you're better off making a telephone appointment for later than having your source become anxious about abandoned house guests or an upcoming meeting.

5. Keep your icebreaker comments brief: "How's the weather back in Boston—as snowy as our papers say?" Personal asides might come later after you've gained rapport. Easterners exhibit a brisk formality and seem to resent small talk. Westerners, midwesterners, and southerners seem to expect a few personal amenities at the start.

6. Don't allow long, unexplained silences on the phone. Note-taking may require explanation: "Please give me a moment to get that comment in my notes. . . ."

7. Provide verbal cues to your listening: "Uh-huh, hmmmmm," and the like (unless you're interviewing for a broadcast actuality).

8. When interviewing on sensitive topics, try to provide credentials and references, naming mutual acquaintances who will vouch for your authenticity. "Your former colleague, Jim Jones, suggested I call you." Similarly, when you conclude an interview, ask for names of others who can help. Your source's name will provide entry to the others.

9. Use caution with quotes and spellings; it's hard to hear above the newsroom din. Ask for names spelled phonetically, B-Boston, P-Portland, and so on, because B and P are easily confused on the phone, as are F and S. Is the name Faulk or Saulk? Sources seldom complain if they know you're trying to ensure accuracy.

10. Above all, be courteous and friendly. And listen.

11. Write a thank-you note, at least for interviews beyond the routine. So rare is a journalistic thank-you note that it will astound people. People will talk about you, and favorably so. The opposite is also true: Word of media discourtesies (not so rare, unfortunately) travels fast.

TAKING NOTES

The human mind cannot do everything at once. Interviewing requires you to listen, think up new questions, keep the interview on track, and take notes, all at the same time. The agency head you're interviewing says she has three reasons for taking a certain action. You take notes as quickly as you can, but by the time you've finished getting down Reason 1, you've missed Reason 2 because your mind was focused on Reason 1. Or you tried to listen to Reason 2 and then forgot most of Reason 1. Now you're too embarrassed to ask her to repeat Reason 2 as she launches into Reason 3. Sound familiar?

The solution? Not easy. First decide what you want out of an interview. If you want every word, use a tape recorder. Note-taking works best for routine news stories and for multiple-interview projects in which you plan to use only small portions of each conversation. Many inexperienced interviewers try to write down everything said, and as a result don't listen carefully.

Journalists tend to develop their own solutions to the problem. Some experienced journalists take lots of notes on big tablets; others take only a few notes in a casual manner, such as on the backs of old envelopes. Their notes may consist of nothing more than key words as reminders—they listen carefully and rely on short-term memory to flesh out the details the moment they leave the conversation. Some reporters try to get direct quotes verbatim and record any numbers or statistics mentioned but rely on memory and key-word notes for the rest.

Some suggestions:

Organize Your Note-Taking.   Chapter 10 on listening suggests that you organize your listening to make a mental note of major points and then supporting evidence. Good notes reflect that. One way is to use one side of a steno pad to record the main points and the other side to record supporting data, including observation, quotations, anecdotes, facts, and figures.

Control Your Interview to Accommodate Note-Taking.   If you're watching for main points and supporting evidence, you learn to ask for information in largely that same way. Imagine this dialogue with, say, a politician.

Q. What do you see as the major economic problems of this region?

A. The governor is our major problem.

Q. Why do you say that?

A. The governor has been stalling for three years now and hasn't come up with a single proposal for improving the economy of this or any other region in the state.

Q. Do you have some specific ideas for improvement?

A. You bet I do! Dozens of them!

Q. Splendid! Could I hear a half-dozen or so of them, please, starting with the most important ones?

The reporter has phrased the last question so that the notes based on the answers will not only contain the main point (the governor's inaction), but continue with supporting points (the politician's solutions), listed in order of importance. You'll find it a lot easier to write a story based on notes organized this way.

Some journalists prefer to listen carefully, then make notes after they have the point clearly in mind. This, too, can be worked into the interview method so long as the respondent knows what you're doing. So you say, "Let me see if I have this correct," repeating your understanding of the point. If it's correct, then: "Okay, let me get this into my notes before we go on."

Develop a Shorthand. When you must get material word for word, a shorthand system helps. Some have taken formal shorthand or speedwriting courses. Most have at least a system of abbreviations and symbols for frequently used words. "Gt7 qts w 4 w > ez wn u no hw" is one reporter's shorthand for "Getting quotes word for word is easy when you know how."

Train Your Memory. Writer Ken Moore, who covers running for *Sports Illustrated*, can't take notes when he's interviewing athletes while accompanying them on training runs. Moore seldom uses a tape recorder—it gets in the way of conversation, he says—but he memorizes the most significant comments and writes them down later. We can all work on memory. Try fixing a quotable remark in memory by rehearsing it a time or two, even talking further about it in the interview.

Type Your Notes. In a long-established newsroom practice, many reporters take notes on the computer terminal, particularly when conducting telephone interviews from the office. In recent years reporters have begun to use laptop computers for taking notes in the field.

Such devices are not the perfect solution to the note-taking problem, however. They do interfere with rapport, particularly with inexperienced sources. They work best with perfunctory interviews with experienced sources such as a police desk sergeant. A school superintendent in Honolulu finds himself annoyed by the clacking noise when speaking to a reporter on the phone. "It isn't the typing that bothers me so much as what it symbolizes," he explained. "It means the fine nuances of conversation are lost. Listening becomes mechanical. It's a linear thing instead of immersion in the conversation. If you so much as burp you activate that darned typewriter."

Introduce Note-Taking Slowly to Inexperienced Respondents. Occasionally you'll find a respondent bothered by any kind of note-taking. Here are three suggestions when you think this could be a problem. (1) Introduce your notes at a routine stage. After icebreaking conversation, ask for routine information, names, ages, spellings, addresses, and write them down. This is no worse than providing information at the driver's license bureau. Eventually they'll get used to your making notes. (2) Listen carefully, repeat your understanding, and then make notes, as suggested earlier. (3) Use gentle flattery; make an agreeable fuss over how much you enjoyed a quotable remark as you write it down.

USING TAPE RECORDERS

Thanks to the growth of broadcast journalism, most news sources have become used to tape recorders. Many sources—celebrities and public officials especially—say they prefer that reporters use recorders, believing they lead to fewer misquotations.

So the question affects print journalists primarily: whether to utilize a tape recorder or simply to make notes on conversations. It remains a controversial question. A veteran newspaper man in Honolulu tried a recorder for the first time after thirty years on the job and had two reactions. First he was enthralled. "I can really *listen* to the conversation," he exclaimed. Second, he painfully learned some weaknesses in his interviewing style. "I talk too damn much. I'm too impatient. I'm always cutting off my source just as he starts to say something."

Recorders can be lifesavers in important interviews. Consider the telephone interview *USA Today* reporter Lee Michael Katz was conducting with Secretary of State James Baker a few years ago. With 80 percent of the interview finished, the paper's computer system crashed, and the typewritten notes disappeared from the screen. The tape recorder saved the day. (Crowe 1993.)

Tape recorders will not solve all interview recording problems. Here, based on the experiences of many print journalists interviewed for this book, are some pros and cons. First the pros:

1. They're a good backup for note-taking, just in case you miss something important.

2. You get quotes verbatim.

3. Freed of note-taking, you can listen more carefully, pick up hints and half-articulated points, sometimes on relistening.

4. The tape preserves things said early in the interview. Reporters often don't recognize the importance of early comments because they don't have a firm grasp on the topic at that point and so they fail to take notes early on.

5. Tapes are useful in legally touchy stories and as a backstop against claims of misquotation.

6. In sensitive interviews—for personality profiles, for example—you can listen repeatedly to catch fine nuances of personality that you might have missed originally.

7. You learn poignant lessons about interviewing by hearing yourself on tape.

Some reasons frequently given *not* to use a recorder:

1. They're inefficient for tight-to-the-deadline reporting—there's barely time to make the necessary phone calls, let alone listen to a tape of the conversations.

2. They're similarly inefficient when you don't expect to use much of an interview—maybe just a quote or two from each of a dozen interviews.

3. They're prone to mechanical breakdown.

4. They're said to intimidate respondents, thus hampering rapport.

5. Transcribing the tape is time consuming.

6. Unless controlled, taped interviews tend to ramble in accord with the nature of informal conversation. The informality begets candor, but the rambling produces disorderly material.

7. Given the routine nature of most news interviews, there's no reason to hear the conversation again.

The negative side contains three myths that should be dispelled. In the hands of a good interviewer, tape recorders seldom intimidate anyone. As noted, experienced sources prefer tapes, and the inexperienced ones tend to take their cues from the interviewer. If you are intimidated by it, they probably will be, too.

Second, tape recorders *can* be used for deadline reporting. Some reporters routinely tape interviews, particularly telephone interviews, still taking notes as they normally would. Whenever a complicated quote rolls by too fast to write down, they merely record the number on the digital counter and later roll the tape back to that point to retrieve the quote.

The third myth deals with mechanical breakdown. True, recorders do break down frequently. Blame yourself, not the machine. To avoid problems, do the following. Buy a good machine. Keep the batteries fresh and have spare batteries at hand. Test the machine before every use. Avoid recording in restaurants, bars, cars, planes, factories (too noisy). Avoid suction cup pickups for telephone interviews; they don't work on some phones and they're prone to breakdown. Rechargeable batteries have a nasty habit—they *suddenly* run out of power rather than gradually as regular batteries do, and they're more likely to lose power when the machine isn't used often. Don't loan your recorder to others—they'll probably drop it from a fifth-floor window and forget to tell you.

What Kind of Recorder?   The machine most used for journalistic interviews is the pocket recorder roughly the size of a paperback book. It uses standard cassette tapes and usually operates on AA batteries or a battery pack. The best machines have a battery condition indicator, a built-in microphone, a plug for a remote microphone, a plug for earphones, an automatic shutoff when a side of the tape cassette has ended, and a digital counter, which resembles an auto mileage odometer. All machines play back the tape on a tiny speaker.

News reporters are growing increasingly fond of the micro-recorder, which is smaller: seldom bigger than a pack of cigarettes. It uses a tiny cassette hardly bigger than a man's thumb ($1'' \times 1\frac{1}{2}''$) good for as much as forty-five minutes on each side. Some machines record at half-speed, giving you twice your forty-five—three hours for both sides of the tape. The playback quality is low, but the small size makes it convenient to slip into a purse or pocket. The price for both this and the pocket recorder runs from $25 to $200.

Using Your Tape Recorder.   Reporters often use recorders at speeches and news conferences as backstops for their note-taking. Recorders are particularly useful for those fast airport lobby interviews where you have no time to sit down. Your celebrity walks briskly toward an appointment or a connecting flight. Or jogs through the streets of your city. You can't take notes but the recorder preserves the conversation.

Taping a face-to-face interview usually involves a certain etiquette. You explain the need for taping the session, and you secure the respondent's approval. Given a choice between your taking notes and taping, most opt for taping, especially when you explain how, freed of note-taking, you can speed up the conversation and listen more carefully. "This way, we can talk like real people."

Most people's concerns center on two areas: (1) What if they want to speak off the record—can they shut off the machine? Yes, some reporters will turn it off. Others say they will honor an agreed-to off-the-record remark whether it's on tape or not. Some reporters decline to hear off-the-record commentary at all. (2) What happens to the tape afterward? It's erased automatically the next time you use it. Some tapes may be kept on file in legally touchy stories. Sometimes an interview may contain material of such historical significance to justify forwarding to a library or museum archives. Most times a respondent simply wants reassurance that things confessed on tape will not be played on the radio or as entertainment at a house party.

Tape recorders can hinder rapport if placed directly between the two participants to an interview. Place your recorder to one side, out of the line of sight between you. Turn it on and let it do its job; avoid the temptation to check its operation. Use your curiosity and charm to sweep your source into the conversation, and soon you'll both forget the tape.

Note-Taking While Taping.   Writing extensive notes while taping negates your claim that you will listen better when freed of note-taking. Some notes can be useful, however. First, they provide nonverbal encouragement; you show what's important by making a note of it. Second, you may wish to note briefly items already covered in the interview just to keep track. You'll also jot down points mentioned in the interview that you want to ask about later, points you might otherwise forget. Third, taped interviews tend to ramble more than those guided by note-taking. In a typical taped interview, for instance, the governor says, "I have three reasons for vetoing this legislation." The discussion of Reason 1 rambles so much that you both forget to cover Reasons 2 and 3. Not so with notes. Write down "3 Rsns for veto" and you'll remember.

Reporters do, however, take extensive notes from taped interviews—back at the office afterwards. Most reporters don't transcribe. They take notes from the playback. A fast typist can almost keep up with a normal conversation, skipping the questions and concentrating on only the worthwhile answers.

The Ethics and Legal Implications of Taping. Laws vary from state to state. The federal wiretap law permits taping of telephone conversations so long as at least one party to the conversation is aware of the recording. This means that in interstate telephone calls, it's sufficient that the reporter knows about the taping. Forty states either have no regulations covering this question or have laws similar to the federal wiretap law. In ten states, however, laws prohibit taping without all-party consent: California, Florida, Illinois, Maryland, Massachusetts, Montana, New Hampshire, Oregon, Pennsylvania, and Washington. (Middleton and Chamberlin 1994.) In Oregon, it's illegal to secretly tape face-to-face conversations without consent, but all right to tape a telephone conversation. Some reporters argue that they see no difference between taking verbatim notes via shorthand and making the same record by tape, and thus they see no ethical need to warn the respondent that the conversation is being recorded.

As in most legal questions pertaining to ethics in publishing, matters are seldom black and white; journalists should err on the side of caution, which means inform your respondent if you are taping a telephone conversation. I've never experienced an instance where doing so has hampered a telephone conversation.

▶ 14

Special Problems

Q. Senator, about your yachting tours to Barbados with the Mafia dons and the dancing girls—

A. I remember nothing, nothing at all!

How do you obtain interviews with busy executives or celebrities? It's becoming more difficult. Once you obtain your interview, other problems may intrude—hostility, evasiveness, poor memory, attempts to manipulate. How can you tell if a person is lying, cope with a respondent who bores you, or ask potentially embarrassing questions?

For twenty years students in my interviewing classes have joined me in seeking answers to such questions. Together we've assembled about 900 conversations with interviewers and sources. Students interviewed not only reporters but other professionals who use interviews: doctors, counselors, police officers, psychiatrists, anthropologists, social workers, fiction writers. The interviewed news sources ranged from cops and coaches to crime victims and beauty queens.

These interviews form the basis for solutions to the special problems cited here. We didn't find solutions for all problems. Sometimes, though, we picked up unique insights. One dealt with the discovery of truth. At the University of Oregon, a young fraternity pledge, Ben Palmer, became a hero when he rescued an unconscious fraternity brother from a fire at the Sigma Phi Epsilon house. Fortunately for Ben, the news media didn't learn of the heroism until a day later, after things had calmed down. Then reporters started coming around. "They wanted to know the truth," Ben Palmer told student interviewer Mark Goldstein, "and this is possible only in a relaxed atmosphere."

How true. To put it another way, truth varies under what we've come to call green, yellow, and red interviewing conditions. A green interview involves happy emotions (or no emotions), and truth flows freely. Most interviews are green. Yellow warns that emotional land mines *might* color the truth. Red denotes highly volatile conditions, major crises where emotional accusations and countercharges explode all around. Condition-red commentary should be taken with grains of salt rather than made into headlines or sound bites.

We did not attempt to quantify those interview reports, but two additional patterns emerged nonetheless. One is the preference of sources and many reporters for the Golden Rule of interviewing: Treat sources the way you would want to be treated if your roles were reversed. In Oregon, reporter Eric Mortenson reflected that view in a conversation with student interviewer Debbie Lair: "I'll tell you what makes it possible to talk to people. It's treating people like real human beings instead of objects for us to gain information from. One rule of journalism is that nobody has to talk to us if they don't want to. I treat people with a sense of dignity that, frankly, a lot of reporters don't. It works. People tell me everything."

The second pattern affirms that most reporters and sources find the interview a pleasant and rewarding experience. Reporters call it the fun part of the job: meeting new people. The remaining insights ranged widely, but out of them we found these suggestions for coping with typical interviewing problems.

HARD-TO-GET INTERVIEWS

So you want to interview Mr. Big, or Ms. Celebrity. Start by looking at your own reputation. Are you known as an honest, hard-working, open-minded journalist working toward altruistic ends for the good of the public? Or as ruthless, crass, exploitative? Your reputation often precedes you. So does that of the medium you represent. Nowhere is that more true than in status-conscious Washington. Women who cover federal government acknowledged in a study that the prestige of a reporter's publication is the first consideration on whether officials will return your call. As one explained, "A certified idiot working for *The New York Times* can get his or her calls returned anytime, anywhere." (Lynch 1993.)

Once past any prestige or reputation problems, you'll find these suggestions helpful for landing hard-to-get interviews.

1. Be enthusiastic about your project—it's infectious.
2. Be persistent. So says entertainment writer Nora Villagrán of the *San Jose Mercury News*. "If the front door is locked, try the back door. If that's locked, try a window." For entertainment celebrities, the front door is the PR person. The back door is the Screen Actors Guild and the actor's agent. The window is a friend, business associate, or relative of the actor. Nora often calls the celebrity's mother. "They like to talk about their kids, and you can ask about their childhood, which is a sure-fire question to ask in celebrity interviews." Sometimes a celebrity will grant an interview just to find out what Mom said. (Villagrán interview 1994.)

3. Be optimistic. Assuming you won't get an interview is a self-fulfilling prophecy.

4. Arrange interviews through an intermediary sympathetic to your purpose. A counselor likes your idea of a story portraying a reformed drug addict, so he agrees to ask persons who have undergone treatment if they'd be willing to talk with you.

5. Write a letter proposing your project. Include clips of past interviews you believe will interest your respondent. Send it by e-mail if possible. Write often.

6. Pose one or more intriguing, ego-flattering questions as examples.

7. Call to verify information obtained from other sources. When Washington reporter Lisa McCormack called realtor Marshall Coyne to verify a quote, he responded gruffly: "You're the first damned reporter who ever called to verify a quote—I like you!" A promising step toward getting your interview.

8. Enlist the interest of aides, secretaries, assistants, and spouses. Explain how important this story will be to the boss: "Everybody else in the industry is quoted in this one, and I'm sure he wouldn't want to be left out."

9. Seek opportunities to meet your source informally after a public speech, press conference, at a social occasion, on the jogging path. A quiet chat that includes an intriguing question can lead to an interview.

10. Offer to drive your all-too-busy source to the airport or to the next appointment.

11. Focus your interview on a topic you know the source will enjoy discussing. Sally Celebrity won't discuss her romantic entanglements but would eagerly talk about her work on behalf of crime victims.

12. Use flattery unabashedly. "Yes, I know you're busy . . . busy people are always the most interesting and important . . . we wouldn't want to talk with you otherwise."

13. Candidly explain the options to reluctant sources involved in public crisis. The details of that crisis will become public sooner or later. When agencies try to cover up they often extend a minor embarrassment into a prolonged scandal. Bureaucrats and business executives become their own worst enemies when they refuse to respond to legitimate inquiries about problems that have come to public attention. Full disclosure now will make this a one-day story, quickly forgotten by the public. Your explanation of this fact of public life can succeed where threats and deceitful tactics fail.

ASKING SENSITIVE QUESTIONS

The term "sensitive question" means either potentially embarrassing or critical questions relating to business or public affairs, or personal questions dealing with traumatic events in one's life.

Embarrassing Questions. This is easier and simpler than most novices suspect. Investigative reporters do not expect to wring confessions out of crooked politicians or shady business executives just for the asking. Rather, they do their homework: documentary research and interviews with other people. They prepare a case against Mr. Shady, and then, in a "confrontation interview," go over the evidence to secure confirmation, denial, explanations, and, if possible, new information. Experienced reporters avoid arguments, angry accusations, and unfriendly demeanor (except on TV entertainment interviews). Surprisingly, some respondents confess their misdeeds, occasionally, it seems, with quiet pride. The journalist thus finds reason to agree with psychoanalyst Theodor Reik about the compulsion to confess: "It is clear that in the criminal two mental forces are fighting for supremacy. One tries to wipe out all traces of the crime, the other proclaims the deed and the doer to the whole world." (Reik 1959.)

Personal Questions. Ask these kinds of sensitive questions only if they are of legitimate concern as part of the story. Your article on AIDS will fall flat if you don't ask people with AIDS to discuss the drug or sexual activity that led to the fatal disease. Your article on Alzheimer's disease needs case histories in which families discuss the trauma of caring for a family member with Alzheimer's. Suggestions:

1. Have a good reason for asking. Explain that through your article you hope others will profit from the respondent's experience—that you've come to educate the public, not to exploit the troubled. If you're convincing, people may tell you the private details you seek.
2. Avoid pressure tactics. Let people decide what they want to tell you. Often they talk candidly because they find it good therapy to do so, particularly if they sense your altruistic purpose and your nonjudgmental attitude.
3. Move indirectly into sensitive areas. If you want to ask about a person's experience with drugs, discuss similar activities involving other people. Respondents often volunteer their own experiences as illustrations of points they want to make.
4. Listen for hints and half-articulated feelings. Sometimes people want to tell you things about themselves but they don't know if you're interested. You, meanwhile, hesitate to ask. People often break the impasse by dropping hints, the way couples do in the early stages of a romance when neither is sure of the other's feelings. They test the climate with hints to see what happens. Your AIDS respondent may speak of a "little problem" in childhood, slipping it in unobtrusively. What little problem? Better ask, because the problem may represent a key element in your report, something you could have missed by not listening or not realizing that your source is ready to talk candidly.

ACCURACY

Beginning interviewers exhibit such anxiety about the interview—establishing rapport, avoiding foolish questions, and so on—that they often neglect the minor details. The result is inaccuracy—names misspelled, titles wrong, points misunderstood, technical details garbled, quotes mishandled.

Most mistakes result from interviewing problems. As noted, oral communication is fraught with peril. People often don't say what they mean and listeners don't catch meanings properly. Little details slip by unchecked or unchallenged. Here are some problem areas:

1. Names, addresses, ages, titles. If you have no other reliable source for these details, then you must ask. The sooner the better. Just say, "Excuse me, I need to check the spelling of your name." Don't apologize. Note the exotic spelling of some first names nowadays: Jon, not John; Janee, not Janie; Tari, not Terry.

2. Major points. As suggested before, repeat back your understanding of main points as the interview progresses.

3. Quotes. Unless you are certain of a comment you plan to quote verbatim, read it back for confirmation.

4. Context. Mistakes often occur because the interviewer does not understand (or worse, ignores) the context in which a source offers a comment. You quote Sally Celebrity saying she hates her mother, but she actually said, "My mother and I have a perfectly normal love–hate relationship, and when at times she tries to run my life or repair the flaws she sees in my character, well, those are times I hate my mother. But there is love, too, especially when she bakes oatmeal cookies and sends them with a note telling me that I'm special. . . ."

5. Corroboration. Mistakes happen because the *source* has the facts wrong. Seek a second opinion or viewpoint, especially if the original source seems unsure.

6. Unwarranted assumptions. Novice journalists tend to make assumptions rather than ask questions. An airplane pilot who had a crash landing told a group of college reporters that his engine had caught fire during an instrument landing approach "just as I reached the inner marker." The young journalists reported the inner marker as something to be sighted visually— "fire occurred just as he *saw* the inner marker." They assumed that it's a visible runway marker when in fact it's a radio beacon. The problem is not confined to novices. When Washington's Mount St. Helens erupted in 1980, an astonishing number of east coast media reported it as located in Oregon. A New York editor explained sheepishly, "It's one of those things everybody knows, so you don't bother to check."

COPING WITH HOSTILITY

Find the reason for the hostility; try to settle matters, and go on with your interview. Oregon sports reporter Ron Bellamy suffered a fruitless twenty-minute fiasco with baseball star Reggie Jackson. Finally Bellamy, seeing that the interview was going nowhere, asked Jackson whether there was some problem with the interview. That released a string of invectives about the biased reporting of a previous interviewer. Bellamy merely listened. Then, remarkably, the interview began anew. Drained of his anger, Jackson talked with new-found candor.

Hostility may also stem from personal problems, such as a fight that morning with a colleague or from worry over the crisis that has made the respondent newsworthy. If you know the reason for the problem, you may be able to defuse it or set it aside. When a doctor complained bitterly about media treatment of medical news, a reporter who had won awards for his medical writing, replied, "I won't blame you for the sins of the medical profession if you won't blame me for the sins of the newspaper profession." The doctor agreed, and the interview turned out fine.

ARE THEY TELLING THE TRUTH?

Truth emerges best through the patient, nonjudgmental listening recommended throughout this text. But it never hurts to utilize the truth-checking devices noted here.

   1. Homework. Good preparation solves many problems when sources realize they can't snow you. Respondents quickly perceive your level of knowledge by your questions. It helps to mention the other sources you have consulted, or will consult, and the documents you've read. Show your preparation in your questions: "Your mother tells me your childhood was not an easy one." Hard for Mr. Big to deny what Mom said—or what else she might have mentioned. Sometimes you'll challenge a questionable statement: "What you told me doesn't square with what I just read in the *Wall Street Journal*—is my memory playing tricks on me?" The latter phrase eases the harshness of the confrontation, but your respondent knows that you'll confirm your memory and will use more care in future comments.

   2. Sources. "Who told you this?" you ask. "Where did you acquire this information?" Aggressive probing along this line intimidates liars but enhances rapport with straight shooters.

   3. Corroboration. Try to find (or ask for) other persons or written evidence to confirm any doubtful statements.

   4. Plausibility. Common sense often suggests whether statements have a ring of truth, and you probe to learn more about those that don't.

5. Time line. Police detectives know that liars have a difficult time keeping the sequence of events in correct order each time they go over them.

NUDGING HAZY MEMORIES

Psychological studies suggest that people remember first things, last things, and unusual things. That's why you remember your first airplane flight, your most recent, and perhaps the one where things went wrong. This helps to explain why people can respond easily to such questions as "What was your most frightening experience?" Memory also operates by association—you remember a joke upon hearing someone tell a similar one. Thus, to remember a long-ago experience, people need cues.

When you seek to discuss past events, come with cues. Some may be news topics of the era. "We're talking about 1995—that was the year of the O.J. Simpson trial—remember?—the year the Republicans assumed control of Congress for the first time in forty years." They may be personal cues: "That was the year of your daughter's wedding, the year you took the Caribbean cruise."

Careful preparation helps. Come to the interview with clippings, letters, and other documents in hand, and give your respondent a chance to review them before you start. In some cases, you may drop off a packet of documents days ahead of the interview. Recollection of long-ago events takes time, even for the most willing of respondents.

Studies of police methods of interviewing witnesses have yielded useful ideas. Witnesses recall events in greater detail when detectives ask them to describe the scene—the weather, the time of day, the lighting conditions, and similar items—before beginning a narrative of what happened. These serve as cues to memory and enhance recall. Officers are advised not to interrupt the narrative but to ask specific questions afterward, and in reverse chronology, starting at the end of the account rather than at the beginning. Combined, the techniques yielded a third more facts than traditional methods. (*New York Times*, 11–15–88.)

EVASIVE RESPONDENTS

Evasion has become an art form that typically employs these devices:

1. Bridging. The respondent makes a subtle transition to bridge your embarrassing question to a safer topic. Your question about a company's pollution problems somehow leads to a diatribe about Congressional inaction.

2. Questioning the interviewer's motives. "Do you ask such a question because you have a statement you want to make? Why don't you go ahead and make your statement, and then let's discuss it."

3. Use of humor. A humorous remark or joke often derails a topic.

4. Intimidation. Sources use a range of tactics, such as belittling the question. ("How can you even think of asking about pollution at a time of industrial crisis?") Other tactics include a blustery, arrogant demeanor, nonstop talking, and even sexual innuendoes with members of the opposite gender.

5. Becoming abstract or academic. Respondents try to lead you down a semantic offramp—"How do you define pollution; what do you think it really means to the American public; what is an acceptable level of pollutants?"

6. Employing a hazy memory.

The solution? Do your homework. Keep the interview on track. Listen carefully to the answers. Ask again if not satisfied. And again if necessary, or ask why the source doesn't answer. On broadcast especially, don't hesitate to cut in whenever a filibuster or a bridging comes up.

Don't assume, however, that the other person is always to blame for problems. Examine your own interviewing procedures to see if your belligerence or tricky techniques aren't the cause of the evasive defensiveness.

OFF THE RECORD

A certain protocol guides your interview with elected officials and bureaucrats, most of it emanating from the experiences of journalists in the nation's capital.

Off the Record. By bureaucratic definition, statements identified as "off the record" are not to be published. They are usually intended for background information, perhaps to enhance the reporter's understanding of events. Or officials may want to avoid premature disclosure of forthcoming events. A police chief, answering questions about drug laws, takes the reporter off the record to tell of a forthcoming raid on a suspected drug factory. The reporter has asked too many perceptive questions, so the chief has little alternative but to announce the raid off the record, and to trust the reporter to keep it secret.

A reporter is not required to agree to off-the-record requests. Some will do so only in exceptional cases (the drug bust being a good example). Some tell sources that if they know something they don't want published, don't say it.

Not for Attribution. Statements so identified—according to Washington protocol—may be used but not identified as coming from the person who said them. Washington bureaucrats often use the terms "on background" and "deep background" to mean roughly the same thing. Thus news columns often contain blind attributions, "According to sources on Capitol Hill." Although attribution has long been a hallmark of news reporting, certain compromises have emerged: A reporter either takes the material not for attribution or doesn't get it at all.

The process can lead to manipulation. A source "close to the governor" announces a new proposal for school tax reform. The source is the governor herself. She is sending up a trial balloon. If the reaction is negative, she may drop the plan without ever having said she was going to do it.

Another example is the "little guy speaks out" scene. A minor bureaucrat, fed up with the problems of an agency, leaks damaging information to the media on condition of anonymity.

On the Record.   If you contact a source, identify yourself as a reporter researching a story, and then start asking questions, the answers are assumed to be publishable: on the record. Experienced sources realize this. Occasionally an inexperienced one will merrily spill out a string of answers and then say, "Of course, you realize this is all off the record—I don't want any of this in the paper." An awkward situation—you negotiate, you explain procedures, and you try to pick up the pieces as best you can. With novice respondents, it helps to explain early in the conversation that you plan to use the answers in your story.

THE NEWS CONFERENCE

The news conference is a necessary means of transmitting information, particularly where officials and celebrities cannot afford the time to grant individual interviews to many reporters. It is not an effective arena for the skilled interviewer. No opportunity exists for establishing rapport. Hostility, tension, and game-playing commonly reign at such sessions, often leading to defensive posturing by the speaker. Follow-up questions, the essence of good interviewing, are hard to ask.

A well-prepared interviewer would be foolish to ask a perceptive question only to hear or read the answer first in a competing medium. Newspaper writers especially tend to hold back, feeling that the news conference inherently favors the broadcast media.

Oregon writer Michael Thoele says he has asked only one question at a press conference in twenty-five years of reporting. That came when another reporter asked a district attorney a question that skirted dangerously close to premature release of information Thoele had worked hard to obtain exclusively. Rather than let the entire news corps stumble unwittingly onto his private gold mine, Thoele quickly asked a diversionary question.

WHAT WILL YOU WRITE ABOUT ME?

Anxious respondents sometimes want to know what you plan to say about them. No right-minded interviewer can tell at the outset of research precisely how an article will turn out. The proper response is, "I don't know." As the conversation goes on, however, good interviewers have a way of subtly telegraphing how the story will appear, largely by the questions they ask. Their respondents are seldom taken by surprise because all comments and issues that seem worthy of note have been discussed in the interview. Consider an example, the "I hate my mother" remark by Sally Celebrity. Some interviewers might appear to ignore the remark at the time but then write it into the lead paragraph of a headline-grabbing story, all to Sally's surprise and dismay. She didn't really mean it the way it sounded, she says. It was a slip of the tongue; it was out of context. She didn't expect it to go into the story. She feels betrayed.

The good interviewer would not let the remark pass without exploring it. Does she really mean it? If so, why the hatred? By such questions you show interest in putting it in your story. If Sally has any second thoughts about the remark, she will bring them up now. True, you might miss a fiery quote, but what good is a fiery quote if the speaker won't stand behind it?

How about allowing sources to read your copy before publication? Most stations and newspapers resist such requests. For one thing, deadlines won't allow it; many news reports barely make the deadline for the six o'clock news or the home edition. Journalists also prefer to avoid hassles with hypersensitive sources who want to quibble over the meaning of every word.

Magazine articles, done at a slower pace, are more likely to be checked with sources. Many magazines employ large research departments to ensure accuracy. Fact checkers routinely call interview sources to verify facts and quotations.

THE BORING RESPONDENT

The respondent bores you. What now? Look within yourself—perhaps you are the bore. Writer Michael Thoele recalls a case in point. His newspaper assigned him to interview a woman from the Red Cross. A boring interview resulted in a boring story. He was twenty-four years old then, inexperienced in both newswriting and in life. He didn't know what to ask. Twenty-five years later he wishes he could do the interview again. It would be a fascinating conversation; he would ask about the Red Cross role in natural disasters, such as floods, because he's covered floods as a reporter. He would ask about the difficulty, often the trauma, of recruiting volunteer helpers and getting them to do their job, because he's learned that recruitment is a major problem. With the self-confidence brought by twenty-five years of experience, he knows he'll find a good story in the conversation.

Within the breast of every living human, an editor once said, lies at least one great story. What's missing is not the story but the skilled interviewer to draw it out.

WHEN YOU'RE UNPREPARED

Reporters often must conduct interviews for which they have little or no preparation. Some enjoy the challenge. "It's like playing twenty questions," says one. If you are truly unprepared, the solution is simpler than you'd expect. You do what any quarterback would do on fourth down and long yardage. You punt. That is, you encourage the source to carry the conversational ball. You play a waiting game. As you listen you (1) pick up cues to orient yourself and figure out the kind of story you might produce, and (2) pick up ideas for follow-up questions. To start the conversation you say something calculated to get the other person talking. It doesn't have to be brilliant. "What brings you to River City, Senator?" Reporters often carry in mind a supply of punting questions. Examples:

What are some of the major problems [trends, changes] in your field nowadays?

When and how did your interest in [fill in the blank] begin?

What concerns are occupying your working hours recently?

What changes would you like to see?

What does the future hold in [respondent's field of endeavor]?

The GOSS pattern also works in these ordeals—what goals are envisioned, what are the obstacles, what are the solutions, where will you start?

▶ 15

Electronic Aids to Interviewing

Q. Sir, what is your view of the world?

A. $E = MC^2$

The 1994 California earthquake violently struck the Northridge area, north of Los Angeles, and soon people all over the world began calling to learn the fate of friends and relatives. Reporter Deborah Crowe, then of the *Tri-Valley Herald*, in northern California, turned to a novel means of contacting earthquake witnesses. The *Herald* is a 25,000-circulation morning paper on the east side of San Francisco Bay, 400 miles north of the earthquake. It's part of a five-paper chain on the East Bay. Crowe wanted eyewitness accounts, especially from any Northridge residents who had hometown connections. She turned to her computer and plugged into a computer communications network. Because several residents from the stricken area also had ties to the network, Crowe obtained the quotes and descriptions without leaving her office—a task she could never have done by phone. Long-distance lines were jammed, and "I wouldn't know who to call," as she explained it. But after posting journalistic inquiries on several "electronic bulletin boards," she found sources contacting her. She was not the only reporter working the computer network that day.

We see here a new journalistic tool. The high-tech revolution has brought computer-to-computer conversations via electronic mail, E-mail for short, and it promises to change the way reporters gather information. A worldwide computer linkup called the Internet has made this possible.

Imagine sending and receiving messages, even conducting "electronic interviews" with sources just about anywhere on earth.

Imagine wanting an expert to comment on a situation you're reporting and finding that expert quickly through a computer query.

Imagine listening to 20,000 public discussions as people from all over the world come together electronically to confer on topics ranging from Holocaust history to TV's "Star Trek." Think of the tips and ideas you could assemble for stories. Journalists can place a finger on the pulse of America—indeed, the world—by listening.

The Internet has opened up three areas of special interest to journalists: (1) electronic interviews, (2) communication through special-interest groups called newsgroups, mailing lists, and bulletin boards, and (3) securing documents from online sources.

THE E-MAIL INTERVIEW

The electronic interview involves an exchange of written messages. As such it supplements, not replaces, the conventional interview. It opens new journalistic vistas, however, such as interviewing people who don't speak or hear well—or not at all. Or hard-to-reach people (busy bureaucrats whose secretaries won't let your calls go through). Or people whose talk rambles but whose writing sings. Or geographically isolated people.

Consider an example. The South Pole qualifies as isolated—among the bleakest, driest, coldest spots on earth. In July 1994, during the depths of the Antarctic winter, reporters became interested in the U.S. Amundsen–Scott South Pole Station where twenty-one men and six women resided in splendid isolation for nine months. Scientists had established a telescope there to take advantage of dry air and twenty-four-hour darkness. That winter journalists contacted several of them, including a University of Chicago astrophysicist named Hien Nguyen, whose infrared telescope focused on the planet Jupiter as four comet fragments closed in for a series of cataclysmic collisions. Telephone contact with the South Pole was tenuous and expensive, but electronic mail flowed easily. Nguyen responded quickly with informal answers to journalistic questions.

Those South Pole interviews touched on many topics. Washington reporter Kim McDonald, writing about a federal proposal to rebuild the South Pole station, e-mailed questions to several residents: What were their most pressing needs in that harsh climate?

"Bathrooms!" came the answer. Bathrooms at the South Pole are occupied twenty-four hours a day, or so it seemed. Where Hien Nguyen worked on the telescope, the nearest bathroom was almost a mile away. "You can imagine how inconvenient that is for us." But Nguyen was philosophical: "Not many of us coming down here were expecting a comfortable life."

His comments, quoted in McDonald's *Chronicle of Higher Education* story, seemed so pleasantly informal that I decided to contact him myself. I wondered how a busy scientist reacted to his new-found media attention. I secured his E-mail address, and on my home Macintosh I wrote him a note. I explained my identity and purpose and posed three questions.

1. Do you find it easy or burdensome to respond to requests for E-mail interviews?
2. Speaking personally, is responding to news interviews worth your time and effort?
3. In your experience, how do E-mail interviews compare with conventional ones?

How eerie it seemed to write to a man I'd never met, click on the "send" button, and watch the message disappear off my screen enroute to its remote destination 10,000 miles away.

His reply arrived the next day. He wrote a chatty response filled with so many insights on journalistic interviewing—how it feels from the other side—that I quote it at length.

First, the frequent requests for E-mail interviews were not burdensome, he said, despite long hours at his job. He just takes a few moments from work "to chat with you guys. It's a privilege to be interviewed!" Second, he found being interviewed interesting and worthwhile. He had good words for the media. "I was amazed by the accuracy in their use of my answers. The matters I'm involved with are either scientific or factual, and relatively straightforward to answer, and so there weren't any apparent hazards." The third question brought a personal response—demonstrating that even written replies can provide anecdotal candor. He wrote:

> *I'm from Viet Nam. Over eastern Asia, there is a popular saying, "Bend your tongue seven times before speaking!" As a result, Asian people tend to be quite passive and make long delays in answering questions. When you ask them a question, no matter how simple it is, you often get a shy smile in return. . . . I have always been amazed by the prompt and accurate response from American people across all ages on TV. Every American seems to be born with some capacity of natural or public speaking. I've been trying to learn to be like that. . . . English is not my mother tongue. E-mail interviews give me ample chance to answer with correct English grammar in my own pace. I would not try to polish my answers, afraid of falling into the oriental fashion of making things too perfect and empty. I have previously been interviewed face-to-face with the University of Chicago News and Media people and with the national newspaper in Viet Nam. Both interviews went surprisingly well. I had fun entertaining their questions with my stories.*

In a personal interview no good reporter would let the last remark pass without a follow-up question: *"What* stories?" I sent a second inquiry. "Oh, I don't remember the stories now," he replied. How disappointing. Yet, as he wrote on, one did occur to him.

> *I was interviewed by the* Chicago Tribune *via electronic "talk," during the impact week, and he asked me what my mom and dad thought about my stay*

here at the pole. I told him that my parents (who are still living in VN; I went back there last December for the first time in 13 years) didn't really know where Antarctica was—that all they knew was that it's very cold (by seeing the South Pole pictures I gave them). My dad was concerned about the climate. He advised me, "Try to get another job after this one, son!" The reporter got a real kick out of it. He used the line in his story!

I'd initiated this E-mail adventure primarily to secure an example for this book, a successful quest because at least four textbook lessons emerge from it.

1. After explaining purpose, ask for precisely what you want and you shall receive.
2. You must recognize cultural differences in interviews; don't be surprised if respondents of Asiatic background are less forthcoming than others.
3. When a source says "I can't remember any stories," don't believe it.
4. Scientists of Asiatic background can write with surprising informality.

The electronic interview is far from perfect. Consider these disadvantages:

- Written messages tend toward stiff formality—the congenial South Pole response notwithstanding. Respondents often strive for dignity and filter out the personal asides.
- You might receive a prompt reply or you might wait days, weeks, or for all eternity.
- Follow-up questions may not be answered.
- Conversational flow is stilted, lacking the interview dynamic that leads to personal rapport—the laughter, the give and take of normal interviewing conversation.
- As interviewer you have little control over the conversation. Sources can easily evade your questions.
- You can't see or hear your respondent, or even tell gender. You can't see the nonverbal mannerisms that communicate feelings: smiles, frowns, laughs.
- You can't respond with smiles, nods, and other affirmations that help build rapport.
- The process favors those who write well and offer quotable nuggets.
- You can't be certain of the other person's identity. "Spoofing," the computer experts call it—using false identification. Savvy reporters verify quotes by telephone after receiving them by E-mail.
- People capable of navigating the intricacies of the Internet do not necessarily represent the population in general. Journalists seeking "person on the street" interviews should not suggest that opinions expressed by this computer-literate population represent the views of average people.

You can alleviate some of the stiffness and formality of the E-mail interview by an electronic "talk" method—"real time chat" in computer parlance. This program puts both parties online at the same time, permitting immediate follow-up questions and answers. The method approaches the informality of traditional interviews.

For all of their disadvantages, E-mail interviews serve a purpose. Sometimes you encounter interesting people on the Internet byways you'd normally never see.

When Washington reporter David Wilson was working on a story about computer hackers, he interviewed an anonymous youth who called himself "Hitman." Hackers are the electronic equivalents of party crashers, sometimes called "crackers," who gain unauthorized entry into private computer systems. Once through the electronic security gates into private networks, they can snoop through private files, even change records such as grade lists. Wilson encountered Hitman in a dark electronic alley of the Internet and proceeded with an interview. Hitman described himself as a sixteen-year-old high school student who had illegally connected with a computer at an eastern university. "A while ago when I was far less mature than I am now," wrote Hitman. "I just had a f– – – the world attitude. I thought a hacker was out to destroy everything in sight and cause havoc. Now it's just for educational purposes." The quote offered a colorful aside in a *Chronicle of Higher Education* news article otherwise populated by academic administrators expressing concern about computer security.

SECURING HELP THROUGH THE INTERNET

Journalists use the Internet to scout for story ideas and to ask for help. Reporter Deborah Crowe's use of Internet contacts to obtain eyewitness accounts of the 1994 California earthquake is one example. To understand the possibilities we must learn more about the Internet.

It is a loose collection of local and regional computer networks run by universities, organizations, government agencies, and commercial units. It started in the late 1960s as "ARPAnet" for military communication, an experiment during the Cold War to develop a communications network that could suffer damage and still function. (Kroll 1992, Shirkey 1994.) Groups meanwhile began to develop local computer networks, which then sought to join the ARPA network to gain access to other local networks. The National Science Foundation developed its own network to permit scientists to reach five supercomputer centers for research needs.

In time the units began to hook up together, many of them adding research files and databases to the electronic potluck. One computer expert, Doug Metzler, suggests thinking of the Internet as chains of Christmas lights. The string of lights at one's home—each light representing a computer—can be wired (or cabled or radio-microwaved) to the lights of another home and eventually to the entire neighborhood, then to another neighborhood, and so on, throughout the world. Each light (computer) can "talk" with any other computer, individually or in groups.

An estimated 23,000 "newsgroups" or "conferences" populate the Internet. They're like bulletin boards on which members post news notices, announcements, and discussion points and to which other members may respond. They represent every interest imaginable: politics, the arts, science, even such exotic groupings as fans of "Star Trek" or "Melrose Place." They're highly specific. "History" comes in more than forty categories, including Holocaust history, ethnic and immigration history, and anti-Semitism history. Some groups have monitors to screen out irrelevant postings, others are free-for-alls. Journalists have their own interest groups including investigative reporters, literary journalism, newspaper librarians, even one called "computer-assisted reporting."

Reporters frequently post notices with newsgroups to ask for help in researching a story. Here's a typical example, posted to a journalism group.

> *I'm looking for leads—past stories, experts, etc.—for a story about how states lease state-owned land to private interests. The lands in question are leased to mining companies, individuals who use them for vacations, farmers/cattlemen, etc. What issues should we pursue?*
>
> Jim Hopkins, *The Idaho Statesman*

Hopkins recalls receiving three or four responses, one of them from the Investigative Reporters and Editors office in Missouri, which sent abstracts of similar stories done by other media. From the abstracts, Hopkins requested the full text of two stories, which he found useful in developing his own story.

Posting journalistic inquiries pays off only about 20 percent of the time, says Hopkins. But sometimes the payoffs are spectacular, providing sources you could find no other way. Writing about wealthy families in Idaho, Hopkins needed an expert in estate planning—preferably one with an out-of-state perspective. An inquiry to ProfNet, composed of some 800 college information offices, produced numerous experts, of which Hopkins selected three for telephone interviews.

Another time Hopkins talked online with teenagers about suicide. He connected to an electronic discussion group composed of teens and identified himself as a journalist interested in writing about teen suicide. Several accepted his invitation to join him in an "electronic conference room." They were all online at the time, scattered through such states as Michigan, Alabama, New Jersey, and Idaho. They talked candidly about stresses on teens caused by parental abuse, broken romances, pressures to succeed in school, and others. All knew friends who had attempted suicide. Hopkins described the discussion in a *Statesman* article. (Hopkins interview 1995.)

Reporter Deborah Crowe's work to secure eyewitness accounts of the California earthquake further demonstrates the versatility of this newsgathering medium. The earthquake occurred on her day off, but she volunteered to use her computer to obtain "local color" from the stricken area. Before leaving home she posted queries via her laptop computer with groups in southern California, including two established to coordinate communication and rescue efforts. Identifying herself as reporter she asked for personal accounts, posing such questions as: What were you doing at the time of the 'quake? . . . What did you feel? . . . Can you describe the scene? . . . and similar items.

Working against a 7 P.M. deadline, she found the responses agonizingly slow; most arrived after the deadline. She did receive a few suitable for quotation in the paper's general earthquake story that evening, and she used the latecomers in a second-day sidebar about computer network groups assisting the rescue work. Her efforts represented such a landmark example of innovative computer methods that she has lectured to reporters' workshops about it. (Crowe interview 1995.)

With the Internet's worldwide connections, it's just as easy to query groups across the globe as across state. From Berlin a freelance magazine writer regularly queries U.S. journalists for help in writing about such issues as dangers faced by German tourists visiting Miami. From Finland, reporter Heikki Kuutti posted a request for ideas about investigative reporting in the United States for an academic project at a Finnish university. From nineteen replies, he quoted several in his 1995 dissertation.

For all the marvels of this Internet source sweep, one should not be overawed. You can achieve similar results by posting notices in your newspaper. "Tell us the most romantic thing that ever happened to you," exhorts a note in a newspaper preparing a Valentine's Day feature. But reporters working the Net find its participants especially chatty—that's what they've come online to do. The sources represent a worldwide selection so that even the most local of media can achieve a worldly feel by quoting people from far-away places.

In addressing queries to newsgroups, journalists should candidly explain their identity and intent. Give your full journalistic credentials. Sometimes a suspicious query will reach a newsgroup. A recent one sought crime victims to tell how it feels to be a victim or a bereaved family member. Because he offered no credentials, however, he received messages like, "Without the appropriate identity, many people who read your post may suspect you of being a ghoul."

PICKING UP NEWS LEADS

Reporters use the Internet to monitor the discussions that go on in the various user groups. "The Usenet is a terrific place to hang out," says Washington reporter Dave Wilson. "It's like sitting in a bar and listening to twenty thousand conversations. . . . It is a terrific way to get sources, a terrific way to get confirmation of stuff somebody else has told you. You post a note on a newsgroup and say I have heard that this is happening, can anyone confirm it? Nine times out of ten you can get someone to confirm it, even eye witnesses—or they can knock it down, too." (Wilson interview 1994.)

Much of the news that emerges from monitoring newsgroups pertains to the Internet itself. Reporters specializing in technology find unique story ideas from issues that confront the Internet, such as online censorship, pornography, government control, advertising, even various electronic scams, including romantic ones.

Washington Post reporter John Schwartz happened on the latter—a story about E-mail courtship gone awry:

> *It started simply, as complicated stories often do.*
>
> *Two women were comparing notes last month on their love lives. Not unusual, except perhaps for the fact that they began their chat in cyberspace. That is, they were communicating through computers and modems on a California-based service called the WELL [Whole Earth 'Lectronic Link].*
>
> *It didn't take long for the two women to realize that their hearts had been broken by the same man—a man who romanced them via electronic mail. . . . (Washington Post, 7–11–93.)*

The man had been courting at least four women at once, maybe more. One of them blew the whistle with a posting. A "Cyber-Scam artist" was on the loose, she said, "Mr. X," whose actions were more sinister than "the thoughtless, casual conduct of a guy out to see how many cyberfeelies he can grab—this man has acted deceitfully and hurtfully, in a calculated way."

Reporter Schwartz saw it as a milestone in the evolution of a new electronic society whose ethical boundaries have yet to be mapped. He pulled the story together by monitoring more than 1,000 often-acerbic postings about the incident. Schwartz talked on E-mail with many of the participants, including Mr. X himself. The WELL observes a policy of not allowing reposting or publication of messages without permission, a policy called YOYOW: "You own your own words." Schwartz obtained permission for each posting he quoted, and Mr. X agreed to a telephone interview on condition of anonymity.

He was hurt by the experience, he told Schwartz. He thought women saw him as a "lightning rod for some generalized female anger about men." He said he thought that relationship fidelity would be different on the network than in the real world. "I was wrong," he confessed. "The cyber world is the same as the real world." (Schwartz interview 1994.)

Another issue directly confronts journalists: How freely can you quote from newsgroup postings, especially when you identify the writer? Is the posting read by hundreds, even thousands, sufficiently "public"—like a soapbox in a public square—that it can be quoted with impunity? And how can you be sure of the source's identity? The rules are still being formulated at this writing.

A New York patent attorney found himself quoted in a newspaper account of the Intel Pentium chip issue in 1994. Intel had offered to replace a faulty computer chip to any computer owner who wanted one, and attorney Carl Oppedahl posted a comment on an Internet newsgroup suggesting that the company should have done so sooner. "It is clear that Intel 'blew it,' " the message said.

A reporter for the *San Francisco Examiner*, writing about the company's announcement, saw the message and quoted it among other E-mail reactions in a news story. But the reporter wrote this disclaimer in the story: "On the Internet, where some people use aliases, it is impossible to verify identities." Later another newspaper used the same quote, but without the disclaimer: "Sloppy journalism," the attorney said. The *Examiner* had done it properly, Oppedahl said in a subsequent E-mail posting. Under the headline, "Intel's decision draws applause on the Net," the story explained that all quotations came from an Internet newsgroup. The *Examiner* reporter was writing *about* the Internet, the attorney said, adding, "He was not cheating the reader, passing off the quotations as real interview material."

Oppedahl explained, "The ground rules for quoting people from what they say on the Internet are just now developing. In my view, he handled things well. Years from now, it may become common knowledge that one can't be quite sure who really wrote something that appears in a net discussion group. Between now and then such disclaimers are very important."

Even confirming identities does not prevent controversy over journalistic ethics. The *Washington Post*'s John Schwartz became the center of just such a controversy.

Yale University computer scientist David Gelernter had been seriously injured in 1993 by a bomb contained in a package he received by mail—one of a series of Unabomber attacks. During his convalescence, he posted a message to some of his faculty colleagues about his recovery. Someone reposted the message and eventually it circulated widely through Internet newsgroups. That's where Schwartz encountered it. He tried to contact Gelernter but was unable to get through, but he did confirm with the Yale computer science department that the message was authentically Gelernter's.

When the article appeared with the quotation, the Internet erupted in acerbic commentary about what many deemed questionable newspaper ethics in quoting from an Internet posting. Schwartz considered himself "seriously flamed." ("Flame" is a computer jargon term meaning attacked with verbal acid.)

Schwartz and Gelernter have since communicated on an amicable basis, according to Schwartz, and Gelernter acknowledged, in an e-mail communication, "I have a lot of respect for John Schwartz, and even at the time the breach of ethics (and I think there was one) seemed to me to lie not with him but with the person who took a note I addressed explicitly and only to my colleagues at the Yale CS department and reposted it."

Time and future court cases may one day establish firmer ground rules for these kinds of Internet issues. Meanwhile, the best procedure is the same verification process newspaper editors use to confirm the authenticity of signatures on letters to the editor where bogus identities are not uncommon.

SECURING DOCUMENTS THROUGH THE INTERNET

Finally, the Internet allows access to vast treasures of databases and daily postings of documents ranging from research data to government reports. Transcripts of White House documents are on line and free of charge to Internet users, among them the full Q–A dialogue of presidential news conferences and interviews, even interview dialogues with President Clinton as he jogged an eight-minute-mile pace.

The list of Internet archival treasures could overflow this book. The problem has been finding what's available and learning how to gain access to it. You can gain much government data free of charge; fees are assessed for some. Private databases are also accessible, some at no cost, others for a fee.

What's there? There are data from the activities of the U. S. Congress, searchable by key words. Also material from courts (including U.S. Supreme Court), from state legislatures, from state and federal agencies from whose files you'll find climate statistics, weather data, flood and earthquake watches, crime reports, census data, NASA space reports and data, historical–archival materials, reports from the U.S. General Accounting Office—and countless others. You can download data such as crime reports and submit them to statistical analyses.

In St. Louis, for instance, the *Post–Dispatch* secured data files containing 120,000 sanitation citations of local area restaurants. Analysis of the citations produced a list of the area's "worst restaurants" from a sanitary point of view. A similar analysis of crimes occurring on city buses in St. Paul, Minnesota enabled the *Saint Paul Pioneer Press* to print a statistical image of the most dangerous bus routes. (Browning interview 1995.)

Databases provide up-to-the-minute listings of new state laws—no more fooling around with books that become out of date the moment they leave the press. The Internet makes it possible to connect to libraries and museums throughout the world, including the Library of Congress. It's not just words. Picture images and sound come from many sources (the Smithsonian, for instance) where databases are loaded with digitized reproductions.

Some newspapers subscribe to a commercial service that contains Federal Aviation Administration records such as aircraft "SDRs" (service difficulty reports) and thus can quickly acquire up-to-date information about the maintenance record of any aircraft involved in an accident.

It boggles the mind to envision the breadth of Internet documentary resources. But avoid the term "Information Superhighway." The Internet is more a complex interlacing of roadways and alleys and dead-end drives where it's difficult for the uninitiated to find their way around. Over the years software tools have been developed to help users navigate the Internet to find useful information. The fastest growing segment of the Internet is an information access system called World Wide Web. The WWW is a vast array of links from one subject to another. Imagine looking up "space travel" in the encyclopedia, and it says "see Apollo" and "see Astronaut." WWW uses the same principle in a point and click format so that if you click on the text, "see Astronaut," you'll instantly jump to that subject. From Astronaut you can jump to other related topics, which explains the term "web." WWW can be accessed using software such as Netscape Navigator and Mosaic, which allow users to view multimedia web pages that integrate pictures, text, audio, and video.

In the process of obtaining this information, you're jumping from network to network in different locales, one a NASA site for technical details on the Apollo missions, another to the files of Harvey Mudd College, one of the few U.S. schools with a major in astronautics.

In conclusion, this chapter represents merely an introduction to journalistic uses of electronic communications. These communications will become more important—eventually to the point where journalists will feel disadvantaged if they don't learn to navigate the Internet. It opens new journalistic horizons. It offers access to people and situations that don't normally appear in the media. One reporter interviewed by E-mail several disabled people who communicate primarily via computer. He found their comments especially poignant—as though they had been bursting to express themselves to someone who would listen. In the years ahead the Internet will continue to grow and expand onto new and unpredictable roadways. Its utility in computer-assisted information gathering will expand along with it.

▶ 16

The Broadcast
Interview

Q. Dr. Zeiss, how do you feel about the world?

A. Based on all available evidence, I'd say it's round, though perhaps not perfectly so.

Q. Sir, forgive me, but I must take issue with you. I disagree flatly.

Principles in this book generally apply to the broadcast interview—at least those done to gather information, such as news reports, and not just for laughs. This book focuses on *information gathering* as the interview's goal, whereas *entertainment* has become increasingly prevalent in the broadcast interview. The higher the entertainment quotient, the less information emerges from the interview and vice versa. The happy medium should favor information without ignoring the pleasure principle.

This is not to dismiss broadcast interviews as mere entertainment fluff. Too much important information comes forth through the work of such interviewers as Ted Koppel, Barbara Walters, Bill Moyers, Larry King, David Frost, and Charlie Rose, and by programs such as "Meet the Press" to justify such a dismissal. But broadcast interviewing has become ever more entertainment oriented with the rapid growth of talk programs, tabloid TV shows, and the lively but frothy dialogue of talk show hosts.

Today's broadcast interviewing covers a spectrum so wide that much of it—the just-for-entertainment interview, especially—lies beyond the purview of this text. You will not learn here how to squeeze laughs or tears out of an audience by staging dialogues with "women who love bad men" or "people whose friends desert them when they lose weight" (talk show topics in 1995). In addition, some entertainment dialogue encourages methods that sink into ethical quicksand, such as the ambush interview, the hidden camera sting, the loaded-questions interview, and the accusatory interview.

What's left, then, is the information gathering interview. As practiced by broadcast professionals, even this often contains elements of entertainment, and properly so. Even the print reporter strives to find, through questions and careful listening, the colorful commentary and the anecdotal accounts of human experience that will both inform and entertain readers.

Two broad categories of broadcast interviewing, then, are entertainment and news/information. How does one tell the difference? Frequently interviewed subjects learn to make inquiries—is the request for an interview from the news division or the entertainment division, home of the tabloid TV shows? The serious ones have learned to grant interviews to news but not to entertainment, sometimes even eschewing offers to pay for the interview.

HOW BROADCAST DIFFERS

Having established that distinction, consider some differences between the way print and broadcast interviewers operate.

Print reporters think of interviewing as a mining process—tons of raw conversational ore for an ounce of gold. Broadcast interviews tend to dive for what glitters. That means short, provocative, usually superficial interviews with personable celebrities or newsmakers. Here are some other differences:

The broadcast interview is dramatic—lights, camera, action—almost a news event in itself, regardless of topic. TV news interviewers do not move unobtrusively through a scene the way newspaper pad-and-pencil reporters do. Often the interviewer is a bigger celebrity than the source (the presence of Dan Rather at a disaster scene can be a headline-making event for local media). The presence of TV cameras, celebrity interviewers, and satellite trucks often alters the nature of the news event.

The on-camera interview calls for a scenic locale, such as the bombed-out building as backdrop for interviewing the fire chief.

It's lively, at least in the hands of a skilled interviewer who seeks information via a colorful conversational exchange, a goal that often involves questions that are spirited but not so provocative as to overwhelm timid performers.

It cuts quickly to the essence of a situation. The sensitive bombshell question will be among the first ones asked.

It's highly focused with a firm and narrow sense of purpose, one that can be realized in four to six minutes.

It is selective, because broadcast favors personable, articulate, and attractive performers.

It fosters self-selection, with stage fright causing potential sources to opt out, especially when facing beautiful, golden-voiced interrogators.

It fosters a performance attitude among respondents who come with strong agendas and who have rehearsed answers to anticipated questions. The more sophisticated among these respondents know the value of the verbal blitzkrieg that leaves little time for penetrating inquiry.

A classic story illustrates the performance aspect. Before an interview, a young BBC reporter warned the minister of housing that he planned to ask some critical questions once the camera was rolling. They talked amiably for a few minutes until the camera started and the first critical question arrived. The minister flew into a rage, attacking both reporter and political opponents, leaving the reporter shattered and practically speechless. When the camera stopped the minister beamed a friendly smile and asked whether he'd done all right. (Tyrrell 1972.)

That was decades ago; have times changed? We have all witnessed similar theatrics over the years, such as then-candidate George Bush's confrontation with CBS's Dan Rather in 1988, a live interview in which Bush bristled at Rather's questions about Iran–Contra dealings, claiming that Rather had ambushed him and had misled him by promising that the interview would focus on why he chose to run for president. Bush even chastised Rather for once having walked off a newscast set in a fit of anger. And we have seen the drama, calculated or not, of such diverse news celebrities as Olympic skater Tonya Harding and Microsoft CEO-billionaire Bill Gates abruptly walking out of interviews done by another erstwhile CBS anchor, Connie Chung.

Consider a final distinction between broadcast and print interviews. Broadcast interviewing resembles living room conversation—formal, theatrical, artificial—but capable of lively discourse. Print interviewing resembles kitchen–family room–workroom discussion, often lengthy, intimate, and candid. That's true, certainly, for interviews done for newspaper and magazine feature articles and nonfiction books if not routine news reports. Given time and freed of the need to perform, even celebrities relax and act normally. Skilled, sensitive broadcast interviewers can reach that level of candor despite the camera, but they rarely do because of time limitations inherent in broadcast. Seldom can they match the depth of a typical *Playboy* interview, some of which are done in installments over weeks or months. The infamous 1976 *Playboy* interview in which Jimmy Carter admitted that he had "lusted in his heart" for women involved no fewer than five interview sessions with journalist Robert Scheer. It's not the type of candor likely to drop out of a typical broadcast interview.

The interviewing styles for print and broadcast do have many similarities, however. Both require a firm sense of purpose, extensive pre-interview preparation, conversational rapport, and keen, nonjudgmental listening.

THREE TYPES OF BROADCAST INTERVIEWS

Broadcast interviews come in three distinct packages: the news interview, the studio interview, and the multi-interview documentary.

The News Interview. The local TV station's ninety-second news item comes largely from the work of local reporters working in the field with camera operators. Once the crew arrives at the scene of a news event, the interview typically proceeds in two stages, a pre-camera inquiry followed by a brief on-camera segment.

The "performance" comes on-camera. The reporter asks questions calculated to elicit an appropriate sound bite that summarizes or provides a personal insight into the topic. With experienced respondents and a simple, clear-cut story purpose, the reporter may skip the preliminary interview. The camera rolls from the beginning and the reporter strives to elicit informal and spontaneous responses. Often the camera operator will shoot the reporter re-asking questions or listening to answers. Technicians will assemble the dialogue at the station.

The Studio Interview. As seen on "Good Morning America," Charlie Rose, Larry King, and similar programs, respondents ("guests") come to the studio for interviews that may last anywhere from a few minutes to an hour. The studio scene is complex. The interviewer must cope not only with the conversation—maintaining eye contact, listening, and thinking up new questions—but with time cues and glowing red lights that signal which camera is on. The confusion bewilders many a beginner. One professional recalled her first television interview: "I was so worried about time cues and which camera to face that I forgot to listen to the answers to my questions. It's hard to ask follow-up questions when you have no idea what you're following up." (Laine 1976.)

Yet it looks easy in the hands of broadcast professionals such as Ted Koppel of ABC's "Nightline." He not only copes with the technical problems but often has guests of violently differing viewpoints located in remote studios around the country. He manages to remain calm, and he invariably picks up on people's comments for follow-up questions. The key, Koppel told *Newsweek*, "is that I listen. Most people don't. Something interesting comes along and—whoosh!—it goes right past them." (6–12–87.) Conducting a live interview also means *editing live* even as the discussion proceeds, according to Koppel. "Editing while you're on the air is extremely tough," he told a writer for *Columbia Journalism Review*. (January–February 1995.) It means separating trivia from relevance, old from new—all in your head while listening and thinking up new questions—and doing it seamlessly as demanded by network broadcast standards.

Radio interviews also call for listening and editing. There the secret of the good interview "is not the quality of the questions you ask, but the quality of attention you pay to the answers." So says one of radio's prime interviewers, Susan Stamberg of National Public Radio. Radio interviews often reach out by telephone. Phone interviews can tap into people's lives wherever they are, allowing more intimate interviews away from the artificiality of a studio. Telephones do not unnerve people the way microphones often do.

The Multiple-Interview Documentary.   Stations put together several interviews, usually splicing them with illustrative scenes. Some are news documentaries, such as a special report on a flood or earthquake or sensational murder trial. The special will show scenes of the event interspersed with interviews with victims and authorities.

Observers say the major documentary is a dying breed, at least on commercial television and especially network television. You're more likely to encounter it on public broadcast. Recent examples include Ken Burns' treatise on baseball in 1994 and his earlier series on the Civil War. Documentaries often focus on celebrities of the past. In 1995 PBS portrayed the late singer Bing Crosby crooning through a series of film clips supplemented by interview snippets with those who either knew him (such as singer Rosemary Clooney) or had studied his career.

In contrast to PBS, time constraints prompt commercial broadcast to confine its documentaries to mere minutes, ten or twelve or at best fifteen, in a "magazine format" such as "Prime Time Live" (ABC) or "Sixty Minutes" (CBS).

ASKING QUESTIONS FOR BROADCAST

Five minutes ago the assignment editor scheduled you to interview Senator Phineas Fogg twenty minutes from now. The topic: the senator's reaction to the President's announcement that, due to Fogg's violent opposition, he had withdrawn his nomination of John Doe as ambassador to Panama.

1. You pick up the news dispatch of the President's decision and check the station's library (or a national electronic database such as Nexis) for anything you can find on the subject, tracking the year-long history of Fogg's opposition to the nomination. With a fistful of documents in hand you're out the door with a camera person who will drive while you study the documents and begin forming tentative questions. Maybe you try one or two questions on the camera operator.

2. You've agreed to meet the senator at an appropriate setting, the steps of the Capitol building, a visual cliché but better than an office scene.

3. You meet your senator ("talking head" in broadcast jargon). A brief "throat clearing" period ensues while the operator sets up the camera—talk of the weather, politics, background questions, but avoiding the subject at hand which you reserve for the camera segment. This example requires no pre-

camera interviewing; your clips have the background facts and the media-savvy senator needs no warmup.

4. Seamlessly, if possible, and with camera now rolling, you edge into the topic at hand, asking the simple, clear question you came for, "Senator Fogg, what's your reaction to the President's decision to withdraw the Doe nomination?"

5. Listen carefully to the answer. Peg your next question on it, if possible. Otherwise use a prepared question, based on your reading of documents, such as "Senator, news accounts suggest that it was Doe's support of the Panama Canal Treaty that prompted your strong opposition—is that a correct analysis?"

6. Listen to see if his answer prompts another question. If not, then try a question calling for a summarizing reaction, one that might yield a good sound bite. An action-oriented or future-oriented query such as "What are the political repercussions for you," or "Where does it go from here?" or "What would you like to tell the President about your preferences for the position?"

7. Finally comes the windup ("Do you have anything to add?") and the thanks-for-your-time speech. Listen carefully to those final thoughts, which may yield a quotable comment or may suggest another story or a fresh angle to this one.

It's a simple process, once you get used to it, so the experienced broadcast interviewers suggest. But some points deserve attention.

Focus.   Stay on target, particularly when glib politicians and celebrities with strong agendas seek to sway the interview to their own ends. Focus starts with *purpose*, which leads to an uncomplicated set of four or five prepared questions all narrowed down to fit the five-minute format.

Preparation.   This may lead to a new approach—new questions that have not been asked before. It requires thorough preparation because you must know what's old before you can tackle the new. The combination of preparation and a lively personal curiosity can claim new ground. Susan Stamberg of National Public Radio frequently springs curiosity-based questions. In one classic example, she asked symphony conductor Seiji Osawa, "Don't your arms ever get tired?" (The answer was "Yes.")

Preparation also allows the interviewer to put authority in the questions, to evaluate answers, devise on-the-spot follow-ups, and to educate the audience should some obscure reference emerge in the conversation that viewers might not understand. Rather than ignoring the reference, you clarify it for the viewers: "When you mention 'Clint,' you're speaking obviously of the actor, Clint Eastwood, who starred opposite you in. . . ."

Interviews often go better if the audience prepares for them, too. That is, as ABC's Barbara Walters' interview specials illustrate, you share some of your preparation—film clips and still photos—to introduce your guest. When Barbara Walters asked actress Debra Winger her attitude toward a love scene in the film *An Officer and a Gentleman*, a film clip illustrated the question. Winger's answer contained a lovely irony—what most viewers took for intense passion in the scene was intense dislike for the actor.

Do not ask for trivial details on a broadcast interview: "Where were you born? Where did you go to college?" If you can't find out through documents, you certainly must ask them before the broadcast and include them in your introduction: "Tonight's guest grew up in Cincinnati and graduated cum laude from Princeton. . . ."

Icebreakers.   The performance aspect of broadcast interviewing often calls for more than the customary icebreaking conversation. Inexperienced respondents are wary of interviews and some even—only half jokingly—ask whether the forthcoming interview will be a "Mike Wallace-type" inquisition. A perceptive TV reporter can tell quickly how the respondent feels about the interview, the nervous ones obvious by their rigid posture, lack of eye contact, sweaty palms, and sometimes by their having overdressed for the occasion. Such people need more than icebreakers—they need immersion in tubs of warm, personalized reassurance—forget the camera and let's just talk.

Phrasing of Questions.   If it's important to keep questions short in all interviews, it's especially so for broadcast. The point is simple: let the guest do most of the talking. That's not easy for reporters with a gift of gab, particularly with less-than-articulate respondents. Sources become more articulate in response to simple questions, careful listening, and enthusiastic feedback. Preface those simple questions with a statement of context if necessary. "Senator Fogg, tomorrow the Senate will vote on whether to confirm the President's appointment of Judge Roe to the Supreme Court. Tell us how you plan to vote and why."

The best questions work off the conversation itself, questions you didn't know you were going to ask. On broadcast, conversational immersion rates better than linear Q–A dialogue. Often the best question is "Why? . . . Why do you say that?" It's particularly effective when something startling comes up, such as Sally Celebrity's announcement that she's swearing off all men.

With timid or nervous respondents, opening questions should arrive like soft pitches: ego reinforcing, easy to answer. "Governor Caxton, your campaign to create more park lands has gained wide support from the media and the public. Why do you think people like your idea?" Once the governor has relaxed you can ask about troublesome things. But if your guest stumbles on a first question, the embarrassment may hamper the entire interview. Some interviewers prefer to give out the first question before air time. The opportunity to think through that first answer helps to calm the guest's pre-interview anxiety. Beware of filibuster answers, though; tell the guest to keep the response brief.

Most interviewers prefer not to suggest the subsequent questions before air time, however, for fear of losing spontaneity. If they know the questions, guests tend to rehearse answers. Stilted conversation results. With articulate guests, surprise questions often bring lively dialogue.

Organization.　　Short broadcast interviews contain only three or four questions, and so they arrive at important points quickly. That often means a less gentle approach to sensitive questions. If the senator is involved in a widely publicized sexual harassment scandal, then that will probably be no later than second on your list of four questions. Maybe first. That's what the audience wants to hear about, and that's what the senator expects, so why delay? Delay leads to viewer frustration and even to the guest's anxiety. On a long interview the key questions might be delayed until number four or five on a list of ten or twelve. Some interviewers like to build suspense by promising to ask certain key questions later in the program—"Senator Fogg's views on marital fidelity after these messages."

The "Ordinary" Respondent.　　Despite earlier comments about the selectivity of interview respondents—only the glib and beautiful need apply—many experienced reporters favor the ordinary person who has an extraordinary story or has witnessed an extraordinary event, and is not jaded by too many prior interviews. They have the most genuine human responses, "unpretentious, even bold, often nakedly emotional," says a former NBC News correspondent, Jim Upshaw. A perceptive reporter can sense when such people are about to express a genuine emotional response. If the camera happens not to be rolling at that moment, better pause or change the subject and bring the respondent back to that emotional moment after the camera starts. It will still be there.

One typical broadcast question should *never* be asked, says Upshaw, who later became a college professor. He recommends banning the phrase *How do you feel about.* . . . "There are more artful and revealing ways to approach this." Some of these include:

- The call for summary: "Give me your personal take on this situation."
- The future action commentary: "Pitch it forward for me—what happens next?"
- The epiphanous experience: "What can you say to other mothers who have lost kids this way?"
- The reflective comment (designed to encourage similar reflection): "Imagine, an innocent picnic at the lake coming out like this!"

To be sure, reporters must listen sympathetically to the answers. They must also ask fresh questions that the source has not heard before. Ask a unique question, get a unique answer. One sign of a forthcoming fresh answer appears when the source takes a few moments to think through the answer rather than glibly pursuing a worn rut. (Upshaw interview 1995.)

▶ 17

Interviewing on
a Newsbeat

Q. Good morning, sergeant; what's new?

A. Well, I've lusted in my heart for women, smoked a marijuana cigarette without inhaling, and haven't the faintest idea how to spell "potato." How come I can't get any publicity about my unsavory past?

Surely matters have changed since 1907 when one John L. Given published a book called *Making a Newspaper.* Maybe not. Describing an exotic vocation, newspaper publishing, Given explained how newspapers gather news. They do not keep a watch on all humanity, he said. Rather, they station watchers "at a comparatively small number of places where it is made known when the life of anyone in the city departs from ordinary pathways or when events worth talking about occur."

Where are those places? Police headquarters. The county clerk's office. The fire station. The courts. City hall, the state capitol building, the governor's office, the White House, Capitol Hill. It does not matter that society and technology have changed since 1907; the principle remains. Newspapers, broadcast news, magazines—all regularly cover newsbeats where they learn of events worth talking about or when the lives of people stray from the routine. From the fire department we learn that somebody's house is on fire. News by definition reflects human nature. What do people talk about? A Honolulu newspaper writer, Bob Krauss, asks this question: You pass ten houses on your way home and one of them is on fire. Which house would *you* talk about?

Though the principle remains the same, times change. Government agencies remain a firm anchor in the beat system, but social and political changes have spawned new areas of interest, such as computer technology, environment, family health, lifestyles. Each has its own set of sources.

Q: Anything new today, Chief?
A: Just the same old routine.

Overlaps occur occasionally. Which reporter covers the sudden outbreak of infectious hepatitis—the family health reporter or the county government reporter whose beat includes the health and sanitation department?

Whatever the answer, covering a beat means keeping in touch with news sources. Some may be government officials, others experts in certain fields (academic researchers, for example). Some may be thinkers: visionaries without portfolio. Some may be secretaries or clerks—or janitors who keep in touch with events by sweeping up people's mistakes. The wise beat reporter will not dismiss anyone as a potential news contact.

HOW INTERVIEWING DIFFERS ON THE BEAT

How does covering a beat change your interview procedures? Probably not much if you follow the Golden Rule of interviewing and treat sources as human beings first and only secondarily as sources of information. Beat reporting represents a long-term relationship, however, not a one-time encounter. Slash-and-burn techniques—alienating news sources through deceit or slanted, inaccurate reporting—may work for one-time encounters but not in the long run. It's not a monogamous relationship. A beat reporter must adjust to an astounding range of personalities, from preachers of political or social dogma to Machiavellian manipulators. These contacts don't always see you as the sincere, lovable person you are. The manipulators will practice their craft on you and when they occasionally force you to guard against their cunning thrusts, they will accuse *you* of being the manipulator, not themselves. You'll also encounter detail quibblers, self-righteous zealots, egomaniacs, and would-be editors eager to tell you what belongs or doesn't belong in the news.

You should not take it too seriously. Consider it a lesson in life, like visiting a zoo. The lessons you learn will serve you when seeking character traits for your novel. Imagine the fun envisioning Ms. Rhinoceros confronting Mr. Buffalo in the county commissioners' office. Do this and you may avoid the cynicism that creeps up on too many reporters after a few months on the beat. You'll also meet many decent, hard-working people on the beat, but they won't stand out the way the zealots do. The latter are so narrowly agenda-oriented that they see neither the broad picture nor the humor so apparent to the journalistic observer.

While you are sizing them up they are doing the same with you. The rapport and trust established on initial contact will affect future interviews, not only with one source, but with many others. Word gets around. A newsbeat—the county building, let's say—contains a small society in which people frequently exchange ideas, experiences, and gossip. The "new reporter on the beat" will enter into the discussion. The interviewing tactics of reporters become magnified over time. "He's sneaky—you've got to watch him all the time." Or, "She seems open and sincere."

Some agencies have ways to handle reporters whose methods are less than open. In Honolulu, a police reporter persisted in surreptitiously reading unauthorized file material. Recalls a police official: "One day we put a lot of junk in that file, including a fictitious murder. He picked it up and got all excited. We let it go just as far as the news desk, and then we called the editor and told him it was all a hoax. We also told the editor why we'd done it. We didn't have any more trouble."

Beat interviews differ from one-shot interviews in another way. Uncovering the news requires knowing what news is—having a working definition. It's one thing to receive an assignment—go interview the governor to see if she plans to veto the education bill. It's something else to be chatting with the governor who during the conversation remarks, "If it weren't for domestic violence, we could cut by 20 percent the police forces in the cities and counties of this state."

Is that news? Possibly. Is it worth pursuing in your conversation? Definitely. What questions would you ask? Start with, "Well, how interesting, governor—why do you say that?" Suddenly the news game is afoot. It requires that you pursue the topic until you're satisfied that the topic fits (or fails to fit) your definition of news.

The definition varies markedly from one medium to the next, a murder being big news in a small town but hardly worthy of mention in a large city unless it involves celebrities or bizarre circumstances. Many reporting texts deal with news definitions in detail. The following simplified definition seeks to illustrate interviewing techniques used to deal with news sources.

By this definition, news depicts something occurring in unmistakable form: a fire, an arrest, a death, a riot, a bill sent to the floor of Congress, a vote, a speech, the remarks of a famous person. Newsbeat watching requires that a reporter identify the points at which news can occur. Some are better at this than others. If a journalist sees a building at a dangerous list, suggests Walter Lippmann in a classic work called *Public Opinion* (1922), she does not have to wait until it falls to recognize news. That may seem obvious, yet a legendary story tells of a novice reporter sent to cover the launching of a ship. He returned empty handed. The story didn't pan out, he told his editor. "Something went wrong and the ship stuck on the ways. They hope to get her into the water tomorrow." The reporter had failed to perceive this deviance from ordinary pathways as news.

Subsequent events have broadened the definition of news, to be sure. Instead of reporting a single murder, reporters employ computers to spot and analyze crime trends. What are the demographic characteristics of people most likely to become crime victims? Or the personal characteristics of the children most likely to commit violent crimes in later years? Instead of reporting a spat in the City Council over zoning codes, a reporting team may explore the entire history, philosophy, and political machinations that protect (or fail to protect) the reader from having an asphalt plant built next to her new home. Those, too, are news by today's standards.

Despite the sophisticated methods, reporters still keep in touch with the watch points, still work to develop news sources, still keep an eye open for those points at which happenings or trends can be fixed, objectified, named, or measured.

THE BASICS OF NEWSBEAT COVERAGE

Few activities intimidate the young reporter as facing for the first time a bureaucratic iceberg such as city hall or the county courthouse. You find it populated with people who speak an exotic jargon. Garbage dumps become sanitary landfills. Dumping trash becomes solid waste disposal. Meetings and hearings bring such opaque jargon as first and second reading . . . declaring an emergency . . . defendant then and there being did then and there unlawfully . . . fiduciary funds, equity transfers, writs of replevin, mandamus, and certiorari, in camera hearings, seismic retrofitting. What do they mean? And how do they become news?

Whatever the field, the beat reporter works to define points at which the flow of political, social, and economic events can be reported. GOSS—the acronym for goals, obstacles, solutions, start—proves useful here because all agencies have goals. The reporter looks for mileposts along the way to those goals—or obstacles that block progress. Among the points at which one might report progress, or the lack of it, are an annual report, a labor dispute, a political altercation, a speech by an official, the announcement of a new budget or a tax increase.

You don't always report progress. Your city establishes a new crime fighting unit deployed nightly to areas with high crime rates for burglary and violence. Is progress being made—is the burglary rate dropping? If the answer is measurably yes, you have a story. If it's no, you still have a story: Despite the employment of an elite crew of officers, burglary and violence remain as high as ever—a newsworthy twist of irony.

Just where are these watch stations, the newsbeats where reporters keep an eye on events? A typical newspaper serving a middle-sized U.S. city will split them up something like this:

1. Emergency services. Police and fire departments, hospitals, medical examiner, ambulance services, jails, Coast Guard.

2. Courts. State, federal, and local courts, also appellate courts, juvenile, probate, and bankruptcy courts.

3. City services. City hall, city council, municipal agencies such as engineering, planning, zoning, civil service, and many others.

4. County government. Tax collection, boards of commissioners, welfare, health and sanitation, elections, environmental controls, housing. State courts are often housed in the county building.

5. State government. Governor, legislature, and state services if the city is also the state capital. Highways, state police, motor vehicles, and so on.

6. Federal. Post office, immigration service, internal revenue, agricultural agencies, law enforcement agencies—these and many more have branches in major cities.

7. Business. Chamber of commerce, business and professional organizations, major local industries, public utilities, financial institutions.

8. Environment. Watchdog organizations, government agencies, research labs.

9. Sports. Professional and interscholastic athletics, outdoor activities, participation sports (golf, tennis, mountain climbing, running, sailing, and so on).

10. Politics. Political organizations, political leaders and candidates, office holders.

11. Education. School boards, student activities, colleges and universities, administrative offices.

12. Social welfare. Altruistic organizations, youth agencies, social betterment groups, government welfare agencies.

13. Agriculture. Farm agencies, granges and other farm organizations, farm research agencies.

14. Transportation. Airports, railroads, waterfront, highways, tourist agencies, hotels, airlines.

15. Entertainment. Movies, theaters, concerts, books, civic events.

16. Medicine and health, science, technology. Research agencies, museums, archival agencies, medical societies, hospitals, college science departments.

Variations exist from community to community. On large newspapers, a reporter's work may be confined to just one of these areas; small papers and broadcast stations have smaller staffs so that beats are combined and coverage is less systematic.

Some new thinking has reorganized the typical beat system into "news teams." In 1994 *The Oregonian* in Portland developed a pioneering program. Politics and government are entrusted to the eight-member *Public Life Team*. Some teams represent tradition (business, education, sports), but others push the boundaries. The coverage of the *Living in the 1990s Team* ranges widely through spirituality, relationships, hobbies and pets, pop culture, even a beat called the "cultural divide" (dealing with the differing values people hold on such issues as homosexuality). The traditional police beat now finds its home with the *Crime, Justice, and Public Safety Team*.

GETTING STARTED ON A NEWSBEAT

Let's assume for discussion that you have been placed on the county courthouse beat, covering county government and the state trial courts. How do you begin? If you're lucky, an experienced reporter will take you around, show you where to find such public documents as court complaints and petitions, and introduce you to important people. But many reporters have had to learn a beat on their own, usually by just diving in. The water is seldom as icy as you imagine.

Plenty of sympathetic and helpful people will come forward to provide assistance once your motives are understood to be honorable. Some are more publicity conscious than others—they seem constantly involved in schemes to get something onto the six o'clock news or to keep something out.

Most people in public life are guided by high principles, and about two-thirds of them are eager, or at least willing, to work with media representatives on news stories. They have their own set of needs, paramount among which is public acceptance of their programs. Highway officials want the public to know about repair projects or new construction. Health officials want to warn about dangerous epidemics of influenza, hepatitis, or sexually transmitted diseases such as herpes or AIDS. A county administrator wants to secure voter approval of a budget. Elected officials sometimes will go to extremes to curry media attention, believing that their political future depends on it.

So as the new reporter on the beat, you're sought out as often as you seek out. You're constantly tested with ideas for publicity. You're bombarded with news releases, tips, suggestions. Pseudoevents—ceremonies, news conferences, demonstrations, inspection tours—are staged for your benefit and the accompanying publicity.

BASIC STEPS FOR A NEW BEAT

Here is a sketch of how a new reporter typically gets started on a newsbeat:

1. Attain a good working definition of news—what it is and how to recognize it when you encounter it.

2. Identify the departments, agencies, and informal sources from which you expect to collect ideas for news and features. Put their phone numbers in your Rolodex. Keep adding new names. These will include all potential sources from chief executive officers to informal sources such as secretaries and janitors. Include home numbers, cellular phone numbers, paging numbers, fax numbers, and e-mail addresses.

3. Read. Prepare as you would for an interview. Read clips of previously published articles from that beat. Read professional journals, such as *Education Week* if you're covering education, or *Law & Order* if you're covering police. Ask to see public documents from various offices: memos, annual reports, brochures, copies of speeches. Monitor bulletin boards.

4. Identify issues and goals—what is the agency trying to accomplish? Identify points at which accomplishment, or the lack of it, can be reported.

5. Establish a "futures book"—an appointment book in which you list all forthcoming ideas and events that you learn of. Asking sources to help you fill out your calendar often turns up ideas for stories. Ask them to consult *their* calendars.

6. Meet your prospective sources, one by one. Leave your business card. Explain your mission. Define news: what you want and why it's important. Discuss plans for regular contact, daily, weekly, or whatever's appropriate. Discuss GOSS—goals, and so on. Together identify potential stories for now and in the future.

7. Continue contact with sources on a regular basis.

8. Never approach a source empty-handed. Come with an agenda of questions to ask, even if hypothetical. When will work start on the new Center Street Bridge? I notice some cement cracks in the Clark Street overpass—are those of concern? Reading *Education Week*, I note that a county in Tennessee has halted school bus services because of a $800,000 budget shortfall—is our own budget shortfall likely to affect buses here?

9. Inform potential sources on the realities of the news business. Not every story will favorably portray a source or agency. Sooner or later events will dictate a story that causes displeasure. Anticipating such events and discussing them before they happen can dispel hard feelings sometimes, particularly if you promise to be open-minded and fair—and your subsequent actions demonstrate those qualities.

A certain amount of bargaining goes on between reporters and sources. Write a story favorable to a source and you stand a better chance of getting tips, leads, and exclusive interviews in return. Any experienced agency head knows, however, that refusal to cooperate—even after being "burned" by an unfavorable story—incurs the risk of more unfavorable stories as reporters seek alternate news sources. Thus a delicate balance of power exists between reporters and officials.

Occasions do exist when reporters must use leverage to secure public information from recalcitrant public officials. They find it wise to use the power of the media in moderation. The reporter who deals honestly and openly with sources seldom has to resort to power tactics. For one thing, you'll find alternative sources of information. When you've pieced together a story from a dozen different sources, *then* try your reluctant bureaucrat again. She may give you an interview just to find out what you know. She may stew and fret about the alleged biases in the information you have. This may reopen negotiations about what information she's willing to provide. A sufficiently enlightened bureaucrat may cooperate even when her heart isn't in it, especially if you refrain from gloating over your apparent victory. Don't claim victory too soon; the statements made under duress are seldom candid. At least you started her talking.

Enlightenment doesn't come easily to some bureaucrats, however, nor does it to some reporters. As a result, strident, adversarial styles of information gathering will continue for all eternity, even if truth suffers as a result.

THREE SOURCES OF NEWS

Systematic beat coverage resembles a three-legged stool. First comes news from press releases, news conferences, meetings, documents, informal suggestions—in short, source-initiated material. Second comes reporter-initiated news: interviews, pursuit of tips and hunches, follow-ups on projects.

The third leg—the one too often overlooked—evolves from the interaction of a reporter and a news source. This produces a kind of intelligence neither party could produce alone. It happens informally. Some reporters call it coffee cup reporting, and one reporter confesses he consumes ten to fifteen cups of coffee a day talking informally with sources on his newsbeat.

It works to the advantage of both parties. One source, a state legislator in Hawaii, explains: "We meet over coffee or in the hallways or during breaks in meetings. The reporters just come around and ask what's the scoop on this bill or that issue. I think this is good because the reporters can ferret out stories that would not always be appropriate in a press release because they might hurt somebody's feelings. This way the public gets a more candid and realistic story." Thus do useful stories emerge, the kind that sources wouldn't volunteer and reporters don't know about. But informal contact allows them to emerge naturally.

The informal give and take also works on the phone, at least after reporters have become acquainted with sources. One newspaper reporter happened to call a woman in community relations at the county courthouse. The conversation, which the reporter characterized as a "fishing expedition," led to two useful story ideas. The story ideas came so casually that the reporter decided to write down the entire conversation afterward as best he could remember it, just to show how informal conversation leads to news—also to show the informal dialogue.

Q. What's new?

A. What's new? Well, same old routine.

Q. Ha! That's what they all say. You've heard this story about a reporter who calls up the courthouse and asks what's going on? Well, the county judge answers and says, "There's nothing going on," and he quickly hangs up. For once he was right. Seems the courthouse was on fire. Everybody had evacuated the building. So they were all standing around doing nothing.

A. Right, right. I get the picture. Hey, I smell smoke!

Q. What?

A. No, I'm kidding. You reporters are so jumpy! Well, if you want to know what's not happening, there's no commissioner's meeting next week.

Q. How come?

A. They're all going to a conference out of town.

Q. Are you going, too? Are you going to give a speech?

A. Didn't anybody teach you not to ask two questions at once? Yes. No. I'm going but I'm not speaking. I'm going to attend a session about how to bridge the credibility gap.

Q. No need. We all know you're an honest woman.

A. Except I lie to my husband and my kids and my friends—

Q. But only because you have so many state secrets, stuff that would really blow the lid off if people knew—

A. Well, no, I don't really.

Q. So, anyhow, who is going to give a speech? Anybody? Or is that two questions?

A. Three. One of the fellows in the Solid Waste Department—he's talking on "Solid Waste and Energy Production." That means burning garbage for electrical energy in case you didn't know.

Q. I know. Is he for it or against it?

A. For it, I hope.

Q. Well, that's worth a story. I'll call him and find out what he intends to say. So who else is going with you on this boondoggle—er, trip?

A. [Gives details. Conversation turns to another department, the Juvenile Department.]

Q. I've just about given up on that department. I used to work years ago in another county and got lots of stories from juvenile. Here, nothing.

A. They're very protective here.

Q. Someday they'll find they'd like more public support—

A. Say, that reminds me, speaking of the courthouse burning—

Q. Oh, no—

A. Seems that the Juvenile Department *is* interested in the public, so they've started some kind of educational programs with juvenile officers going out and talking to parents' groups about juvenile problems—what youth is all about today, what to look for in the way of problems, drugs, alcohol. Maybe there's a story there.

Q. Right. Could be. I'll check into it.

Does the dialogue seem almost too casual, too personal with its teasing references to honest women and jumpy reporters? It's almost as though this were a personal conversation, not business. Don't overlook its importance. The pair clearly enjoy chatting informally, but as the conversation goes on, both are alert to hints and reminders that can lead to the business at hand: fishing for news.

Fishing for news? Watery metaphors dominate the definition of the newsgathering process, it seems. Beat coverage is like throwing a net across a salmon stream. Newsgathering is like hand-line fishing from leaky rowboats. Extreme comparisons, to be sure. Yet each contains some truth. The court reporter, for example, casts a net by inspecting all the court papers that come through the court clerk's office, selecting those deemed most newsworthy. In some agencies where there is little regular dialogue between reporters and sources, newsgathering does indeed resemble a catch-as-catch-can affair.

BLIND QUESTIONS FOR BEAT COVERAGE

Once they get to know their beats, reporters don't often have to resort to "blind" questions for news coverage, the ones that are purely fishing expeditions. Tips and leads and follow-ups will keep you busy. Sometimes, though, having a set of universal questions can expand your view. Here are some examples of questions you can ask of a news source when nothing else appears on the horizon:

1. What kinds of problems cause you the greatest concern right now?
2. What projects are you working on?
3. When members of the public talk with you, what concerns are on their minds? What do you tell them?
4. What stories could the paper (or station) run to help you meet your goals?
5. What new trends are evident in your field? What is your department doing to adjust to these trends?
6. Do you have a vision for what this department might be doing five or ten years from now?
7. If you had more money, what new projects would you start?
8. Do you ever ask yourself, what should the department be doing in the future? What stands in the way of doing it?
9. What research is going on?
10. What personnel changes are being made or contemplated?
11. What experts or consultants are being brought in, and for what purpose?
12. What new equipment is being purchased, and for what purpose?
13. What significant statistical trends have been spotted?
14. How will outside forces (economic, political, legal) affect your department?
15. What publications, reports, or memoranda are being prepared, for whom and to what end?
16. Are you or members of your department planning any trips, conferences, speeches, or meetings in the weeks ahead?
17. Who are some people in your department who have the most interesting jobs, the most unusual insights into human nature, or have achieved the most remarkable goals?
18. If, as you suggest, absolutely nothing noteworthy is going on in your department, could the organization (or taxpayers) save money by eliminating it?

Question 18 seems harsh, so perhaps you should get to know your source before you try it. I used it several times, and got remarkable results. One agency director approached days later with no fewer than twenty ideas for stories, of which half struck me as pretty good, and several of which eventually appeared in print. "Your question stimulated our thinking," the director said, "and we got to wondering, just why are we in existence? So we came up with these ideas as part of the answer." So heed the lesson: Don't be afraid to pose challenging questions.

► 18

Multiple-Interview Projects

Q. Tell me, Senator, who would be some other good sources of information to talk with about your proposed legislation?

A. No one! Talk to no one but me; believe no one but me!

"Triangulating the truth"—a phrase often used by careful journalists—means seeking evidence from at least three sources familiar with the topic. Those sources may not agree. Now what? You may have to form your own journalistic perception of reality. Now you have a fine struggle to identify "truth," defined here as simple factual reality. You're like a jury arriving at a verdict. Do you average, so to speak, the many comments and place reality somewhere in the middle? Or do you give more weight to some sources than to others? Your truth, your reality, may then rest on one side or another instead of dead center. It's not easy.

Triangulation puts more responsibility on the reporter. Reporters find it easy to quote a single source even when they disagree with the source's views. Not so easy is finding your own perception of reality after interviewing a dozen sources with contradictory views, some reflecting your ideas, others not. It requires a certain purity of soul. Going into a project, you must have no overt biases, no agenda other than gaining your view of reality. Simple things become more complex when you begin to triangulate. Not easy, true, but more challenging and exciting.

Permit me a personal example. I confess a certain small-boy thrill watching a big airplane take off. Working in Honolulu one time, I decided to try to write an article about it—the departure of Flight 180 for San Francisco. Talk to a pilot: You move the throttles forward causing the Boeing 747's four engines—exerting 174,000 pounds of thrust—to pull the craft down the runway, and upon reaching airspeed you ease the plane off the runway. Make a right turn after takeoff to avoid flying over a congested area. Fly the route shown on your chart as the Blue Fin Departure. With luck Departure Control will override Blue Fin and give you vectors that represent shortcuts. Simple. But one-source interviewing produces a narrow perspective.

Talk to others—triangulate the truth—and it's far from simple. In a sense, the departure began eleven months earlier when the first passenger reserved space. The story builds from there. They've overbooked the flight, but no-shows will probably solve the problem. Flight attendants hold a preflight meeting and select one of them as the "head flight attendant." They're all business, but they take a moment to answer my questions, some of them calculated to draw on their vast experience. (Many have worked for the airline twenty years or more.) How does the Hawaii flight compare to others? Hawaii, they say, is the "doomsday flight," so called because of occasional illnesses among passengers and no place for emergency landings. They say that tongue-in-cheek, of course. Working SF–Honolulu ranks vastly superior to New York–LA. Hawaii-bound passengers are happy. The unhappiest passengers, by contrast, fly from Chicago to Washington, D.C. or New York to Palm Beach. They don't know why typical passengers on those routes are so grim.

As passengers check in for Flight 180, airline personnel decide to deny boarding to what they consider an inappropriately dressed young woman from Los Angeles—she's wearing a translucent beach cover-up and—quite obviously—nothing underneath. A dog breaks loose from its travel cage. Agents help chase it down the airport corridors. They forget about the woman.

On the plane, now being boarded, the head flight attendant announces to the captain, "Four red lights in the pit!" Trouble. Ventilation in an area deep in the belly of the plane isn't working. The pit serves as storage for in-flight meals. Attendants work there, so the plane can't depart with faulty ventilation. Call maintenance. The captain has another concern. If the flight doesn't depart on time, he may have to take a less-preferred altitude and routing to San Francisco. This could add as much as two minutes to his flight time, burning more fuel and requiring reprogramming of the plane's two navigational computers.

And so on. Twenty-three sources contributed to this story—including mechanics, air traffic controllers, and passenger agents. As it turned out, Flight 180 departed the gate on time, with both the dog and the scantily clad woman on board—and the pit properly ventilated. Because of traffic delays on departure, however, the captain failed to obtain his preferred altitude and routing. Strictly routine, as the airline folks like to say. The experience in this multi-interview project taught me the reality of modern jet flying—getting a big plane aloft is far more complex than I had imagined. The project also yielded a fine learning experience. The major lesson? Multi-interview projects are fun.

As projects go, this was simple compared to the prize-winning work of business writer Peter Rinearson of *The Seattle Times*. He wrote a seven-part series of articles that dealt with making one airplane fly. Rinearson undertook to tell the story of the airplane manufacturer's development of the Boeing 757, another commercial jetliner. At first he thought the job would take three or four weeks. As it turned out, he spent six months of seventy-hour weeks, consulted 325 categories of sources, conducted extensive taped interviews with seventy to eighty people, and amassed some two thousand pages of transcribed notes from his interviews.

Rinearson found the task so complex that he developed a computer database just to keep track of the information. He seemed to thrive on detail. Making the 757 fly started on a sun-drenched day near the Miami International Airport. Two men shook hands as they sat in the back seat of a car just as it jiggled over some railroad tracks—and that led to the birth of the 757. No novelist would dare to include that symbolism—critics would call it too contrived. But that's the way it happened. The series, titled, "Making It Fly," reads like a novel. It won several writing awards including the Pulitzer Prize for feature writing.

Not all are that extensive. Yet today's significant works of nonfiction writing—books, magazine articles, and newspaper reports of Pulitzer Prize caliber—derive from extensive interviewing and observation. For example, J. Douglas Bates, in his book *The Pulitzer Prize*, provides three gripping accounts of projects done by the three finalists for the 1990 prize for "local specialized reporting." They are gripping because they show how the three reporters persevered against obstacles and hostile sources. They published articles that brought changes for the better. New Mexico reporter Tamar Stieber's research on a link between a rare blood disorder and a certain drug started with a bad interview with a hostile respondent. It could have ended there with a less-persistent reporter. Instead, she doggedly pursued interview after interview. The articles led to banning the faulty drug and captured a Pulitzer. (Bates 1991.)

THE NATURE OF MULTIPLE-INTERVIEW PROJECTS

By definition, the multiple-interview project is a journalistic endeavor that involves more than one interview. Most news articles come from multiple sources, even the simplest ones. The police reporter contacts witnesses to the bank robbery to bring readers a more vivid account. A journalist writing a comprehensive magazine article about AIDS interviews everyone from researchers to patients. One survey of newspaper reporters suggests that the newspaper features that most satisfied their authors involved many interviews, up to one hundred, including many by phone. (Norris 1987.)

Project interviewing differs from both beat reporting and the single interview. No longer are you at the mercy of an uncooperative or manipulative source. What one person refuses to tell you, another will. Even lack of cooperation from the subject of a biographical profile need not kill a project, as writer Gay Talese demonstrated when he wrote an article for *Esquire* about Frank Sinatra. When Sinatra refused to cooperate, Talese interviewed others around him and spent time hanging around the edges when Sinatra and his entourage appeared in public. The journalistic result of such activities goes by various names—comprehensive reporting, depth reporting, saturation reporting, literary reportage, to name a few.

Multiple-interview projects represent more than many separate interviews. Rather, they are intricately related. From early interviews the journalist learns a good deal that can be applied to all subsequent interviews. A fact learned in, say, interview number 17 may change the complexion of all subsequent interviews and may even cause you to reinterview earlier sources.

SPECIAL REQUIREMENTS OF
THE PROJECT INTERVIEW

Here are some points to consider when embarking on a multiple-interview project:

Guard Your Reputation.   In communities where people know each other, your presence as a journalist gives them something to talk about. After the first interview, your reputation will precede you. That will make subsequent interviews easier or harder depending on the perception of the first.

The interviewer who believes in fairness, completeness, and nonjudgmental listening has little to fear from the talk. The reverse applies—bad vibes travel on express lanes. Subsequent sources will become more wary and guarded as the project progresses. It may not progress at all if matters become too negative.

Discretion is the key. Take great care to avoid gossip. Don't spill to subsequent sources things confided to you in previous interviews. Don't take sides among the power factions inherent in such communities as factory workers, Rotary Club members, or Alcoholics Anonymous. Each faction will work hard to recruit you to its point of view. Finally, make clear just how you plan to use the information people give you. Will you quote them? By name? If so, they may not speak as freely and candidly, especially if you're seeking personal information. Some may speak candidly in any event, but they have a right to know the rules by which you plan to abide.

Work with Key People.   Every group has its leaders, some official, others unofficial. To illustrate, suppose you're developing a story on police detectives: What are they really like compared to their film and television portrayals? You'll negotiate with the police chief and the head of detectives to get their approval. Less clear is the need to consult a person we'll call "Big

Jim." He's the informal leader. The other detectives take their cues from him. If Big Jim says you're okay, then you're okay. If you're smart, you'll identify Big Jim as the leader and interview him first, hoping that he will approve your mission.

Why do people like Big Jim hold sway over a group's opinions? An interesting question. Intelligence, character, skill, courage, charisma, wisdom, communications ability—all these cause some people to emerge as informal leaders. They can make or break your project.

Physical size has little to do with this leadership status. When sociologist Elijah Anderson began a three-year observation at Jelly's, a South Chicago ghetto bar, he enjoyed acceptance only after he met Herman, a small, brown-skinned janitor who patronized Jelly's regularly. Herman, the street-wise former pimp, hustler, and junkie, introduced Anderson to his friends as the "cat gettin' his doctor's degree." In short, Herman's approval enhanced the project. (Anderson 1978.)

Collect Fragments.   What one respondent doesn't tell you, another will. This fact enables you to relax and enjoy the conversations without putting too much pressure on yourself and your respondents. That, in turn, often produces informal conversation that leads to more candor and more information. Listen for colorful fragments that drop out of the conversation. They will ultimately build up a mosaic of information consistent with whatever theme emerges out of your research. To write of the drama of getting an airliner on its way, little human things happen such as runaway dogs and scantily clad passengers arriving straight from the beach. Those kinds of examples make your story interesting to the casual reader. You have to recognize their importance and listen for them.

Often they're important in symbolic ways. Consider Peter Rinearson's article on the development of the Boeing 757. It began with the handshake in the back seat of the car just as it jiggled over a set of railroad tracks, a fact mentioned early in the *Seattle Times* story. The handshakers were Frank Borman, then president of Eastern Airlines, and E. H. (Tex) Boullioun, president of Boeing's commercial airplane division. Roy Peter Clark later interviewed Rinearson about how he obtained that remarkable bit of information, since he was not there at the time. Rinearson replied:

> *I asked Borman—this is a verbatim quote—"I'm really trying to recreate that car ride. Was it a car like this?" (I was in a car with him at the time.) "Was it a limo?" And he chuckles, "No, we don't have limos at Eastern. It was a private car or rental car. I don't know. There were three of us in the back seat. I was sitting on that side and Tex was on this side. It was cramped and crowded and there were other people around, but I don't believe anyone else knew that we had shaken hands." I said, "Was it a short ride?" He said, "It was about a four-minute ride from my office to the terminal." It was Borman who remembered the railroad tracks. "On that trip where you and*

Boullioun shook hands, do you remember if it was a nice day?" "Beautiful sunny day. As I recall, as a matter of fact, we had just gone over the railroad tracks that separate the terminal side from the office side, just halfway between."

I wasn't going to take literary license here. I went to as extreme a length as I could to pin things down. The specific dialogue is Boullioun's recollection of the conversation. In single-spaced typewritten pages of transcript I have close to 200 pages with Tex Boullioun alone. (Clark 1984.)

As Rinearson's comment suggests, interviewing for such detail involves a certain tedium. It is not easy to recreate scenes based on interviews. Rinearson obtained sufficient detail to dramatize the point at which a new airplane was conceived through the agreement of the now-defunct Eastern Airlines to purchase the new craft. As they rode in the back seat of the car, Borman told Boullioun he liked the airplane design and was willing to gamble on it. Rinearson's story captures the moment:

"All at once Borman had a flash that a 175-passenger airplane was what Eastern wanted," Boullioun recalled. "He said, 'If you'll build that, we'll go.' "

Boullioun replied, "You've got it."

And so, with a handshake—just as the car jiggled over some railroad tracks—the Boeing 757 was born. (Seattle Times, 6–19–83.)

Use Informal Observation and Interviewing. Some writers conduct a large part of their research without formal interviews, believing that they receive more candid information. It's a little like participant observation. Sit in the flight deck of the airliner with the captain just before takeoff and dramatic incidents emerge on stage like a play: "Red lights in the pit!"

Magazine writers seem especially adept at informal information gathering. It happens because magazines often deal with the joys and problems of daily living rather than with public affairs. The author of a *Reader's Digest* article on "intuition" spent much research time simply bringing up the topic whenever he met people socially. Almost everybody he asked had had some experience with it and could relate interesting anecdotes. Often they didn't even know they were being interviewed. Their names did not appear in the story, but their comments added to the fund of knowledge assembled by the author.

Don't be afraid to state your identity on such occasions, however. At social events, some magazine writers routinely announce to anyone close at hand the nature of a current writing project. No matter what the topic—divorce, children, widowhood, whatever—word gets around. People approach to volunteer information, experiences, and points of view. Often journalists obtain ideas for stories by listening to what people are talking about. Edward Kosner, former editor of *New York* magazine, recalls attending a party filled with elegantly dressed New Yorkers. What were they talking about? "Cock-roaches!" That prompted the magazine to produce an article on cockroaches.

Some magazines specialize in such mundane matters as preparing meals, buying a new house, and raising children. Magazine writers often draw on their own life's experiences for source material. That, too, is a multiple-inter-view project. I spent eight years researching an article on child care, simply by observing and talking with my own children. Through this observation I felt I had gained a worthwhile insight: Kids are psychologically and physi-cally tougher than most parents think. I gained that notion by watching my then nine-year-old son struggle with—and finally succeed in—climbing a ten thousand-foot mountain. I wrote an article, "A boy went up the mountain—a man came down" (*Parents*, April 1973), suggesting that parents shouldn't protect children from hardships that offer them a chance to mature. Later I published an article on how executives should handle news media inter-views, including a list of the "ten most dangerous questions" typically asked by the media. (*Hemispheres*, March 1994.) People asked how long it took to write that article. Thirty years.

Trading Information. As you learn more about a topic, you yourself be-come the expert, strange as that may sound. Eventually you find people granting you interviews largely to find out what you know. Your candor en-courages their candor. Short of violating confidences, this seems an equitable tradeoff. In such instances, the respondents' questions will prompt you to talk more than you ordinarily would. Although you should guard against dominating the conversation, you can use your talk to good advantage. By this time you have enough information to develop hypotheses. That is, you test ideas that represent possible thematic thrusts of your material, perhaps via questions like this in a conversation with a detective:

Q. Mind if I try an idea on you?

A. Go ahead.

Q. I wondered what you think of one of the conclusions I've been working out in my mind after interviewing a dozen men and women in the Criminal Investigations Division. First, detective work is not at all like you see on tele-vision—no thrill-a-minute shootups or knockdown brawls—in fact it seems more like the work of a scholar, a professor, maybe, tracking down leads, con-ducting interviews. Somebody said damned if it isn't a lot like housework—routine drudgery like being up to your elbows in soap suds punctuated by occasional moments of sheer excitement. What do you think?

That is an example of the creative question discussed before—a hypothetical framework to explain the facts and ideas you've thus far uncovered. Such conceptual questions have a valid function, particularly when asked of sources well acquainted with the overall picture. They may not agree, so you discuss it further. Perhaps one convinces the other, perhaps not. By submitting your ideas to this kind of testing, you emerge with a stronger, more valid result. If your theories are solid, fine. If not—if people can poke holes in them—then you're not ready to pull everything together into a final synthesis. You need more research—which means more interviews.

▶ 19

The Personality Interview

Q. Ms. Celebrity—may I call you Sally?—just what is it that makes you tick?

A. [Laughs.] Are you kidding? I haven't the foggiest notion.

Think of the personality interview and you probably think of celebrities—film stars, political leaders, great athletes. Secondarily, you may think of unknown people who lead extraordinary lives or have heroic stories to tell—the amputee who climbs a high mountain or the high school swim champion who rescues a child from a raging river. But have you considered the fact that *all* interviews are personality interviews?

Personality interviews do come in two broad categories. One observer, describing the content of the typical national magazine, calls the first category "little things about big people"—the celebrity profile. He calls the other *human interest*: "big things about little people"—the unknown hero. (Hubbard 1982.)

But all interviews involve personality because they involve people. Too many writers, though, squelch the personality by what they select or omit from the interview. Consider an example.

One time I set a class in magazine writing to work interviewing editors on the subject, *Why beginning writers fail.* Over several weeks we brought six editors to the classroom in person or by speaker phone, including the former editors of *Runner's World* and *Ms.*

The editors often dropped acid remarks about the dumb things beginning writers do: "You wouldn't believe the kind of trash we get in the mail." One editor even opened a batch of query letters (proposals for articles) in the classroom and began reading them, just to show what an editor goes through.

"So . . . tell me something interesting about one of your personalities."

Most students wrote creditable stories based on the interviews. A typical opening paragraph ran like this:

> What's the biggest mistake beginning magazine writers make? Editors agree—it's failure to read the magazine for which they hope to write. "You wouldn't believe the kind of trash we get in the mail," lamented one editor interviewed for this article.

Then came Camille's article. Camille Domaloan began her article in a way that not only dramatized a beginner's mistake but captured a personality:

> Jack Hart, editor of The Oregonian's Northwest Magazine, *sits in front of a magazine class at the University of Oregon. Today, Hart is here as an educator, teaching a lesson using bad examples—a stack of query letters. Choosing one he reads it aloud.*
>
> Dear Mr. Hart: Many people go to San Juan Island for one thing—to see a live whale. . . .
>
> *"Already," Hart tells the class, "I'm not very excited here. 'Many people.' That's about the most abstract of modifiers; it's certainly the most abstract noun you can use in reference to human beings. This is not a*

professional writer. This is not somebody who knows how to evoke imagery with concrete references."

One sentence into the query letter, and the writer is already on shaky ground with this editor. As Hart continues to critique the query aloud, it becomes evident that the proposal is doomed.

They are usually spotted between May and September.

"What? The people or the whales? Already we've got a thing with pronouns here in the second sentence," says Hart.

However, while you are not guaranteed to see a whale you are always welcome to visit the whale museum in Friday Harbor.

"Now we have a change from third person to second person, willy-nilly, by the third sentence."

Because the museum is so unique. . . .

"What? Unique can be in degrees? It's a little bit unique or so unique?"

Hart shrugs and puts the query aside. He admits that the idea of the museum has potential as a Northwest travel story. "But," he says, "I'm not going to screw around with this writer, and I'm probably not going to read any farther than this. Someday, somewhere along the line, a good writer will query me on the whale museum—and we'll make a story out of it."

The writer has been rejected three and one-half sentences into the query letter. . . .

The scene captures personality in action—a stern editor passing merciless judgment on the quality of writing. How ironic is the editor's admission that the topic has merit—only the writing brings rejection. It contains a lesson. Call it the three-and-a-half-sentence rule: That's all the space you have to gain a favorable impression for your idea.

An equally important lesson looms for interviewers. No longer can we consider the personality interview a separate entity from all other interviews. Newspaper editors, eager to place their writing "closer to our readers," demand that even routine news articles strive to capture the human dimension.

For the interviewer, the key to capturing human drama lies in observing and listening—especially knowing what to listen for. All students sat through the same interviews, yet only Camille listened for drama. Only Camille sought to show a personality in action. *Show, don't just tell* what editors demand of writers. The interviewer seeking irony and drama—and recognizing them when they slip fleetingly past—will acquire better material than those less certain of their listening goals.

Personality interviews, to sum up, find their way into just about every medium, from book-length biographies to short sketches. Personification attracts larger audiences and thus has more social impact than does abstraction. Stories do not always focus on honorable people. More and more, journalists are interviewing the pariahs of society—child molesters, spouse abusers, armed robbers, and others—to understand them better while seeking solutions to the violence they foist upon society.

TYPES OF PERSONALITY INTERVIEWS

As noted, the two basic categories are "personality" (celebrities) and "human interest" (ordinary people). Some examples will help to explain.

Personality.   As celebrities go, they don't come much bigger than singer Whitney Houston, with 66 million album sales to her credit. But it's the little things that count in a profile written by Lynn Norment in the May 1995 issue of *Ebony*, "Whitney and Cissy." Cissy is Whitney's mother. The article focuses on motherhood. Ordinary stuff, except when it's about somebody famous. What kind of kid was Whitney? Shy. In public school kids used to tease her about her nice clothes and "pretty hair." Conditions improved when she transferred to private school in sixth grade: "I didn't have to fight anybody and I didn't have anybody who wanted to fight me. I hated hiding." In adolescence she rebelled a little, earning her first and only "real spanking," Mom says, "when she wanted to do what she wanted to do." Whitney hated doing dishes and housework and wanted to wear stockings like the other girls.

Now Whitney is a mother herself (of Bobbi Kristina, two at the time of the interview) who is "very outgoing like her father," and whom she worries about when the babysitter is late delivering her back home.

In other words, ordinary domestic stuff, the stuff people enjoy reading because it shows the celebrity not much different from the rest of us. Bashful folks love to hear that somebody famous was a shy kid, too.

Human Interest.   This lures us into magazines and newspapers to find extraordinary actions by ordinary people. You find them frequently in major disasters. When the catastrophic explosion destroyed the federal building in Oklahoma City in 1995, we read of heroic rescue exploits, the plight of survivors, and the impact on victims' families. Thus we hear about one Randy Ledger, a maintenance worker, injured so severely that he could not talk his first days in the hospital. "But he had things he needed to say," according to an Associated Press story (4–21–95). He put them in writing. He thanked the nurses "for their gentleness." When they asked, he told his parents they could stay in his apartment ("Sure! Clean it!"). And the most touching: "I worry about forgiveness for the things I do. Jesus forgave those who crucified him. It's very hard, but I'm trying to forgive them that did this to the kids."

The quintessential little-people saga is the popular *Reader's Digest* feature, "Drama in Real Life." Dramatic events unfold, such as a hostage crisis focusing on two people, one a woman hostage, the other a deputy sheriff. They are both little people who assume heroic dimensions by the end of the account. ("Don't Move! I've Got a Bomb!" by Michael Bowker, January 1995.)

But the human interest feature is not limited to earth-shaking events. In 1995 the *Boston Globe* published a feature on several teenagers who had overcome adversity. One of those featured, Gina Grant, was quoted as saying, "The secret of success is not to dwell on the past." She achieved subsequent notoriety when Harvard University withdrew its acceptance of her because she failed to include in her application the fact that she had killed her mother years earlier. At that point, she became the subject of a feature in *People Weekly*.

People Weekly thrives on celebrities. Actor Brad Pitt graces a cover as "The Sexiest Man Alive" in the January 30, 1995 issue. But another half of *People Weekly* thrives on the little-known people, such as Dan Hirchman, age ten. He took up contract bridge at the age of four. In six years he'd become the youngest life master in the fifty-eight-year history of the American Contract Bridge League. A champion at bridge, in other words, an achievement so noteworthy that little things could be said about him—he eats Oreo cookies, doesn't like school ("It's boring"), and doesn't cry when he loses.

One veteran interviewer observes that the little people often offer bigger rewards. Author–interviewer Studs Terkel says his tape recorder "can be used to capture the voice of a celebrity, whose answers are ever ready and flow through all the expected straits. I have yet to be astonished by one. It can be used to capture the thoughts of the noncelebrated—on the steps of a public housing project, in a frame bungalow, in a furnished apartment, in a parked car. . . . I am constantly astonished." (*Working* 1974.)

USES FOR THE PERSONALITY INTERVIEW

Television turns every respondent into a personality, no matter what the topic under discussion. So the American public has formed impressions through the years: the charismatic John F. Kennedy, the ingenuous Jimmy Carter, the smooth-talking Ronald Reagan, the agile-minded Bill Clinton.

In print the projection of personality becomes more difficult. It depends largely on the writer's ability to capture on paper the personality traits seen so clearly on the screen. Yet print has the advantage of a wider variety of presentations at greater length and detail. Print can focus sharply on the characteristics of greatest interest to specialty audiences. In specialized magazines, a personality interview of a famous woman may focus on feminist issues for *Ms.*, on management issues for *Working Woman*, and on outdoor issues for *Outside*. Only the book-length biography allows room for all of those.

Consider these typical types of print personality interviews:

1. Q–A dialogue, such as those seen in *U.S. News* or *Playboy*.
2. Sidebars and sketches. Both magazines and newspapers give glimpses of people involved in some topic of public interest. If the topic is safety around busy airports, an interview with an air traffic controller—presented

in a short article alongside the main one—makes the problem more personal and dramatic.

3. Thematic interviews. The interview and the resultant article focus on a single issue or theme. The interview with singer Whitney Houston covers a narrow topic—motherhood. The answers, examples, and anecdotal illustrations demonstrate the personality in this limited context.

4. Case histories. Sometimes the interview becomes so narrow and thematic that it focuses on a single incident or series of incidents. The personality emerges through the dramatic illustration of activities described. "Can This Marriage Be Saved?" a long-running feature in the *Ladies' Home Journal*, stands as an example. Readers learn much about character traits through the discussion of marital discord.

5. The "guest soloist" interview. Like a singer in front of an orchestra, the guest soloist interview focuses on a prime example—the single impoverished family in front of a broader discussion of poverty, for instance. The story thus contains the human drama of one family's problems, backed up by statistics, research studies, and quotes from social workers and academics. The success of such a project depends on selecting someone articulate and appealing.

5. The profile. *The New Yorker* pioneered the profile in the 1920s. Its writers, not content merely to record the words of a celebrity, elected to write personality portrayals based on extensive research, including wide-ranging interviews. The interviews include not only the celebrity but also family members, friends, enemies, business associates, subordinates—anyone who can add insight or anecdotal detail. The result is more comprehensive and more believable. It includes the dark side of the person's character, thus delivering a more honest portrait. Most profiles contain, overtly or implicitly, a thematic statement: a notion of a central characteristic about the person. She's spurred by ruthless ambition. . . . He's so insecure that he must dominate the lives of those around him. . . . Publicly she's a happy-go-lucky clown, but privately she's a melancholy person—and so on.

PROBLEMS OF COPING WITH PERSONALITY

If the personality interview were seeking only the routine facts of a person's life—date of birth, college degrees, career history, habits, and hobbies—it would be simple. But for the full-blown personality story you are seeking two aspects beyond the routine.

First you must try to understand what the person is like: the essential character. This would be simple enough if concrete answers were available. They aren't. You won't gain much by asking Sally Celebrity. She just lives a life composed of countless odd-shaped fragments like a giant jigsaw puzzle. They defy any journalistic attempt to piece them together.

And Sally C. is as confused as anyone. You may be the first person to inquire of such things. You often become involved in an exchange of ideas that may lead to some joint conclusions. Or they may lead nowhere. The complexities of writing about people are perhaps best summarized by the late French novelist and biographer, Andre Maurois: "Except in those rare cases in which [the biographer] is writing the history of a man whose life happens to have constructed itself, he is obliged to take over a shapeless mass, made up of unequal fragments and prolonged in every direction by isolated groups of events which lead nowhere." (Whitman 1970.)

The second problem with the personality interview is the need to illustrate character once you have established some order to that shapeless mass. Your writing comes out flat and lifeless unless you can portray the personality in action, a living, breathing, thinking, doing human being.

Keen observation of the person in action—the stern editor responding to writers' queries, for example—will help. So will careful interviewing to obtain anecdotes, action narratives, and instances.

In essence, then, you are seeking to portray a personality in much the same manner as an actor plays a role. Any acting, according to a concept called the Stanislavsky Method, must rest on a foundation of understanding three aspects of character:

1. Who am I, and why am I here?
2. Where did I come from, and how did I get here?
3. Where am I going?

Your interviews and observations should seek the answers and the examples to illustrate them.

CONDUCTING THE PERSONALITY INTERVIEW

Virtually everything said in this book applies to the personality interview. Preparation? Definitely! Study everything you can about your subject. Sharpen your mental and physical faculties. Interview friends and relatives. Listening? Yes, listen with the third ear for inner voices and half-expressed ideas. Observation? Of course. Look for everything that could be significant, particularly in a symbolic way. One writer of personality articles makes it a point to look for what the person considers humorous, taking particular note of jokes told and cartoons tacked on the office bulletin board. Another writer believes that peoples' fantasies reveal who they are, and he probes in that direction.

Purpose? This is the most important. Without a keen sense of purpose, many personality interviews become mere shots in the dark—a few random questions, a quick search for some (often hastily contrived) unifying theme along which to unravel the miscellaneous information collected.

Here are some additional principles that seem particularly important to interviews designed to ascertain and assess personal characteristics.

1. Heed the advice of biographers: Find the dark side of the most honorable of characters and the bright side of the most despicable of characters.

2. Take time. A full personality profile can seldom be assembled in limited time. Catherine Drinker Bowen, in her *Adventures of a Biographer,* suggests that an interviewer behave like a woman invited to waltz: "She must follow easily, no matter how intricate the side steps. A little tactful steering can put the conversation back on track, but there is no room for forcing or impatience."

3. Use observation. Spend time with your subjects to view typical events.

4. Interview for beginnings. Use them to start a life's history. When did the famous round-the-world sailor first take an interest in sailboats? When did the politician first awaken to the world of public affairs? People often tell charming anecdotes in response to such questions. Ask about childhood, often the most revealing beginning of all.

5. Interview for crossroads. As life continues, people make decisions, big or little. Some of them represent dramatic changes. Did the notorious criminal have a difficult time deciding whether to rob that first bank? Did the business executive have a hard time deciding on a risky course of action, one that might endanger the company's future? What were the steps, the counterarguments, the sleepless nights that led to the decision? Such a decision recounted in narrative detail can provide both suspense and character. Even simple decisions—what to have for lunch—can reveal a celebrity's character, particularly if she's indecisive.

6. Interview for epiphanies. Out of experience comes learning. It cannot be otherwise, and so the personality interviewer seeks to discover the lesson whenever possible. Questions like, "What did you learn from losing your job (or failing the exam—whatever)?" often bring worthwhile insights.

TWENTY PERSONALITY QUESTIONS

Most interviewers have favorite methods, special questions, to encourage their subjects to speak candidly about themselves. Studs Terkel likes to ask, "When did the window open?" as a means of starting respondents off on a philosophical discussion of how they came to hold a certain set of beliefs. "Was there any one time, was there one teacher, one influence, or was it an accretion of events?" (Brian 1973.)

The example illustrates a truism about human nature: how people come to hold beliefs that guide their actions. The interviewer must trace them back to their source. As Terkel suggests, the beliefs usually come in one of two ways—a sudden discovery, often resulting from an explosive or traumatic experience, or an accretion of events composed of tiny incidents, like building an ocean beach a grain of sand at a time.

Susan Kissir, a California freelance writer who interviews entertainment personalities, keeps an entire arsenal of stock questions.

> *What one word describes you best?* Richard Simmons: "Whimsical." Alan King: "Aggressive." Steve Guttenberg: "Dangerous." Kissir typically follows up the answer: "Oh, really? Why?" Guttenberg replied, "Because I'm unpredictable—and dangerous."
>
> *What's your biggest weakness as a person?* Guttenberg: "I don't say *no* enough."
>
> *What do you think the public would be amazed to learn about you?* Actress Annie Potts: "People would be surprised at the lack of glamour in my life."
>
> *What's your biggest fear?* Richard Simmons: "That there will be no gymnasium in heaven."

To judge the impact of such questions, imagine answering them yourself. If you think you could deliver an interesting answer to any or all of them, then you can anticipate how another person might respond.

One student first criticized such a list of "stock questions" as simplistic and boring. He confessed later that his interview with a fire chief was getting nowhere until he plugged in his first stock question: "Were you ever frightened in a fire?" Of course he was, many times, the chief responded. He told several dramatic tales to illustrate just how scared he was, all to the delight (and surprise) of the interviewer.

What kinds of answers could you give to the following questions?

1. What were the best times of your life (or of your involvement with the topic under discussion) and the worst?

2. What things, circumstances, etc. make you angry? Sad? Happy? Frightened?

3. What makes you laugh? Or cry?

4. What were the major events of your childhood? What childhood experiences explain what you are today—your successes, failures, your beliefs, opinions, your personality, your character?

5. What are your best character traits?

6. What are your worst faults? Make a list. (One time after an interview a woman wrote down her "ten worst faults" and mailed them to me. The list started with "As you know, I talk too much. *Your* worst fault is listening too eagerly!")

7. What kinds of material goods do you surround yourself with? What meaning can you attach to them? If your house caught on fire, what would you try to save? (Ancient love letters, old photos, and computer disks are commonly mentioned.)

8. What do you read (books on your shelf and magazines)?

9. Who are your heroes, your "ten most admired people," and why?

10. What are your major goals and problems, both professionally and personally, and what are you doing about them?

11. What kinds of people do you surround yourself with—from your spouse or significant other to friends, colleagues, subordinates?

12. Where and how do you spend leisure time?

13. What issues, concepts, philosophies really matter to you, both personally and professionally? What would you fight for, die for? Why? What actions have you taken (or will you take) to support your beliefs?

14. What's a typical day like for you?

15. What do you dream or fantasize about?

16. How do you react to common problems? If somebody insults you do you fight back, ignore it, or what? How do you behave at a party where you don't know anyone? What happens if somebody pushes ahead of you in the cafeteria line?

17. What have been significant mileposts in your life? (The usual response covers marriage, childbirth, divorce, changes of location and employment, but ask about unexpected events, chance encounters, inspiring teachers, and so on.)

18. What do you regret in your life; what are you proudest of?

19. If you could erect a billboard to explain the essence of your character, what would it say?

20. How would you like to be remembered?

REMEMBERING THE INTERVIEWER

That brings us to a final point on personality. How shall we as interviewers be remembered? If you erected a billboard to pinpoint the essential personality of the good interviewer, what would it say?

Some research evidence suggests that the personality traits of the good interviewer are warm, supportive, nonjudgmental, understanding, tolerant. One study found the characteristics of the good interviewer to be most like those of ministers and accountants—and least like those of doctors and managers. That makes sense—ministers represent tolerance and understanding, accountants represent precision and detail, whereas doctors and managers represent authoritarian qualities. Another study suggests that in social research, interview respondents had trouble even remembering persons who had interviewed them weeks earlier. That's not good news for egotists.

Anyway, your billboard could run the gamut from "warm" to "precise" if not "memorable." Mine would say "eager listener."

▶ 20

Ethics of the Interview

Q. Tell me the truth about yourself, just between you and me, whisper it in my ear.

A. Thanks, but when I'm ready to tell the truth, I'll shout it from the rooftops. That way no one will notice.

What are the rights of news sources? Journalists employ no "Miranda Warning" to begin an interview, no statement assuring a source that "you have a right to remain silent and if you give up that right, anything you say can and will be used against you."

Only in recent years have the ethics of the interview received broad public discussion. Print interviewers have long conducted interviews in private with only the published result showing. The growth of television news and talk shows allowed the public glimpses of the interview process itself. Then, in 1995, the public saw a famous CBS news anchor, Connie Chung, coaxing House Speaker Newt Gingrich's mother to say precisely what her suddenly famous son thinks of first lady Hillary Clinton. "Why don't you just whisper it to me—just between you and me?"

Millions of viewers shared the ensuing moment—Newt's mom using the B-word—and many began to question the ethics of that interview and interviews generally. What does "just between you and me" really mean? Is it like "off the record"? Did Chung betray a confidence, a sort of "contractual promise" to edit out of the taped interview that improvident remark? And can anyone claim that this was important news affecting the course of public policy? No, we have here nothing more than entertaining fluff.

As noted, the 1990s brought interviews aimed more toward entertainment than information. Tabloid journalism, both print and broadcast, focused ever more on the indiscretions of celebrities. Soon even traditional news media began tagging along the gossip-laden byways. Meanwhile, the tone of

"As a reporter, I should warn you that anything you say can, and will, be used against you in my story."

some interviews became ever more bombastic—loaded or baiting questions that lead to defensive, emotional, or petulant responses. That's entertainment. To those you can add ambush interviews and hidden-camera stings. Skater Tonya Harding alleged that a network had "wired" her estranged mother—had her wear a hidden microphone to obtain quotes from Harding, though the quotes, if any, were not used. (*TV Guide*, 4–29–95.)

It gets even worse. Consider an extreme example. Marla Hanson, the New York model who became a news celebrity as a crime victim, visited a New York club one evening with a boyfriend. Their conversation became quarrelsome. Later she was astounded to find a detailed account of the evening published in a weekly tabloid newspaper. Apparently an eavesdropper, exploiting Hanson's new-found celebrity status, had sold an account to the tabloid. (Hanson interview 1991.) Sleazeball journalism? Definitely. A further victimization? Yes.

Would the legitimate press ever indulge in such tactics? Many newspapers and broadcast stations do have codes of ethics. A survey of 304 of them showed that 49 percent of television news operations and 44 percent of newspapers have written codes that spell out guidelines for reporters. They universally condemn deceptive practices such as eavesdropping. (Black 1995.)

The codes tend to agree on three principles, as defined by the Society of Professional Journalists.

1. Seek and report the truth.
2. Act independently of external pressures.
3. Minimize harm to all concerned.

Some principles apply to publishing policies only indirectly related to interviewing. To minimize harm, for example, most media will not identify a rape victim or publish pictures of mangled bodies in a crime or accident scene. They will think twice about invading a family's private grief in routine crime cases, although this seldom holds true in sensational cases involving celebrities. Often, though, they may balance some private harm against a greater public good, such as an account of a teen suicide or a violent crime written in such detail that the public gains a useful lesson about violence. Ethical decisions often represent a delicate balance between public good and private harm.

Acting independently of pressures means avoiding conflicts of interest such as writing stories about urban development when the reporter owns stock in a downtown office complex, or accepting a valuable gift from an organization that the reporter writes about regularly. It means refusing to cave in to economic pressures such as threats to withdraw advertising if a firm's labor troubles are publicized.

That leaves "seeking truth" as the principle most directly related to interviewing. Most problems fall into one or more of these four categories:

1. Deception
2. Betrayal
3. Distortion
4. Invasion of privacy

DECEPTION

Deception means obtaining information under false pretenses. Seeking truth, however one defines that elusive term, stands as a noble goal for all journalistic enterprise. But just how far should you go in pursuit of truth? Eavesdrop on celebrities' conversations? Peek into bedroom windows? Paw through a bureaucrat's garbage in search of revealing documents? Pretend to be a coroner's assistant to gain access to crime scenes that bar reporters? Steal documents from an administrator's file? Pose as a waitress at a truck stop to obtain unguarded views of truck drivers? And can you in fairness quote people telling you things they would not have said for public consumption?

Interesting questions. Consider a classic example. In his book *The Opinion Makers* author William Rivers describes a newly elected public official who refused to discuss his views with the press. A reporter chanced to meet the official in a bar one day and struck up a conversation. Soon the official was disclosing candidly his perspective on the issues and his vision for the future. The reporter revealed his identity only at the end of the conversation. After the story appeared, the reporter acknowledged the questionable ethics but argued that any news the official would discuss with a chance acquaintance at a bar could scarcely be kept out of the public press.

Did the end justify the means? Did the official have a responsibility to talk with the news media? You could argue either way, of course—journalistic ethics are a house built on shifting sands. Among key questions always asked in such discussions is this: Can you get the information in some other way? A quiet chat might persuade the reluctant official to express his views more candidly in the future in exchange for withholding the information acquired by deception. Even that may seem sleazy to some.

In the 1990s hidden camera interviews became increasingly popular with broadcast journalists, even as newspapers shied away from them. In 1979 the *Chicago Sun-Times* was a candidate for a Pulitzer Prize for stories about payoffs demanded by sanitary inspectors at the Mirage Tavern, a bar the *Sun-Times* had opened specifically to document the payoffs via hidden cameras. But members of the Pulitzer advisory board questioned the ethics of the deception, and they declined to recommend a *Sun-Times* award. (Goodwin-Smith 1994.)

What do media codes of ethics say about deception? "Impersonation undermines the trust that should be implicit in our relationship with the public. . . . the use of entrapment or criminal methods cannot be condoned." (*Philadelphia Inquirer*.) "Under all but the most extreme circumstances, people have a right to know when they are talking to a reporter." (*Beaumont Enterprise*, Texas.) "The people we interview should understand they are speaking to a reporter and that their comments may be published. We should be particularly sensitive to the emotional or ignorant source, the person who is not accustomed to dealing with the press or who doesn't appreciate the implications of his or her statements." (*Grand Forks Herald*, North Dakota.)

The Society of Professional Journalists suggests a code that prohibits hidden cameras and impersonation unless the revelations are of "profound importance. . . . vital public interest" and can be obtained no other way—and only when the journalists involved are willing to disclose fully the deception and the reasons for them. (Black 1995.)

BETRAYAL

Betrayal here means disclosing a confidence or reneging on a promise. In recent years discussion has focused on the reporter who seems sincere, caresses the source with eye contact and smiles and nods, seems to hang on every word—but publishes a devastatingly negative story, quoting candid admissions made under the spell of warm interview rapport. *New Yorker* writer Janet Malcolm called the issue to public attention in a two-part article (subsequently published as a book) titled "The Journalist and the Murderer." She wrote this acerbic opening:

> *Every journalist who is not too stupid or too full of himself to notice what is going on knows that what he does is morally indefensible. He is a kind of confidence man, preying on people's vanity, ignorance, or loneliness, gaining their trust and betraying them without remorse. (3–13–89.)*

The Malcolm article portrayed the relationship between author Joe McGinniss and Jeffrey MacDonald, a former Green Beret physician accused of murdering his wife and two small children. A jury eventually convicted MacDonald.

The journalist befriended his source—spent months with him, sat daily through his court sessions. He reassured him that he believed in his innocence. He even wrote letters of support to MacDonald in prison after his conviction. Then he published a book that portrayed MacDonald as a psychopathic killer.

Was this a betrayal? MacDonald certainly thought so. He had signed a royalty-sharing contract with the author, granting full cooperation through the murder trial in return for income that would help pay his legal expenses. He filed a $15 million lawsuit from prison. A jury split 5–1 in favor of MacDonald, and the author eventually settled out of court for $325,000.

Considerable soul searching ensued among the nation's journalists as summarized by Fred Friendly, former director of CBS News, who reviewed Malcolm's book in the *New York Times Book Review* (2–15–90). Malcolm's views of journalistic betrayal "constituted an inning of wild pitches," Friendly said, even while praising it for bringing the issue to public attention. "Her critique, no matter if exaggerated, should force all of us in the news business to reexamine our methods and manners." He suggested that journalists carefully explain the rules of interviewing to sources, particularly the inexperienced ones. They, basking in the glow of sudden celebrityhood, may not recognize the journalistic booby traps that await them.

DISTORTION

Distortion means misrepresentation of a source's views, sometimes intentionally but more often the result of sloppy, incomplete reporting. Better preparation, more careful listening, and greater attention to detail can eliminate much of the misunderstanding that lies behind distortion.

The simplest element of distortion is the misquotation. A long-standing debate among journalists and academics has centered on just what quotation marks mean. Consider this quote from the governor, responding to a question about crime: "I'm glad you asked the question about crime, because, ah, it is my firm belief that either we build more prisons or we, ah, ah, well, that when we, I mean we build or we pry ever more bodies, mangled bodies, I should say, of innocent victims off the streets."

Clear away the rhetorical underbrush of that ad-libbed response and we get this: "Either we build more prisons or we pry ever more mangled bodies of innocent victims off the streets."

Some would argue that the latter rendition is just what the governor said, but is edited for clarity. It has not changed meaning—may even have enhanced it because of the greater clarity achieved through simplicity.

Others argue that the quote must be 100 percent verbatim or should not bear quote marks. Besides, they say, if the governor is a fumbler in her spontaneous remarks, news reports should duly illustrate that quality.

Fine, goes the retort, but our responsibility is to our readers, which means quickly getting off the page and into the readers' minds the essence of the governor's comment. If the reader must reread a garbled comment, we've failed. And so on, a never-ending debate.

A middling view holds that a reporter should indeed touch up a direct quote for grammar and construction and read it back to the governor for approval. Perhaps it comes down to one rigid rule: Use the speaker's own words and don't change the meaning. Use caution in stripping away meaningless verbiage. If the message is so garbled that it defies direct quotation, consider paraphrasing the comment—that is, capture the governor's comment in your own words.

Media practices vary. Magazine fact checkers routinely read quotes back to sources, but daily news organizations frown on the practice. In magazines and books, what passes for direct quotation is usually reorganized and condensed. *Playboy* magazine edits and reorganizes its "Playboy Interview" pieces. Author Studs Terkel says he condenses a typical hundred-page interview transcript to fifteen pages for the books based on his oral history interviews. Terkel compares the process to refining raw ore to recover the pure gold. Television stations edit sound bites. Author John Hulteng cites in his book on media ethics his experience as a source for a network news broadcast. From a six-minute interview, only a fifteen-second segment was broadcast—one question and one answer. But the answer was one he'd provided to an earlier question, not the one broadcast. Hulteng concludes, "These built-in characteristics of the television news field lead, certainly, to some distortions." (Hulteng 1976.)

Such distortions are more inadvertent than deliberate—oversimplifications of complex realities. Often the complexities of public events defy simple descriptions, and the seven-second soundbite becomes little more than frosting on a hastily baked ninety-second minicake. Other distortions result from superficial interviews, often by inexperienced reporters. Some reporters enter an interview not with an open mind but with certain underlying assumptions, and they peg their questions on them. Questions based on erroneous assumptions lead to distortions.

Selection of respondents represents another typical media distortion. The President (a Democrat, we'll say) has made a startling declaration of policy—which Republican do you call for response, the senator whose acid tongue produces predictably quotable fireworks? Or the more balanced but verbose one? Wouldn't the newscast be more lively with Senator Acidtongue than Senator Monotone? Acidtongue's quoted belligerence, unfortunately, may produce distortion. As President Bill Clinton told ABC's Peter Jennings in a 1994 interview, "People tend to get their news in a negative and combative context."

Even an interviewer's own enthusiasms can affect a conversational exchange. It happened to me as a source. When writing the first edition of this book, I spent a sabbatical leave in Hawaii. A college student interviewed me about my leave, and the dialogue proceeded along these lines:

Q. Why did you choose Hawaii?

A. I had an opportunity to work for the *Advertiser*, the morning paper. That gave me a chance to observe reporters at work and to interview them about how they conducted interviews for their articles. Also I had an opportunity to do interviews myself and write stories for the paper—sort of field testing my ideas about interviewing.

A second interviewer, a veteran UPI reporter, approached the same topic this way:

Q. Hawaii! [Chuckles.] Holy smoke! You must have really pulled some strings to get yourself sent to *Hawaii* for nine months!

A. There's a funny story about that. We spent an earlier sabbatical in Chicago in the winter of sixty-seven—a terrible winter with a blizzard in January that was the worst on record. My wife hates midwestern winters. She insisted that our next sabbatical be in a warm climate. So I sought out a nine-month newspaper job so I could write a book about interviewing. I applied only to papers in the south, from Miami to Honolulu, and Honolulu said come on over!

Reporter 1 asked a straight question and received a straight answer. Reporter 2 issued a challenging comment, and received an anecdotal response—a more candid and interesting one.

That's a benign example. Can you imagine how reporters with agendas can easily manipulate interviews? Their subtle biases affect their questions and, more important, their responses to answers. Frowns and inattention greet politically left-wing answers, let's say, smiles and nods greet right-wing responses. Those reporter reactions can affect a source unsure of his own political views.

You may find it hard to avoid such distortions—a happy bias (e.g., you *love* the mayor's proposal for new parks) being just as much a distortion as a negative bias. Maybe they are not distortions so much as different and new glimpses into the personality of the person interviewed. They may even represent the personality of *both* interviewer and source, particularly in features, documentaries, and personality profiles.

It's difficult, therefore, to condemn all "distortion," just as one cannot condemn classic impressionistic paintings—they are a personal statement by the artist and not expected to project photographic reality. In a similar way, an interview done by a skilled questioner can produce a level of candor unreachable by ordinary inquiry. They can even achieve a level of art—the combined personal statement of interviewer and respondent.

And, to be frank, journalism itself is impressionistic reality. The very definition of news contains a natural bias toward the unusual, the dramatic, the ironic, the departure from routine. This point came to the attention of one news source, David Rust, who won a $3 million lottery jackpot in Iowa. He was pleased to accept interview requests because, as a social worker, he thought he could discuss an agenda calling for greater support of the state's social programs. It turned out that the news media had no interest in that agenda. But one television station found a curious little drama especially interesting. One of Rust's children asked for fifty cents for lunch money, and millionaire Rust found he had no cash available. This happened in the presence of the TV crew. "Guess what was on the news that evening?" said Rust. (Rust interview 1990.)

INVASION OF PRIVACY

When it comes to celebrities involved in sensational cases, the behavior of the news media "wolf pack" remains a sorry sight. The shouting, jostling reporters and camera crews not only distort the reality of the incident being recorded, but often their presence becomes a news event in itself.

Some reporters become overly aggressive. Model Marla Hanson recalls that it wasn't long after doctors stitched up the razor cuts on her face before a TV crew stood at her bedside asking questions. (Hanson interview 1991.)

And they ask insensitive questions. Cissy McClure, mother of Jessica McClure, the baby who had fallen into the well in Midland, Texas in 1987, said she will never forget the time a reporter stuck a microphone in her face and asked, "How do you feel about having your baby in the well?" She doesn't recall her reply, but she remembers what she thought: "I wanted to turn that question around and ask the reporter, 'Well, how would *you* feel if *your* baby was in the well?'" (McClure interview 1991.)

The invasion of privacy seems particularly acute in the case of ordinary people swept up in a killer wave of media interest, only to retreat to obscurity weeks or months later. They must cope with countless requests for private interviews, which are time consuming and repetitive. Caroline Dow, a journalism professor in Indiana, even changed the way she teaches her courses as a

"Turn around, Ms. Celebrity, the public needs to know if the rumors about the tattoo are true."

result of frequent interviews she and her husband fielded about a research project they'd done. She found reporters often ill-prepared for the interview. They asked the same often-simplistic questions. Now she tells her students to prepare something *new* to ask when interviewing veteran sources. (Dow interview 1991.)

   Given a choice, the new celebrities prefer one-on-one interviews to press conferences or impromptu street or hallway interviews but find it impossible to grant every request. Often, though, a novel approach together with a reputation as a thorough, accurate reporter will succeed.

Consider the news media ordeal of Melissa Rathbun Coleman. In 1991 she became the first female enlisted soldier to be taken prisoner of war. She spent her twenty-first birthday as prisoner of the Iraqi forces during the Persian Gulf War.

She became an instant celebrity. On Coleman's release, *Life* magazine featured on its cover the petite, smiling soldier receiving a big, nonmilitary hug from General Norman Schwarzkopf. The media sought out and quoted her every remark, including her crack about being the only soldier ever to gain weight as a prisoner of war—"I gained one pound; everybody else lost weight."

That was before the reserved Melissa Coleman discovered the full dimensions of her celebrity status and the demands it would make on her. She hated the shouted questions during chance encounters with the media wolf pack. "Melissa, how do you feel? . . . Were you attacked? . . . Were you raped? . . . Did you try to escape? . . . Were you scared?" Reporters followed her, hounded her, as she and her husband walked down the hallways of a military hospital.

She tried to avoid their questions. But, reflecting on them in a telephone interview months later, she volunteered a personal response to such a question as, "Were you scared?" "Well, gee," she said, recounting her thoughts whenever a reporter posed such a question, "would *you* be scared if you got captured by the enemy in a wartime situation and you're the first female and you're alone in this country? I think you would be." (Coleman interview 1991.)

A perfectly fine answer—but not the kind she felt comfortable shouting back to the wolf pack—an example of why truth is ill-served by bullhorn journalism. Stationed at Fort Bliss, Texas after her return, she received 125 requests for interviews, Phil Donahue, Sally Jessy Raphael, and Maury Povich among them. She turned down the celebrity talk shows and almost all the others.

Then along came a request from David Sheppard of the local *El Paso Times*. He made it clear that he wanted to write a detailed chronology of her ordeal. He wanted her to recall the pain and the terror of the capture and imprisonment.

To this she said okay.

How ironic—recalling the wartime horror in detail versus fielding a few questions from the wolf pack. Coleman says she agreed to Sheppard's request because an Army public information officer had cited his reputation as a thorough, accurate reporter and because she found him "just real pleasant—and he talked to me at first about what he wanted to write and everything."

Reporter Sheppard later cited his belief that she wanted to tell her story but only to the right reporter. Sheppard has a guiding philosophy of interviewing: "Melissa is 'real people.' When interviewing real people I think of how I would feel in their place, and I conduct the interview the way I would want to be interviewed." (Sheppard interview 1994.) "Unreal people," such as wily politicians and bureaucrats, may call for aggressive interviewing tactics, Sheppard explained, but talking with real people requires sincerity and careful listening.

Sheppard insisted that the interview be held in an informal setting and they settled on the apartment shared by Coleman and her husband, Michael. They talked informally for a time about mementos of the war (she showed him her yellow Iraqi prisoner suit). They talked about her religious faith that served her through the month-long prison ordeal. From there the conversation focused on her imprisonment, proceeding along chronological lines, Sheppard occasionally probing for detail. He had her recall experiences she'd mentally blocked out. She told him about her wounds—flesh wounds in an arm and a leg—something she hadn't even told her parents.

The only critical juncture in the interview came with the question of whether the Iraqi captors had harmed her physically. She hesitated only a moment before making it clear that she had not been mistreated, according to Sheppard.

Coleman had long complained bitterly about the invasion of her privacy by the media. "I'd rather be back in that Iraqi prison than the prison the news media have put me in," she once remarked. But she had no complaints about Sheppard's intimate and revealing article. "It was a good story," she said.

A MEDIA SOURCE'S "BILL OF RIGHTS"

How about a Bill of Rights for news media sources? One organization has proposed a document worthy of note. The National Association of Convenience Stores (NACS), found its members the target of hostile interviews and hidden-camera stings after the U.S. Surgeon General had identified convenience stores as a source of illegal sales of tobacco products to minors. The NACS issued a nine-point "Bill of Rights as a Media Source." News sources, it says, have the right:

1. To know the interview topics in advance.
2. To know the angle of the story and the planned use of the interview.
3. To know whether others are being interviewed for the story.
4. To state and restate your key points.
5. To keep some control over the interview environment.
6. To keep the interview process orderly, even the "ambush" interview.
7. To interrupt if false statements are being made and to receive equal time to respond to accusations.
8. To refuse to give genuinely proprietary information.
9. To remain silent if the interviewer's question is hypothetical.

To these one could add the "right to remain silent—period." That this does not appear on the list suggests that stonewalling the media is no longer a suitable option for most prospective sources.

SUMMARY

In an ethically ideal journalistic world, journalists would always remain open and sincere about their intentions and, in return, respondents would always be equally candid about themselves.

That the journalistic world is neither ideal nor perfect should not deter journalists from starting with an idealistic premise: The more open and candid you are, the more candid the respondent will be. The excesses of media interviewing methods will not disappear overnight, probably not ever. As the debate rages over the ethics of interviewing tactics, perhaps we can all strike a small blow by adhering to certain reporting principles suggested by retired Professor Dean F. Rea, who taught journalism at various colleges in Montana, Oregon, and California. Professor Rea advocates what he calls *FACT* reporting, an acronym for Fairness, Accuracy, Completeness, and Temperance:

> *Fairness* means that you will be honest and aboveboard, that you will not indulge in trickery, that you will try to obtain all sides to any story. You'll be open-minded and tolerant.
>
> *Accuracy* means that you will go the extra mile to be sure that what you publish or broadcast is correct in every detail. You will contact more than one source for corroboration—triangulating the truth. You will not make dumb mistakes such as misspelling someone's name.
>
> *Completeness* means not only getting all sides of a story but interviewing and interviewing and interviewing until sources are telling you nothing you don't already know.
>
> *Temperance* means using restraint and common sense and good taste, avoiding blowing up minor details grotesquely out of perspective.

As we in the media work more and more in the public eye, we should err on the side of openness, candor, honesty, sincerity, and altruistic motives and not on the side of deceit.

▶ 21

Ten Steps
toward Truth

Q. Compared to the novel, how close is journalism to truth?

A. If truth is the touchdown, journalism has reached the fifty-yard line, third down and seven yards to go. At least we have the ball.

Ask Susan Kissir about truth in journalistic packaging. She is a former student with whom I've kept in touch. She has established a career as a freelance writer. She has interviewed entertainment celebrities such as actress Annie Potts, and actor–directors Danny DeVito and Keith Gordon. I asked Susan if she'd ask some of her show biz celebrities to discuss their perception of news media interviews. She said she'd been probing that topic herself off and on with questions like "What's the most annoying question a journalist has ever asked you?" Actress Linda Kozlowski (*Crocodile Dundee*): "Just when they try to be too, too, too, too personal. Then I turn bright red and blush and say 'I don't want to talk about that.' "

Susan Kissir sent me transcripts of a dozen taped interviews with celebrities who talked about interview experiences. One time she asked Keith Gordon a question he enjoyed.

Q. [Kissir.] In what ways do you find directing more fulfilling than acting?

A. [Gordon.] Wow! These are good questions. I'm not used to this. Most people don't ask those kinds of things. It's great. I have to think about these.

Q. Oh, I've only just begun. They get harder.

A. No, but it's good; I mean, so few interviews—they're usually like, "Who have you slept with?" and all this stuff, and I'm like, "What does this have to do with the movie?" I mean, these are very thoughtful questions.

Q. Thanks.

Later in the conversation, Gordon cited another common annoyance with interviews: "There's a lot of sleazy publications in the world, and sometimes they like to start by reading you nasty quotes that have been said about you and then say, 'Well, how do you feel about that?'" Such comments by frequently interviewed celebrities cast an uneasy shadow over journalistic interviewing and the resultant products on broadcast and in print. Not all interviews lead to truth, defined throughout this book as "simple factual reality." That definition, admittedly, evades the age-old question, "What is truth?" Philosophers have debated that for two thousand years, and the definitive answer remains elusive. This chapter tries to answer a simpler question—how does an interviewer achieve a greater level of personal candor—truth of sorts—in the sources' responses? For the answer, let's look at some stories.

A police officer spoke to our interviewing class one day and presented a predictable party line about police–student relations. Then a young man in the class remarked, "You probably don't remember me, but you visited my apartment one day when I reported a burglary. I remember how caring and sympathetic you were. Of course, I could tell you thought I was a silly fool for leaving my apartment door unlocked all weekend, but—"

The officer chuckled. He relaxed. He told the class a story about his participation on the riot squad during the tense days of student rebellion in the early 1970s. In the midst of one campus melee, he angrily held his baton over an obstreperous student, ready to give him a swat. He described the agony of decision—to hit or not to hit. In the end his anger drained away, and he lowered his baton without striking. He went on to tell the class a totally unrehearsed and sometimes-faltering account of his emotions on that long-ago day.

"I'm telling the truth now," he said.

So on that memorable occasion, the class came a step closer to truth, with personal candor overriding the facade. How did it happen? When an interviewer treats a source as a human being—"I remember how caring and sympathetic you were"—the level of candor in the responses will rise.

So "handle with care" is *Step One* in the quest for truth. Please consider nine more steps.

Step Two.   Stop exploiting celebrities with fabrications and distortions. Try to present them as they really are. Susan Kissir insists that celebrities are interesting in their own right; why make up things about them? Her transcripts contain numerous celebrity complaints about distortions. Consider this dialogue with actress Annie Potts of the TV series "Designing Women."

Q. [Kissir.] Oh, here's one last question. I read in some article that you drive a Harley.

A. [Potts, speaking furiously.] That is such bullshit.

Q. God, how do these things get into print?

A. I don't know. Nothing could be further from the truth. *Life* magazine called me up and said they were doing a big spread on people who drive Harleys. I said, "Are you out of your mind? I don't even approve of motorcycles." And they said, "No, no, it's just for fun. A bunch of famous people are going to be shot on top of Harleys. It's mostly like a fashion layout." So I said, "Sure, I'll do *that*." So I did this thing for them. They ended up not doing the story, but they ran a picture of me in a little capsule in the front and quoted me as saying that I lived for Harleys.

A. You're kidding.

Q. I remember the girl talking to me and I think she said, "Can I get a quote from you about motorcycles?" And I said, "I hate them. I don't approve of them. I told you that in the beginning." And she said, "Well, just say something like what motorcycles have done for my career." And I said—sarcastically—"Oh, they've *made* my career." Completely sarcastically, and of course they pulled that out like I said that. I hate that.

Q. It's pitiful.

A. Unfortunately, so many things like that have happened that one becomes very guarded. You hate when you hit a really good, honest journalist who's really asking questions, but you're so guarded because you think, "They're going to take this out of context and say something terrible." . . . I hate that. To me, now it's all become like the *National Enquirer*. The facts are *so* screwed up.

Annie Potts gave an even worse example. A magazine writer spent three days following her around and, in an interview, asked, "If you were on death row what would you ask for as your last meal?" Potts replied, "Probably potato chips and sour cream." She added, "Did you hear about the old woman in North Carolina on death row who asked for Cheez Doodles?" The published article said that while others admire politicians or athletes or musicians, Annie Potts admires (and then named a woman executed for murdering her boyfriend). Potts was furious. "This is just the most outrageous and unethical journalism that I can even imagine." (Kissir 1990.)

Why do such distortions occur? It is possible, of course, that the actress's own memory of events is flawed. The *Life* article in 1988 appeared to be a spoof on celebrity bikers, but people took it seriously—as shown by the many requests to Potts's publicist by professional photographers. They wanted to photograph her on a Harley–Davidson. In any event, when enough celebrities complain of media distortions—as they do in Kissir's interview scripts—you can hardly blame them for being wary of interviews.

Nora Villagrán, another former student (the one who fell down the stairs en route to interview folk singer Joan Baez), agrees that truth is the primary goal of any interview, including those with celebrities. Villagrán continues to write for the *San Jose Mercury News* specializing in entertainment celebrities. She had a second interview with Joan Baez. When she called for the appointment, she asked an assistant to remind Baez that "I was the reporter who fell down the stairs." Baez remembered and granted the interview.

Villagrán says her agenda in any celebrity interview is to "get at the truth." That means trying to capture the essence of a person's character as best she can determine it through the interview. "I don't walk in thinking I'm going to trash or embarrass them. If I did, it would not be giving the truth about that person."

Step Three. Avoid asking "tough questions" if by that term you mean harsh, antagonistic questions calculated to make your victim squirm. Instead of demanding to hear the truth as an inalienable First Amendment right, try to create an interview atmosphere that allows truth to flow naturally. Case in point. In the interview with Joan Baez, Nora Villagrán had received instructions from her editor: Don't come back without a comment about folk singer Bob Dylan, with whom Baez was linked romantically in the 1960s. But Baez's public relations person warned her not to ask about Bob Dylan—"She doesn't like to answer questions about Dylan." How to resolve the dilemma? As it happened, Villagrán's brother had long possessed a picture of Dylan and Baez together. Villagrán borrowed it. Toward the end of the interview she handed the photo to Baez with the comment, "I grew up with my brother who had this picture of you and Bob Dylan—"

"Oh, I haven't seen this picture in years," responded Baez. "I've always loved this picture. I remember the day it was taken. We had an argument and. . . ."

And she proceeded to talk about Dylan voluntarily. Sometimes the best questions are not questions at all. Truth flows more smoothly when people tell you things of their own volition.

Step Four. Employ a genuine curiosity to bring you closer to truth. Nora Villagrán, in her quest to find the essence of a celebrity's character, lets her curiosity delve into childhood. "What kind of little girl [boy] were you?" The response frequently elicits confessions of a psychological nature. Novelist Ron Ruiz (*Happy Birthday Jesús*) told Villagrán of a lifelong torment brought on by his Mexican-American heritage and the resultant drive to compensate through achievement.

Susan Kissir's interviews reveal a similar curiosity, ranging from "describe yourself in one word" to asking about the personal elements of celebrity life, including childhood traumas, insecurities, and idiosyncrasies. (Actress Demi Moore prides herself on being on all the worst-dressed lists. Annie Potts goes to the grocery store wearing torn sweat pants.)

Step Five. Try getting closer to people. Have you thought of baking cinnamon rolls for your sources for past favors? That's mostly symbolic; common human courtesy will do or maybe flowers or a thank-you note. In the tiny town of Cottage Grove, Oregon newspaper reporter Janelle Hartman started covering the fire department. For two months relations between the reporter and the firefighters remained cordial but standoffish. Only routine news resulted, and Hartman never seemed to make the breakthrough to the personal candor she'd hoped for.

Then one day she backed her car out of a parking place and nearly smashed into a parked car. The fire crew chuckled at that. But noting that the incident had shaken her, they yelled, "Come in! Have a cup of coffee." She joined them in the fire station's day room. The relationship thawed. They became among her best informants. They offered great news tips about events around town. They started calling her "Scoop." She could hardly believe her good luck. One time, to show her gratitude, she baked a batch of cinnamon rolls. To her surprise—she confesses to being a lousy cook—they turned out fine. The firefighters devoured them and asked for more—"trade you a hot news tip for a cinnamon roll." She moved to a nearby city shortly thereafter, but the fire crew continued to serve as news sources.

That said, it must be acknowledged that reporters can become *too* close to their sources so that bias creeps into their reporting. The history of journalism even contains instances of reporters becoming romantically involved with sources. A rotten idea. Treating sources as real people, showing respect for their candor, avoiding disrespect for their station in life, expressing appreciation for their help—those represent the elements of cultivating people-sources.

Step Six. "Walk a hundred miles in the Reeboks of a bureaucrat." The comment was coined by Honolulu attorney Janice Wolf who spent twelve years as a newspaper reporter before going to law school. In 1986, law degree in hand, she took a job as administrative director of the Hawaii Judiciary, an organization embroiled in political controversy and tainted by scandal for such lapses as favoritism, fiscal mismanagement, and improper hiring practices. But reforms were under way, at least on paper, and part of her job was to oversee the changes. With her newspaper background and savvy, she thought she could enlist the help of Hawaii's news media in the reformation.

But the media appeared to have little interest in that role, preferring instead to prey on so juicy a target in efforts to uncover still more instances of scandal. Wolf fielded more and more antagonistic interviews. "I learned early on that I definitely did not like talking to reporters on the phone," she said. One of her first interviews came by phone, an interview dripping with belligerence. "He showed a total lack of understanding of what he was talking about, accusing me and the Judiciary of horrible things, and I got off the phone feeling terribly upset, feeling that I had been treated unfairly—actually quite shaken by it all."

So shaken that when she chanced to meet a state official later that day—Andy Chang, who had been one of *her* sources as a reporter years earlier—

she exclaimed, "I'm so sorry, Andy!" Chang was the director of Social Services and Housing (SSH).

She explained that the telephone interview experience was a first-rate epiphany because it was then that she realized that some of her own reporting had been self-righteous and antagonistic. "I was really sincere about it," Wolf recalled. "I saw all the times I had written all those vicious stories about what the SSH had done or not done. At the time I was convinced of the rightness of my stories. But I remember coming out of this telephone interview all of a sudden challenging all the stories I had written in twelve years as a reporter, and—oh, my God, is that the way I was perceived as a reporter?"

The problem, she's come to believe, lies in the often-intense feelings of moral indignation by reporters who perceive a wrong and proceed to expose it via newsgathering methods narrowly focused on confirming their original perception. An investigative reporter on TV ran an expose about a luau held by the chief justice at his home at state expense in connection with a convention of judges. It was presented as a great scandal. Later the reporter learned that, prior to the event, the proposal for a luau had been approved by the judicial ethics committee as an official function, justifying the use of public funds. The reporter refused to air that seemingly significant detail in a later program because, as he told Wolf, he didn't agree with the ethics committee's decision. Such experiences caused Wolf to view every request for an interview with anxiety. "I was terrified every time I talked to the press."

There were occasional exceptions. "Reporters are more likely to get information by not being antagonistic," she says. "If I sensed either sympathy or understanding in an interview, I tended to be much more open, and I spilled my guts a lot more readily—sometimes to my detriment. But when I perceived hostility, I clammed up. My response was that I'm not talking to this guy. Being 'tough' in the interview process may elicit less information than a softer approach." (Wolf interview 1990.)

Wolf left that position after three years, calling it a stressful but fascinating experience. As for the news media, the world needs more "blank slate" reporting, she says, by reporters interested in but not emotionally involved in the topic, thus free to pursue all aspects including historical and political context.

Step Seven.   Subdue your ego. Control your theatrics. On broadcast, the *respondent* should be the featured soloist. Have you ever wondered how much is truth and how much is broadcast theatrics whenever a broadcast celebrity encounters a news celebrity? Dan Rather versus George Bush in tonight's bout, for example, or Connie Chung versus Bill Gates.

Even Bill Gates, founder of Microsoft and the world's richest man, according to *Forbes*, cannot match Connie Chung in name and face recognition. In 1994 Chung interviewed Gates for an "Eye to Eye" segment on CBS. Chung's questions—often statements of negative things others had said about him—seemed calculated to draw more fiery theatrics than substance: "You're described as a take-no-prisoners kind of guy."

She quoted a competitor who had brought a patent infringement lawsuit against Microsoft: Playing with Gates is not just hardball, he'd said—"I'd say it's more like a knife fight." Upon hearing Chung relay that remark, Gates' patience wore thin. "I've never heard these things. You're saying like a knife fight—that's silliness; that's childish. I mean, why be a mouthpiece for that kind of silliness? Why doesn't he just say—because it has nothing to do with the patent lawsuit, it has to do with creating a kind of David versus Goliath thing. . . . Well, I'm done." Whereupon he walked out of the interview.

Why are theatrics so often the goal of the broadcast interview? To what extent do theatrics equate with truth? Would the real Bill Gates please stand? The real Bill Gates appeared more evident in a videotaped interview done by the Smithsonian Institution. Gates discussed his childhood interest in computers and demonstrated some of the earliest personal computers arranged on a table before him. There you see a Bill Gates full of boyish enthusiasm reliving earlier times. All questions of him were asked *off camera* by an anonymous interviewer. How simple and elegant—and more historically significant. Would we stand closer to truth if TV celebrities asked their questions from off-camera? One on-screen celebrity at a time, please.

Step Eight.   Peg your questions toward altruistic and democratic ends. You've read the term "altruistic" before in this text—it means concern for the welfare of others. The term "democratic ends" assumes that open discussion of public issues, based on information provided by a free press, will lead to a sound system of self-governance—Truth and Falsehood grappling on the open forum, to paraphrase John Milton. Whoever knew truth to be defeated in a free and open encounter?

In recent years, however, the American news media have come under attack as a threat to democracy. James Fallows dramatized the point in his book, *Breaking the News: How the Media Undermine American Democracy.* Fallows, an editor for *The Atlantic Monthly*, says the media have failed to provide the necessary tools to allow the democratic process to proceed. They have undermined it with their insistence on "conflict and spectacle, building up celebrities and tearing them down, presenting a crisis or issue with the volume turned all the way up, only to drop that issue and turn to the next emergency." (Fallows 1996.)

The problem, and thus the solution, may rest more with editors than the reporters who strive to deliver what editors want. If they want gossip and accounts of cat fights from the public arena, then your questions will be pegged toward that end. But one newspaper editor—and she's not alone—spends considerable time thinking through the question, "What kinds of stories can we develop that would most help our readers perform their roles as professionals and as citizens?" This editor, Virginia Edwards, runs a specialized weekly, *Education Week*, directed to educators and school administrators. Does the principle also apply to mainstream media? That, says Edwards, is where she learned it—as regional editor and education writer for *The Courier-Journal* in Louisville, Kentucky.

To the reporter, this brand of truth-seeking means taking a more positive and constructive attitude when seeking information. Seek the information that citizens can use, not that which merely titillates.

Step Nine. Truth would flow more smoothly if journalists monitored more systematically the winds of change in society. This means keeping a perceptive ear to the ground to hear what people talk about not only in board rooms and executive offices, but in the State House cafeterias and employee lounges, the front steps of row houses, and the living rooms of "ordinary people." Ideas worthy of public discussion come from everywhere.

I am constantly astounded by the insights and ideas that come from the students who attend my classes. A pacifist woman enrolls in ROTC, the army officer training program on campus. What an interesting paradox: a pacifist working to become an army officer. Another student, the president of a group that oversees sororities on campus, quixotically attempts to get fraternities to stop serving alcoholic beverages to underage students. What a courageous quest. A man of twenty-seven gives up a high-paying business position because he found it meaningless materialism. Now he's back in school, impoverished, trying to fulfill a long ambition to become a writer. A young woman volunteers for a campus rape crisis telephone hot line, and tells us (in a classroom interview) that the typical trauma call to the crisis center does not involve a recent attack, but one that had happened weeks, months, even years before. The trauma hits the victims much later, and that's when they call. We're astounded; we didn't know that.

Why is no one writing about such things? Because (1) they don't know about them or (2) they don't recognize them as remarkable. They are merely the things people talk about.

A few journalists have the knack for drawing people out. One is Frank Allen, dean of the School of Journalism at the University of Montana. When he worked for the *Wall Street Journal*, he did the kind of news monitoring he later began to teach to students. Basically, he talked to everybody. He struck up conversations with people he met on commuter trains and buses, at airports and employee cafeteria lines, and with other parents at the Little League baseball games. Checking into a hotel for a conference, he seldom failed to toss a few friendly questions to the hotel clerk or the elevator operator: "What makes this a good place to work?" Frank Allen, a quietly gregarious man, just can't stop striking up conversations with most anyone and slipping in gentle questions, some of which lead to ideas for news and feature articles.

His methods are not unique. In Honolulu veteran *Star–Bulletin* reporter Helen Altonn calls it "just chit-chat." "There's a pot of coffee going all the time in the governor's executive office and in most of the department offices," she explains. "Once you've gotten established with them, you can just go in and say 'Hi,' and have some coffee and just chit-chat. That's where good stories come from. You find yourself constantly saying things like, 'Oh, that's really interesting . . . I didn't know that! . . . that might make a story— I'd like to hear more about it.' "

This old-fashioned monitoring produces good stories, but it may be a lost art. Today's reporters seem more assignment oriented; you talk with the governor only when you're working on a specific story that requires her comment.

Lost art? Maybe these comments are unduly alarmist. Let's hope so. Failure of ongoing reporter contact with society would leave only press-release journalism and newsroom-initiative journalism by editors whose limited contacts offer a narrow view of reality. Both contain biases. The informal interchange with sources contains more potential for truth.

Step Ten: The Final Solution. How prepared are you to tell the truth about *yourself*? Think about that, because sources may turn the tables at any moment. Actor Eric Stoltz once remarked to Susan Kissir, "It's always strange doing interviews because I never get to ask *you* personal, revealing questions." A Kissir interview with Danny DeVito, however, turned out differently.

Q. [Kissir.] If you had just one word to describe yourself, what would it be?

A. [DeVito, after long silence.] That's very difficult. I don't know. How about you?

Q. Driven.

A. Are you talking about me?

Q. No, me. I don't know you well enough—

A. Are you driven?

Q. Yeah.

A. What are you driven by?

Q. Ambition.

A. A desire to get ahead?

Q. Or passion. I don't know.

A. Do you have a boyfriend?

Q. Uh, four.

A. *Four boyfriends!* You're a driven sex maniac! [Laughs uproariously.]

Q. No, no—

A. *Four guys!* How do you balance them?

Q. Well, I'm going to give them all up—quit turning this on me, Danny. *I'm* the interviewer!

"But enough about me—let's talk about you!"

A. No, I want to know—it's very interesting. *Four guys?*

Q. Well, no; I'm ending things with a couple of them. It's just gotten a little complicated.

A. Do you live with anyone—you don't live with anybody, so you just, like, balance these guys—

Q. Well, no. It's just—

A. Do they know each other?

Q. Well, no. Listen, it's not how it sounds.

A. You've got four guys. And you're *driven*. Boy, I'll say! [Laughs.]

Q. No, not by them. I'm sick of them. I don't care if I never have another boyfriend in my life.

A. Oh, really?

Q. I'm driven by a desire to interview people like you and figure you out and then write about you.

A. Oh, really? Great—that's good.

Q. Okay, back to you, Danny. . . .

Danny DeVito revealed quite a bit about himself in that interview: If he weren't an actor, he said, he'd probably be a gardener. . . . He always loved movies and, as a kid sitting in the dark eating popcorn, he often identified with a favorite character on the screen, thinking to himself, "I think I could do that!" . . . He enjoys being recognized in public, shaking hands, giving autographs, but he thinks it's tough on his children when they're with him. He never did describe himself in one word.

But the dialogue reveals certain characteristics even closer to truth than those factual tidbits. The dialogue reveals—indeed, dramatizes—the feisty, capricious, teasing nature of the real Danny DeVito. As a byproduct, it also offers a lively sketch of Susan Kissir, the good sport, submitting to DeVito's caprices as she struggles to reassert control of the interview. Sometimes truth emerges best from a fair tradeoff.

APPENDIX A

Interview
Exercises

Any class or workshop group using this book will find that the best learning comes from interviewing experience. This appendix contains ten practice interviews designed for classroom or workshop use. They are the best of the many practice exercises we have tried in twenty-five years of teaching interviewing classes at the University of Oregon and in workshops in many parts of the United States, Canada, and New Zealand.

The best experience comes after a class or workshop has been separated into interview pairs—the interviewers given an assignment to interview the respondents on a particular topic that can be covered in a few minutes. Such an interview is a useful experience in itself, but the best comes after the group reassembles to discuss the experience. The discussion leader should pose certain questions. Did the respondents have an enjoyable experience? (Yes! Definitely. They got an opportunity to be listened to, and they usually felt free to talk about themselves.) Was the purpose of the interview made clear to the respondent? (Often not.) What did the respondent like best about the interview? (Usually the chance to talk about oneself.) Worst? (Usually uncertainty about the concept or purpose of the session.) Did the respondents learn anything that they will incorporate into their own interviews—or did they at least have some advice for the interviewers? (Yes—and the suggestions often covered nonverbal points, such as frowning too much or slouched body posture, taking notes too excessively, and absence of eye contact.)

The practice interviews in this chapter usually work best in groups up to twenty persons. Half the class will perform as interviewers, the other half as respondents. The interviews are brief, usually not more than ten minutes. They are among the most successful ones developed in our interviewing seminars—"successful" in that they often turn up common interviewing faults in dramatic ways that students can easily perceive.

The sessions seem to work best under these five principles:

1. Interviews must be "real"—role playing should be held to a minimum. Students should not assume the role of governor or county sheriff because most students have had few experiences that would qualify them to think, talk, and act like governors or sheriffs. Participants in these exercises should portray no one but themselves, and the questions should elicit information that is real, not hypothetical. However, exercises that call for respondents to be evasive or taciturn or even a little hostile seem to contain the seeds of good learning experiences. If the respondents are asked to answer questions briefly and not volunteer any information (a hard thing for most people to do, by the way), then interviewers are forced to rely more on their interviewing skills rather than having information handed to them with little effort.

2. Presentation of an interview assignment must be done out of earshot of the respondents to avoid adulterating the interview. Similarly, any classroom preparation for the interview should be done with the respondents out of the classroom.

3. Classroom or workshop atmosphere for post-interview discussion must be psychologically safe for even the most timid students; caustic criticism and sarcasm must be discouraged. I've found college students remarkably good at treading the fine line between empty platitudes of praise on the one hand and hurtful or mean-spirited criticism on the other. The best students will try sincerely to be helpful and quick to praise, but careful to make constructive suggestions for improvement.

4. Each participant should fill out a personal background questionnaire to be made available to interviewers for pre-interview preparation. Among the points to be covered:

   a. Name, address, age, hometown, occupation [if not a student].
   b. List favorite sports and hobbies.
   c. Cite an especially interesting place you've visited.
   d. Cite your plans for the future.
   e. List one or two of your favorite *publishable* "fantasies."
   f. List a favorite childhood activity.
   g. Cite a frightening or embarrassing experience in your life.
   h. List one or two topics about which you have specialized knowledge [e.g., expert knowledge of antique cars, or ghost stories, or fly fishing, or the writings of Samuel Johnson, etc.].
   i. Cite an interesting fact about yourself that few people know.
   j. Cite the best thing that ever happened to you.

This tiny questionnaire has a remarkable ability to elicit character-revealing facets about persons—facets often unknown to their best friends. This is especially true when responding to items *e* through *j*. Participants filling out such a questionnaire must be warned that the answers are in the "public domain," subject even to possible class discussion. And yet they continue to cite extraordinary aspects of their dreams, fantasies, and good and bad experiences. It's almost as though most people's true inner character lies just beneath the surface, waiting to be discovered.

5. A post-interview questionnaire should be prepared to permit each respondent to comment on the following points and perhaps offer suggestions for improvement. Each respondent's completed questionnaire goes directly to the interviewer.

1. Was the purpose of the interview made clear?
2. Were questions clearly and succinctly stated?
3. Were the questions relevant to the stated purpose?
4. Was the interviewer a good listener?
5. Was rapport good? (Did you feel comfortable answering the questions? Did you feel free to be honest and candid, or were you guarded in your answers?)
6. Did any personal or nonverbal mannerisms please or annoy you (such as eye contact, body posture, too much talking, interrupting, note-taking, etc.)
7. What constructive suggestions can you offer for improvement of the interviewer's technique?

CLASSROOM OR WORKSHOP INTERVIEW EXERCISES

Exercise 1.   Interviewers ask their respondents to enumerate the specific material possessions they surround themselves with and which they prize the most—clothes, trinkets, jewelry, computers, cars, back issues of *Cosmopolitan*, anything that helps to define character. *Purpose*: Encourage interviewers to seek concrete details that help to characterize or define a personality. *Suggestions*: This is among the more successful exercises we've used over the years, provided the interviewers are well briefed on what's expected. I usually put it in the context of a personality feature in which a writer seeks to develop a "flashby" paragraph that characterizes a person through the possessions. The paragraph would cite a characteristic and then support it by flashing a list of possessions. Thus: "Jane Doe says she loves to read mystery stories, and so her most prized possessions include the complete works of Arthur Conan Doyle, creator of Sherlock Holmes, along with thirty other volumes ranging from a book of Sherlock Holmes party games to a well-thumbed *Sherlock Holmes Cookbook* that tends to fall open to the page containing a recipe for a meat pie dish called "Colonel Warburton's Madness . . ."

The exercise offers interesting challenges on how to approach and explain the topic. In this, as in all exercises, the interviewer takes notes and writes a paragraph based on the interview while the respondent fills out the post-interview questionnaire.

Exercise 2. Same as Exercise 1, except interviewer asks for "heroes": the kinds of people the respondent most admires and why. The list can contain anyone, including celebrities, living or dead, or lesser-known persons such as friends, teachers, relatives. An alternative is to ask for "least-admired persons." Or try a Barbara Walters-style zinger, such as "If you woke up in a hospital, whom would you like to have in the bed next to you—and why?"

Exercise 3. Solicit the expression of an opinion on a topic about which the respondent feels strongly in order to obtain lively, character-revealing quotations. *Purpose*: Encourage interviewer to find ways to bring out a personality through quotes. *Suggestions*: Prepare by using the background questionnaire for clues. Interviewer may experiment with provocative questions—or possibly silence. See Chapter 12 (Quotations) for further suggestions.

Exercise 4. Same as Exercise 3, except interviewer also attempts to find a specific instance or anecdote that further illustrates the strong opinion. *Purpose*: Encourage development of skills in obtaining anecdotes. *Suggestion*: See Chapter 12 (Anecdotes).

Exercise 5. Explore a topic that holds some sensitivity to the respondent, such as a frightening or embarrassing experience or a private fantasy. *Purpose*: Learn to cope with people's feelings. *Suggestions*: You have to play it by ear when dealing with sensitive issues. Start by referring to the respondent's background card described earlier. Most student respondents freely discuss such things, or they wouldn't have listed them on the card. Warm rapport helps. See Chapter 14 on "sensitive questions."

Exercise 6. Explore with the respondent the "specialized knowledge" listed in the personal background card. *Purpose*: Interviewers are usually thrust into an area about which they have little knowledge, which forces them to ask background and filter questions to gain understanding. *Suggestions*: It looks more intimidating than it really is. Most respondents enjoy playing the role of teacher on a favorite topic, especially if they have a good "student."

GENERAL INTERVIEW ASSIGNMENTS

The more extensive interviews done outside the classroom or workshop offer greater challenges. Such interviews work better, however, if they are more than hypothetical. Purely hypothetical interviews tend to gain less-than-serious attention from both interviewer and respondent. So most of the ones done by our interviewing classes have a practical purpose wherein members of the class take on a legwork assignment for a comprehensive editorial project. For example, members of a class interviewed graduating seniors for a writer preparing a story on the difficulties of college graduates finding employment during a period of economic recession. Another time they interviewed businesswomen in the community for a newspaper feature. They interviewed professors about topics ranging from students' excuses for late papers to teaching methods of prize-winning teachers. They've conducted personality interviews to be placed in the biography file of a daily newspaper.

Each student conducting such an interview prepares a "file": semiorganized notes similar to those provided by magazine correspondents that are combined with other files for a roundup story. The file is not a finished story, just notes on specific details, facts, figures, quotes, instances, anecdotes. For an example of a student-produced file, see Appendix B on page 211.

Here are some standard ideas for extended interviews:

Exercise 7.   Interview a working journalist on the ways in which he or she utilizes the interview. (Alternative: Interview other persons who regularly use interviews, such as a social worker, doctor, nurse, counselor, employment recruiter, police detective.) *Purpose*: Students gain ideas about interviewing by learning how the professionals do it. The best files can be duplicated for distribution to the class, thus giving the assignment a useful purpose, which in turn will make it easier to arrange and conduct.

Exercise 8.   Interview someone who has been interviewed recently by the media. *Purpose*: Learn how it feels to be interviewed. *Suggestions*: Locate a respondent by watching interview programs on TV or obtaining clippings from a local newspaper. This project, like the interview with interviewers, has a practical purpose: Information can be shared with the entire class. Useful insights often emerge about how respondents feel about their interviews. The best papers, or excerpts from them, can be duplicated for the class. The class should strive for a wide range of respondents—from officials who often speak to the media to private citizens for whom a media interview is a once-in-a-lifetime experience.

Exercise 9.   Interview someone about a past event, such as a senior citizen who participated in some major event—fought in World War II or Vietnam, perhaps, or survived a great flood or tornado. *Purpose*: Develop techniques of memory stimulation; gain interviewing experience. *Suggestions*: Once stimulated, most people love to talk about the past. Examine Studs Terkel's books, such as *Hard Times* (recollections of the 1930s depression) or *The Good War* (recollections of World War II).

Exercise 10.   A see-it-in-action interview. Find a respondent who's willing to have the interviewer observe as he or she does a task involving action. *Exam-*

ples: A coach or athlete during a game, a judge or attorney during a court-room session, a police officer or police dispatcher, a lively classroom teacher. *Purpose*: To sharpen observation powers and writing techniques in narration and description. *Suggestions*: Select a respondent engaged in the kind of action where your presence is unlikely to interfere or change anything. You have to work in your questions as best you can because often you cannot interrupt the action. Review Chapter 11 on observation.

Miscellaneous Exercises.   Lots of other exercises are possible—asking about interesting places visited, about plans for the future, about childhood events, or about the areas of expertise listed in the background questionnaire. Newswriting classes offer other possibilities. One useful exercise calls for dividing the class into interviewer–respondent pairs. Each respondent receives a mock police report to study and digest. Each interviewer must obtain information for a news account not by inspecting the report but by asking questions. If respondents are instructed to be closed-mouthed public information officers—"give answers only to specific questions; volunteer nothing"—then interviewers must work harder and thus gain more from the effort.

Another interesting exercise is to have four or five members of the class form a "legislative council" empowered to make a decision, such as whether the instructor should give a midterm exam in place of a difficult writing assignment. The council completes its brief (five minutes or less) deliberations in private but with a tape recorder running. When it has made a decision the remaining students are instructed to get the story by interviewing separately one or more of the participants, asking for details of how the council arrived at its decision and who said what. After the students have written news stories about the decision, they listen to the tape. The disparity between the witness accounts gained through the interviews and the actual discussion as revealed by the tape is sometimes dramatic. Reporters often find that what they obtained through interviews was a mere fragment of the total story. They sometimes learn that witnesses do not recall specific details accurately. A useful lesson thus emerges for all concerned, including members of the council.

APPENDIX B

Sample Interview Report

The interview report or "file" is essentially a set of semiorganized notes from the conversation. It includes a brief biographical sketch of the respondent along with the comments, quotations, and anecdotes that are the heart of the interview. The following report is a condensed version of a report done by a student in an interviewing class at the University of Oregon presenting notes from an interview with a local newspaper columnist. (Note: This report appeared in the second edition of *Creative Interviewing*, published in 1989. No student report has surpassed it in quality since then, and Bishoff, still with *The Register–Guard* as this edition goes to press, claims he has learned nothing new about interviewing since this report.)

Respondent

> *Don Bishoff, columnist,* The Register–Guard, *Eugene, Oregon*

Interviewer

> *Hedda Hoiland*

Topic of Interview

> *"The real world of newspaper journalism—with emphasis on interviewing technique"*

Background

> *Age fifty-one, he obtained both bachelor's and master's in journalism from Northwestern University, Evanston, Illinois. He worked for his hometown*

newspaper in Richmond, Virginia. At The Register–Guard *he has worked a total of twenty-eight years, fifteen as a regular reporter, seven as an editorial writer, and six as a columnist. His column is noted for its lighthearted, featurish approach to community topics, and Bishoff has a rule he tries to follow as he produces his column: "Don't be dull!"*

HOW THE FEATURE WRITING STARTED

In the early 1960s when Don Bishoff first worked for the paper, his editor, Donn Bonham, suggested that Bishoff dress as a rabbit the night before Halloween, go trick-or-treating, and then write a story about the experience. Bishoff rented a huge bunny suit, borrowed a potato sack from a supermarket, and set out on the expedition. A photographer went along.

At one house an elderly man came to the door. "I said 'trick-or-treat,' and he just said 'Whoosh,' shut the door, and turned out the lights," Bishoff says. "I just stood there while he flipped the light on and off, and I heard him say to his wife, 'There is a full-grown man out there dressed up as a rabbit.' "

The pair went on to another house where the woman opening the door screamed and slammed the door. "We could see her through the window running through her house and grabbing the telephone." Bishoff recalls that the photographer got cold feet and said, "Hey, let's get out of here; she's calling the cops." Bishoff suggested that they stay on and see what happened. Five minutes later two police officers arrived and asked what's going on.

"I explained that we were from *The Register–Guard*, and we were doing this feature story on Halloween. He asked for ID, so I reached down inside the rabbit suit, got my wallet out, and the photographer got this great picture of a cop checking a rabbit's ID."

Recounting the event a quarter-century later, Bishoff says, "I did anything in those days." He says he'd never have thought of anything like the rabbit adventure on his own; his editor, Bonham, came up with those off-the-wall feature ideas. But he decided he liked feature writing, and, triggered by Bonham's wild ideas, he did a lot of it.

"It's a real cliché to say, but I've always liked people; people intrigue me. I've said to others that this is the greatest continuing education job in the world. Every time I interview somebody about whatever it is that he or she is interested in, I come away a little more educated." And because of his esoteric information, he always wins Trivial Pursuit games at home.

He approaches feature writing from "the tree falling in the forest" theory. If a tree falls and there is no one to hear it, is there any sound? "It seems to me that an unread story is a tree falling in the forest. If nobody bothers to read it, it's all for naught. It is as if it never happened. So I try to make every story as interesting as possible."

ON GETTING IDEAS FOR COLUMNS

Bishoff claims he has trouble finding ideas for his column; most of them come as suggestions from readers, other staff members, and editors. Humor is one source of ideas he considers important. "Be able to see how essentially absurd life is, and look for the absurdities. Also be able to laugh at life."

His former editor, Bonham, once gave him a $500 bill with instructions to visit small stores, buy something trivial, and try to pay for it with the $500 bill. Bishoff went to a tiny grocery store, found a 35-cent cantaloupe, and gave the grocer the $500 bill.

"He looked at me, and I watched him getting furious. 'Do you really think a lousy little market like this has got change for a $500 bill?' he hissed. 'Why don't you take this to the bank?' "

"But the bank doesn't sell cantaloupes," Bishoff recalled replying, beating a retreat without the cantaloupe.

"Just think of what's the most absurd thing you can think of and then just test the human reaction. One thing I lament today is that we take ourselves too seriously, and we don't do enough stories for the fun of it."

Among the absurdities, Bishoff frequently writes about all the red tape bureaucracies produce. "Bureaucracies get too caught up in themselves and forget why they are there in the first place."

IMPACT OF HIS WRITING

Bishoff doubts that his columns carry much influence around the community. In his seven years as an editorial writer, he wrote constant items of advice about what the City Council should or should not do, and only once did the council follow that advice, he says. "My batting average as a columnist isn't much better than that."

But once he wrote about a tavern located in Noti, a rural community west of Eugene. Visiting the tavern he saw a variety of signs—NO SHOES, NO SHIRTS, NO SERVICE, and by one big NO was scrawled in the word "Niggers." Elsewhere was a sign, "Viva Apartheid."

Bishoff's column describing the place led to the state labor commissioner filing charges against the owner for violation of the state's civil rights laws. The owner was fined $5,000, but by that time he had sold the tavern and disappeared. No one has seen him since, says Bishoff, but occasionally Bishoff receives a postcard addressed to Don Bishit. One showed a photo of a dart board with Bishoff's picture in the center, nailed with darts.

The column also resulted in additional ordinances by the county, and it influenced new school programs in the local schools to educate students about civil rights. But that's the exception, Bishoff says. Mostly his column is to entertain.

ON WRITING

A good column is organized around three elements: A lead to entice the reader in. Then give the reader some meat, some substance, upfront. Finally, give the reader a kicker at the end.

Young people interested in feature writing should become good news reporters first, he says. Learn your trade. "Feature writing is nothing but news writing with a twist, but first you have to learn how to deal with the facts."

Even news stories could benefit from feature treatment, he says, such as a *Time* magazine type of lead that captures anecdotally a dramatic moment in the news event and then presents the hard facts starting with the second or third paragraph.

INTERVIEWING

Good quotes brighten up a story. "I'm a believer in letting people tell their own story," he says. When he wants to interview someone for a column, he always tries to put himself in that person's situation. "I think about how I would feel if somebody from the newspaper called me and said, 'I want to write about you' and started asking me a bunch of questions. I think I'd get real paranoid."

So he tries to put people at ease by saying, "Look, just start from the beginning, and I'll walk you through it and ask you questions as we go along." He also tries to end the interview with a question such as, "Is there anything we haven't talked about that you think I ought to know?" or "Is there an angle we haven't looked at?"

"Frequently people will come to think about something and sometimes that will produce the best stuff of the interview." He also tells respondents that if they have second thoughts or want to talk to him some more or come back to say something in a better way, they are welcome to give him a call or send him a note. "Not everybody can come up with a brilliant statement right off the bat."

Sometimes he has to interview people he strongly disagrees with. In most cases he will tell them so in the interview. If there is an element of hostility there, he will try to say to them, "Look, if you don't talk to me it will look worse than if you do. I want your full and best shot of explaining why you do it this way. We may agree or disagree if that was the right way."

He explains, "I'd like people to think that I'm fair, that I may end up disagreeing with them, but that I at least give them their shot in print to tell their side of an issue."

Sometimes he gets a suspicion that the respondent is lying. He will then phrase the question in two or three different ways to cross-check what the person is saying. Then afterward he will double-check the information independently. If it turns out that the respondent hasn't been telling the truth, he'll call the person and confront him or her.

Bishoff usually uses a tape recorder for interviews. He worries about becoming TRD (tape recorder dependent), but he also takes good notes to avoid the kind of situation he found himself in one time—interviewing a political candidate using a recorder, only to discover later that he'd put the batteries in backwards. Bishoff calls the tape recorder the luxury of a columnist; a reporter fighting a deadline will not be able to use it for interviews.

For telephone interviews, Bishoff takes notes directly on his computer as the conversation is progressing. Before conducting any interview by phone, he writes down every conceivable question on his computer. He also has the opportunity to scroll back over them at the end of the interview.

The list of questions also helps him remember such key questions as the respondents' age and how they spell their names. Bishoff admits he has a terrible time getting names spelled right. A former city editor devised a system for him.

"When I finish writing, I make a double-spaced printout of my column, and I go through and circle every proper name and indicate above where I have double-checked." It seems to have solved the problem. He no longer gets nasty notes from the copydesk. He suggests it as a procedure that journalism students would find useful.

Bishoff says he feels comfortable using the telephone for interviews. This may be so because he worked for the City News Bureau of Chicago in his graduate year at Northwestern University. The bureau was a small one, owned by the four Chicago papers published at the time. The bureau then handled only police news. Four reporters had to cover the entire city. They would go to the main police stations and use the phone to reach the precincts. They were given $1.50 worth of dimes at a time when phone calls were 10 cents. "The first trick was to get the desk sergeant to let you use the extra phones there so that you didn't have to use this pitiful handful of dimes," Bishoff says.

Having to approach people on the phone doesn't come naturally to everyone, he says; "I was almost apologetic about being a reporter and having to bother the people I called." But because everything had to be done by phone, the inhibitions soon disappeared. They disappeared to such an extent that Bishoff recounts a shady spot in his past. During his time at the City News Bureau, he said, it was strongly rumored that everybody hated reporters and that no one would talk to them. Therefore reporters would seldom identify themselves as such but would take on false identities such as officials or police officers. "My standard identity was 'Officer Fischer from the 35th Precinct.'"

He would call up crime victims to get details for his "police report." "One time I was calling this crime victim, talking to her on the phone, and I heard the doorbell ring in the background. I heard some conversation, and then a man's voice came on the phone and said, 'Who is this?' I said, 'This is Officer Fischer from the 35th Precinct,' and he said, 'This is Officer Sloan from the 35th Precinct—and we don't have any Officer Fischer.' I quickly hung up the phone."

"I think we knew at the time that it was totally unethical, but we were convinced by the people who preceded us that this was the only way. It was sort of tacitly approved by our bosses. Their only concern was to get the story. Today I'd never do anything like that, and I work for a paper that would instantly fire anyone who tried."

But Bishoff calls the Chicago experience "the greatest experience in the world, although I hated every minute of it at the time."

Bibliography

Abel, Elie. *Leaking: Who Does It? Who Benefits? At What Cost?* New York: Priority, 1987.

Adler, Ronald B., Lawrence B. Rosenfeld, and Neil Towne. *Interplay: The Process of Interpersonal Communication.* New York: Holt, Rinehart and Winston, 1980.

Anderson, Elijah. *A Place on the Corner.* Chicago: U of Chicago P, 1978.

Anderson, Nels. *The Hobo: The Society of the Homeless Man.* Chicago: U of Chicago P, 1923.

Babbie, Earl. *The Practice of Social Research.* 6th ed. Belmont, CA: Wadsworth, 1992.

Barkalow, Capt. Carol, and Andrea Raab. *In the Men's House.* New York: Poseidon, 1990.

Bates, J. Douglas. *The Pulitzer Prize.* New York: Birch Lane, 1992.

Belknap, Nuel D., and Thomas B. Steel. *The Logic of Questions and Answers.* New Haven, CT: Yale UP, 1975.

Belsey, Andrew, and Ruth Chadwick, eds. *Ethical Issues in Journalism and the Media.* London: Routledge, 1992.

Benjamin, Alfred D. *The Helping Interview.* 4th ed. Boston: Houghton Mifflin, 1987.

Berner, R. Thomas. "Literary Newswriting: The Death of an Oxymoron." *Journalism Monographs*, No. 99, October 1986.

Biagi, Shirley. *Interviews That Work.* 2nd ed. Belmont, CA: Wadsworth, 1992.

Borden, Sandra L. "Empathic Listening: The Interviewer's Betrayal." *Journal of Mass Media Ethics* 8.4 (1993): 219–226.

Bostrom, Robert N. *Listening Behavior.* New York: Guilford, 1992.

Bowen, Catherine Drinker. *Adventures of a Biographer.* Boston: Little, Brown, 1959.

Brady, John. *The Craft of Interviewing.* New York: Random House, 1977.

Breakwell, Glynis M. *Interviewing.* London: Routledge, 1990.

Brenner, Michael, Jennifer Brown, and David Carter. *The Research Interview: Uses and Approaches.* London: Academic Press, 1985.

Brian, Denis. *Murderers and Other Friendly People.* New York: McGraw-Hill, 1973.

Briggs, Charles L. *Learning How to Ask.* New York: Cambridge UP, 1986.

Broughton, Irv. *The Art of Interviewing for Television, Radio and Film.* Blue Ridge, PA: TAB Books, 1981.

Buckley, William F., Jr. *On the Firing Line: The Public Life of Our Public Figures.* New York: Random House, 1989.

Buckwalter, Art. *Interviews and Interrogations.* Stoneham, MA: Butterworth, 1983.

Burger, Chester. "How to Meet the Press." *Articulate Executive*. Boston: Harvard Business Review P, 1993.

Carnegie, Dale. *How to Win Friends and Influence People*. New York: Simon and Schuster, 1936.

Cerotsky, Barbara. "Nonverbal Communication in the Journalistic Interview." Master's Thesis. U of Oregon, 1989.

Chang, Peter. "Effects of Interviewer Questions and Response Type on Compliance." *Journal of Counseling Psychology* 41.1 (1994): 74–82.

Cheney, Theodore A. Rees. *Writing Creative Nonfiction*. Berkeley, CA: Ten Speed Press, 1991.

Christians, Clifford G., Kim B. Rotzoll, and Mark Fackler. *Media Ethics*. 3rd ed. New York: Longman, 1991.

Clark, Roy Peter, ed. *Best Newspaper Writing 1984*. St. Petersburg, FL: Poynter Institute for Media Studies, 1984.

Cochran, Wendell. "E-Mail: Land of 1000 Sources." *American Journalism Review* 15.4 (1993): 11–12.

Cohen, Akiba A. *The Television News Interview*. Beverly Hills, CA: Sage, 1987.

Cook, Timothy E. *Making Laws & Making News*. Washington, D.C.: Brookings Institution, 1984.

Cormier, William H., and Sherilyn N. Cormier. *Interviewing Strategies for Helpers*. 3rd ed. Monterey, CA: Brooks-Cole, 1991.

Corry, John. *My Times: Adventures in the News Trade*. New York: Putnam, 1994.

Crowe, Adell. "Winning at Phone Tag." *Second Takes*, published by *The Oregonian*, Portland, December 1993.

Dexter, Lewis A. *Elite and Specialized Interviewing*. Evanston: Northwestern UP, 1970.

DiBella, Suzan, M., Anthony J. Ferri, and Allan B. Padderud. "Scientists' Reasons for Mass Media Interviews." *Journalism Quarterly* 68.4 (1991): 741–749. Winter 1991.

Dillon, James T. *The Practice of Questioning*. London: Routledge, 1990.

Donaldson, Sam. *Hold On, Mr. President!* New York: Random House, 1987.

Dowling, Colette. *The Cinderella Complex*. New York: Summit Books, 1981.

Downs, Cal W., G. Paul Smeyak, and Ernest Martin. *Professional Interviewing*. New York: Harper & Row, 1990.

Driscoll, Dawn-Marie, and Carol R. Goldberg. *Members of the Club*. New York: The Free Press, 1993.

Epstein, Laura. *Talking and Listening*. St. Louis: Times Mirror/Mosby College, 1985.

Fallows, James. *Breaking the News: How the Media Undermine American Democracy*. New York: Pantheon, 1996.

Fisher, Anne B. *Wall Street Women*. New York: Knopf, 1990.

Franklin, Jon. *Writing for Story*. New York: Atheneum, 1986.

Friedman, Howard S. "The Modification of Word Meaning by Nonverbal Cues." *Nonverbal Communication Today: Current Research*. Ed. Mary Ritchie Key. Berlin: Moulton, 1982. 57–67.

Garrett, Annette. *Interviewing: Its Principles and Methods*. Rev. by Margaret M. Mangold and Elinor P. Zaki. 3rd ed. New York: Family Service Association, 1982.

Getzels, J.W. "The Question–Answer Process." *Public Opinion Quarterly* 18 (1954): 80–91.

Gibson, Rhonda. "The Importance of Quotation in News Reports on Issue Perception." *Journalism Quarterly* 70.4 (1993): 793–800.

Gilleland, LaRue W. "Gilleland's GOSS Formula." *Journalism Educator* 26 (1971): 19–20. See also *Editor & Publisher* 18 Sept. 1971: 54.

Given, John L. *Making a Newspaper*. New York: Henry Holt, 1907.

Goldstein, Tom. *The News at Any Cost*. New York: Simon & Schuster, 1985.

Goodwin, Gene, and Ron F. Smith. *Groping for Ethics in Journalism*. 3rd ed. Ames: Iowa State UP, 1994.

Gorden, Raymond L. *Basic Interviewing Skills*. Itasca, IL: Peacock Publications, 1992.

Gottlieb, Marvin. *Interview*. New York: Longman, 1986.

Graesser, Arthur, and John Black, eds. *The Psychology of Questions*. Hillsdale, NJ: Erlbaum, 1985.

Hall, Edward T. *The Hidden Dimension*. Garden City, NY: Doubleday, 1966.

———. *The Silent Language*. Garden City, NY: Doubleday, 1959.

Harper, Robert G., Arthur N. Wiens, and Joseph D. Matarazzo. *Nonverbal Communication: The State of the Art*. New York: Wiley, 1978.

Harragan, Betty Lehan. *Games Mother Never Taught You*. New York: Rawson, 1977.

———. *Knowing the Score: Play-by-Play Directions for Women on the Job*. New York: St. Martin's, 1983.

Harrigan, Jenni A., Thomas E. Oxman, and Robert Rosenthal. "Rapport Expressed through Nonverbal Behavior." *Journal of Nonverbal Behavior* 9.2 (1985): 95–110. Summer 1985.

Heim, Pat, and Susan K. Golant. *Hardball for Women*. New York: Plume, 1992.

Hennig, Margaret, and Anne Jardim. *The Managerial Woman*. Garden City, NY: Doubleday, 1977.

Hentoff, Nat, et al. "The Art of the Interview." *(More)*, July 1975: 11.

Hilton, Jack. *How to Meet the Press*. New York: Dodd, Mead, 1987.

Hilton, Jack, and Mary Knoblauch. *On Television! A Survival Guide for Media Interviews*. New York: Amacon, 1980.

Hirsch, Robert. O. *Listening: A Way to Process Information Aurally*. Dubuque, IA: Gorsuch Scarisbrick, 1979.

Hopper, Robert. *Telephone Conversation*. Bloomington: Indiana UP, 1992.

Hubbard, J.T.W. *Magazine Editing*. Englewood Cliffs, NJ: Prentice-Hall, 1982.

Huber, Jack, and Dean Diggins. *Interviewing America's Top Interviewers*. New York: Birch Lane, 1991.

Hulteng, John L. *The Messenger's Motives*. Englewood Cliffs, NJ: Prentice-Hall, 1976.

Hunt, Gary T., and William F. Eadie. *Interviewing*. New York: Holt, Rinehart and Winston, 1987.

Inbau, Fred E., and John E. Reid. *Criminal Interrogation and Confessions*. 4th ed. Baltimore: Williams & Wilkins, 1986.

Jensen, Marlene. *Women Who Want to Be Boss*. Garden City, NY: Doubleday, 1987.

Kahn, Robert L., and Charles F. Cannell. 1957. *The Dynamics of Interviewing: Theory, Technique and Cases*. Malabor, FL: Krieger, 1979.

Kaiser, Artur. *Questioning Techniques*. San Bernardino, CA: Borge, 1985.

Keir, Gerry, Maxwell McCombs, and Donald L. Shaw. *Advanced Reporting*. New York: Longman, 1986.

Kestler, Jeffrey L. *Questioning Techniques and Tactics*. 2nd ed. Colorado Springs: Shepards/McGraw-Hill, 1992.

Killenberg, George, and Rob Anderson. *Before the Story*. New York: St. Martin's, 1989.

King, Larry. *Tell It to the King*. New York: Putnam, 1989.

King, Larry, and Bill Gilbert. *How to Talk to Anyone Anytime, Anywhere*. New York: Crown 1994.

Kissir, Susan. "Annie Potts Speaks Her Mind." *Spotlight on Video* June 1990: 8–12.

Klick, R. E., and W. Nuessel. "Congruence Between the Indicative and Communicative Functions of Eye Contact in Interpersonal Relations." *British Journal of Social and Clinical Psychology* 7 (1968): 241–246.

Knapp, Mark L. *Essentials of Nonverbal Communication.* New York: Holt, Rinehart and Winston, 1980.

———. *Interpersonal Communication and Human Relations.* Boston: Allyn & Bacon, 1984.

Kroeger, Brooke. *Nellie Bly: Daredevil, Reporter, Feminist.* New York: Times Books, 1994.

Kroll, Ed. *The Whole Internet.* Sebastopol, CA: O'Reilly & Associates, 1992.

Lahrer, Adrienne. "Between Quotation Marks." *Journalism Quarterly* 66.4 (1989): 902+. Winter 1989.

Laine, Margaret. "Broadcast Interviewing Handbook." Research paper, School of Journalism, U of Oregon, 1976.

Lee, Irving J. *How to Talk with People.* New York: Harper & Brothers, 1952.

Lesher, Stephan. *Media Unbound.* Boston: Houghton Mifflin, 1982.

Lippmann, Walter. *Public Opinion.* New York: Macmillan, 1922.

Loftus, Elizabeth F., and James M. Doyle. *Eyewitness Testimony.* New York: Kluwer Law Books, 1987.

Lynch, Dianne. "Washington's Newswomen and Their News Sources." *Newspaper Research Journal* 14.3–4 (1993): 82–91. Summer–Fall 1993.

MacHovec, Frank J. *Interview and Interrogation.* Springfield, IL: Charles C. Thomas, 1989.

Mackoff, Barbara. *What Mona Lisa Knew.* Los Angeles: Lowell House, 1990.

Magee, Bryan. *The Television Interviewer.* London: MacDonald, 1966.

Maharidge, Dale, and Michael Williamson. *Journey to Nowhere.* Garden City, NY: Doubleday, 1985.

———. *The Last Great American Hobo.* Rocklin, CA: Prima, 1993.

Malandro, Loretta, and Larry Barker. *Nonverbal Communication.* 2nd ed. New York: McGraw-Hill, 1989.

Malcolm, Janet. *The Journalist and the Murderer.* New York: Knopf, 1990.

Maltz, Daniel N., and Ruth A. Borker. "A Cultural Approach to Male–Female Miscommunication." *Language and Social Identity.* Ed. John J. Gumperz. Cambridge: Cambridge UP, 1982.

Mann, Merlin. "Journalistic Interviewing: Evaluation of Interview Effectiveness by Interviewers and Respondents." Ph.D. dissertation, U of Missouri, 1991.

Mayberry, D. L. *Tell Me About Yourself: How to Interview Anyone From Your Friends to Famous People.* Minneapolis: Lerner 1985.

Mayo, Clara, and Nancy M. Henley, eds. *Gender and Nonverbal Behavior.* New York: Springer-Verlag, 1981.

Mead, Margaret. *Coming of Age in Samoa.* 1928. New York: Morrow, 1983.

Medley, H. Anthony. *Sweaty Palms: The Neglected Art of Being Interviewed.* Rev. ed. Berkeley: Ten Speed, 1992.

Mehrabian, Albert. *Nonverbal Communication.* Chicago: Aldine-Atherton, 1972.

———. *Silent Messages.* 2nd ed. Belmont, CA: Wadsworth, 1981.

Middleton, Kent R., and Bill F. Chamberlin. *The Law of Public Communication.* 3rd ed. New York: Longman, 1994.

Millar, Rob, Valerie Crute, and Owen Hargie. *Professional Interviewing.* London: Routledge, 1992.

Milwid, Beth. *What You Get When You Go for It.* New York: Dodd, Mead, 1987.

Mincer, Richard and Deanne Mincer. *The Talk Show Book.* New York: Facts on File Publications, 1982.

Mischler, Elliot. *Research Interviewing.* Cambridge: Harvard UP, 1986.

Moore, William T. *Dateline Chicago.* New York: Taplinger, 1973.

Morris, Jim R. "Newsmen's Interview Techniques and Attitudes toward Interviewing." *Journalism Quarterly* 50 (1973): 539–42; 548.

Morrison, Ann M., Randall P. White, and Ellen Van Velsor. *Breaking the Glass Ceiling.* Reading, MA: Addison-Wesley, 1987.

Nichols, Ralph G., and Leonard A. Stevens. *Are You Listening?* New York: McGraw-Hill, 1957.

Norris, Timothy M. "Face-to-Voice: A Survey of Face-to-Face and Telephone Interviewing in Daily News Work." Master's Thesis, U of Oregon, 1987.

Patterson, Miles L. "Nonverbal Exchange: Past, Present, and Future." *Journal of Nonverbal Behavior* 8.4 (1984): 350–359. Summer 1984.

———. *Nonverbal Behavior.* New York: Springer-Verlag, 1983.

Paul, Nora. *Computer Assisted Research.* 2nd ed. St. Petersburg, FL: Poynter Institute for Media Studies, 1994.

Plimpton, George. *Open Net.* New York: W. W. Norton, 1986.

———. *Out of My League.* New York: Harper & Brothers, 1961.

———. *Paper Lion.* New York: Harper & Row, 1966.

———. *Shadow Box.* New York: Putnam, 1977.

Poyatos, Fernando. *Paralanguage.* Philadelphia: Benjamins, 1993.

Rankin, Paul T. "The Measurement of the Ability to Understand Spoken Language." Ph.D. dissertation, U of Michigan, 1926.

Reik, Theodor. *The Compulsion to Confess.* New York: Farrar, Straus and Cudahy, 1959.

———. *Listening with the Third Ear.* New York: Farrar, Straus, 1952.

Rice, Stuart A. "Contagious Bias in the Interview." *American Journal of Sociology* 35 (1929): 420–23.

Riley, Sam G., and Joel M. Wiessler. "Privacy: The Reporter and Telephone and Tape Recorder." *Journalism Quarterly* 51 (1974): 511–15.

Ritz, David. "Inside Interviewing." *The Writer* Mar. 1993: 15–17.

Rivers, William. *The Adversaries.* Boston: Beacon Press, 1970.

Rivers, William L., and Wilbur Schramm. *Responsibility in Mass Communications.* New York: Harper & Row, 1969.

Rogers, Carl R. *A Way of Being.* Boston: Houghton Mifflin, 1980.

———. *Client-Centered Therapy.* Boston: Houghton Mifflin, 1951.

———. *Counseling and Psychotherapy.* Boston: Houghton Mifflin, 1942.

Rogers, Carl R., and F. J. Roethlisberger. "Barriers and Gateways to Communication." *Harvard Business Review* July–Aug. 1952: 46.

Rosensteil, Tom. "Yakety-Yak: The Lost Art of Interviewing." *Columbia Journalism Review* Jan.–Feb. 1995.

Roshco, Bernard. *Newsmaking.* Chicago: U of Chicago P, 1979.

Rowe, Chip. "Talking to Ourselves." *American Journalism Review* 16.2 (1994): 44–48. Mar. 1994.

Royal, Robert. F., and Steven R. Schutt. *The Gentle Art of Interviewing and Interrogation.* Englewood Cliffs, NJ: Prentice-Hall, 1976.

Sabato, Larry J. *Feeding Frenzy.* New York: The Free Press, 1991.

Scanlan, Christopher, ed. *How I Wrote the Story.* 2nd ed. Providence, RI: The Providence Journal, 1986.

Schudson Michael. *The Power of News*. Cambridge: Harvard UP, 1995.

Shirky, Clay. *The Internet by E-Mail*. Emeryville, CA: Ziff-Davis, 1994.

Sigal, Leon V. *Reporters and Officials*. Lexington, Mass.: Heath, 1973.

Sincoff, Michael Z., and Robert S. Goyer. *Interviewing*. New York: Macmillan, 1984.

Slavens, Thomas P., ed. *Informational Interviews and Questions*. Metuchen, NJ: Scarecrow Press, 1978.

Spradley, James P. *Participant Observation*. New York: Holt, Rinehart and Winston, 1980.

———. *The Ethnographic Interview*. New York: Harper & Row, 1979.

Stauffer, Dennis. *Mediasmart: How to Handle a Reporter*. Minneapolis: MinneApple Press, 1994.

Stavitsky, Alan G. *Independence and Integrity: A Guidebook for Public Radio Journalism*. Washington: National Public Radio, 1995.

Steele, Bob. "Doing Ethics: How a Minneapolis Journalist Turned a Difficult Situation into a Human Triumph." *Quill* Nov.–Dec. 1992: 28–30.

Steil, Lyman K., L. Barker, and K. Watson. *Effective Listening*. Reading, MA: Addison-Wesley, 1983.

Stempel, Guido H. III, and Bruce H. Westley, eds. *Research Methods in Mass Communications*. 2nd ed. Englewood Cliffs, NJ: Prentice-Hall, 1989.

Stewart, Charles J., and William B. Cash. *Interviewing Principles and Practices*. 7th ed. Madison, WI: Brown & Benchmark, 1994.

Sudman, Seymour, and Norman. M. Bradburn. *Asking Questions*. San Francisco: Jossey-Bass, 1982.

Tannen, Deborah. *Talking from 9 to 5*. New York: Morrow, 1994.

———. *You Just Don't Understand*. New York: Morrow, 1990.

Terkel, Studs. *Division Street: America*. New York: Pantheon, 1967.

———. *Working*. New York: Pantheon, 1974.

Tolor, Alexander, ed. *Effective Interviewing*. Springfield, IL: Charles C. Thomas, 1985.

Tyrrell, Robert. *The Work of the Television Journalist*. New York: Hastings House, 1972.

Vargas, Marjorie Fink. *Louder Than Words*. Ames: Iowa State UP, 1986.

Wallace, Mike, and Gary Paul Gates. *Close Encounters*. New York: Morrow, 1984.

Walters, Barbara. *How to Talk with Practically Anybody about Practically Anything*. New York: Doubleday, 1970.

Wax, Rosalie H. *Doing Fieldwork*. Chicago: U of Chicago, 1971.

Weaver, Carl H. *Human Listening: Process and Behavior*. Indianapolis: Bobbs-Merrill, 1972.

Webb, Eugene J., and Jerry R. Salancik. *The Interview, or The Only Wheel in Town*. Journalism Monograph No. 2. Columbia, SC: Association for Education in Journalism and Mass Communication, 1966.

Webb, Eugene J., Donald T. Campbell, Richard D. Schwartz, Lee Sechrest, and Janet Belew Grove. *Unobtrusive Measures*. Boston: Houghton-Mifflin, 1981.

Weiser, A. "How Not to Answer a Question." *Papers from the 11th Regional Meeting of the Chicago Linguistic Society*. Eds. R. E. Grossman, L. J. San, and T. J. Vance. Chicago: Chicago Linguistic Society, 1975.

Werner, Elyse K. "A Study of Communication Time." Master's Thesis, U of Maryland, 1975.

Whitman, Alden. *The Obituary Book*. New York: Stein and Day, 1970.

Whyte, William Foote. *Learning from the Field*. Beverly Hills, CA: Sage, 1984.

———. *Street Corner Society*. Chicago: U of Chicago, 1943.

Wicks, Robert J., and Ernest H. Josephs Jr. *Techniques of Interviewing for Law Enforcement and Corrections Personnel.* Springfield, IL: Charles C. Thomas, 1972.

Wiemann, John, and Randall Harrison, eds. *Nonverbal Interaction.* Beverly Hills, CA: Sage, 1983.

Wilkens, Joanne. *Her Own Business.* New York: McGraw-Hill, 1987.

Wineberg, Steve. *Trade Secrets of Washington Journalists.* Washington, D.C.: Acropolis, 1981.

Wolvin, Andrew D., and Carolyn G. Coakley. *Listening.* 4th ed. Madison, WI: Brown & Benchmark, 1993.

Wood, John. "A Conversation with the Playboy Interviewer." *Writer's Digest* Oct. 1991. 28–32.

Zunin, Leonard, and Natalie B. Zunin. *Contact: The First Four Minutes.* Los Angeles: Nash, 1972.

Interviews

Allen, Frank, School of Journalism dean, April 14, 1995

Altonn, Helen, reporter, April 26, 1995

Belli, Melvin, attorney, Nov. 2, 1991

Browning, Dan, editor, Jan. 18, 1995

Coleman, Melissa, soldier, Dec. 2, 1991

Crowe, Deborah, reporter, Jan. 24, 1995

Dow, Caroline, professor, June 8, 1991

Downs, Diane, prison convict, Sept. 27, 1991

Forbes, Steve, paramedic, Sept. 13, 1990

Franklin, Jon, professor, April 11, 1995

Grunder, Anita, geologist, Feb. 11, 1991

Guibord, Jackie, police officer, April 1, 1991

Hanson, Marla, model, May 2, 1991

Hartman, Janelle, reporter, June 8, 1994

Hoffman, Tham, nurse, Mar. 11, 1991

Hopkins, Jim, reporter, Jan. 10, 1995

Leslie, Melody Ward, writer, Oct. 9, 1996

Kesey, Ken, author, June 30, 1991

Kevorkian, Jack, medical doctor, June 19, 1991

Kissir, Susan, writer, Oct. 15, 1990

McClure, Cissy, mother of Jessica McClure, Texas well rescue, Sept. 25, 1990

McDonald, Kim, reporter, Aug. 26, 1994

Millikin, Capt. Steve, Tailhook Association spokesman, Jan. 29, 1993

Nguyen, Hien, astrophysicist, Aug. 26 and Sept. 7, 1994

Olson, Gretchen, writer, Jan. 21, 1995

Rathbun, Joan and Leo, parents of Melissa Coleman, Sept. 5, 1991

Rust, David, lottery winner, Oct. 30, 1990

Schwartz, John, reporter, Jan. 4, 1995

Sheppard, David, reporter, Sept. 8, 1994

Stavitsky, Al, professor, Jan. 9, 1995

Villagrán, Nora, feature writer, May 19, 1994

Uphaw, Jim, professor, Jan. 24, 1995

Voda, Patti, nurse, Mar. 11, 1990

Wells, Denise, country music fan, Sept. 4, 1990

Wilson, David, reporter, Aug. 26, 1994

Wolf, Janice, attorney, July 6, 1990

Index